Additional Parenting Books From the
American Academy of Pediatrics

Caring for Your Baby and Young Child: Birth to Age 5
(English and Spanish)

Heading Home With
From Birth to

Mommy Calls: Dr. Tanya Answers   Questions
About Babies and Toddlers

The Wonder Years: Helping Your Baby and Young Child
Successfully Negotiate the Major Developmental Milestones

Raising Twins: From Pregnancy to Preschool

Your Baby's First Year
(English and Spanish)

New Mother's Guide to Breastfeeding
(English and Spanish)

Food Fights: Winning the Nutritional Challenges of Parenthood
Armed With Insight, Humor, and a Bottle of Ketchup

A Parent's Guide to Childhood Obesity: A Road Map to Health

Guide to Your Child's Nutrition

ADHD: A Complete and Authoritative Guide

Waking Up Dry: A Guide to Help Children Overcome Bedwetting

A Parent's Guide to Building Resilience in Children and Teens:
Giving Your Child Roots and Wings

Sports Success R$_x$! Your Child's Prescription for the Best Experience

Less Stress, More Success: A New Approach to Guiding Your Teen
Through College Admissions and Beyond

Mental Health, Naturally: The Family Guide to Holistic Care
for a Healthy Mind and Body

Caring for Your School-Age Child:
Ages 5 to 12

Caring for Your Teenager

Guide to Your Child's Allergies and Asthma

Guide to Toilet Training
(English and Spanish)

For more information, please visit the official AAP Web site for parents,
HealthyChildren.org/bookstore.

CyberSafe

Protecting and Empowering Kids in the Digital World
of Texting, Gaming, and Social Media

Gwenn Schurgin O'Keeffe, MD, FAAP

American Academy of Pediatrics
DEDICATED TO THE HEALTH OF ALL CHILDREN™

American Academy of Pediatrics Department of Marketing and Publications

*Director, Department of Marketing
and Publications*
Maureen DeRosa, MPA

Director, Division of Product Development
Mark Grimes

Manager, Consumer Publishing
Carolyn Kolbaba

*Director, Division of Publishing
and Production Services*
Sandi King, MS

Editorial Specialist
Jason Crase

Print Production Specialist
Shannan Martin

Manager, Art Direction and Production
Linda Diamond

Director, Division of Marketing and Sales
Kevin Tuley

Manager, Consumer Product Marketing
Kathleen Juhl

Published by the American Academy of Pediatrics
141 Northwest Point Blvd, Elk Grove Village, IL 60007-1098
847/434-4000
Fax: 847/434-8000
www.aap.org

Cover design by Wild Onion Design, Inc.
Back cover photo by David Fox, Photographer
Book design by Linda Diamond

*CyberSafe: Protecting and Empowering Kids in the Digital World of Texting, Gaming,
and Social Media* was created by Gwenn Schurgin O'Keeffe, MD, FAAP.

Library of Congress Control Number: 2010903969
ISBN: 978-1-58110-452-3

The recommendations in this publication do not indicate an exclusive course of treatment or serve as a standard of medical care. Variations, taking into account individual circumstances, may be appropriate.

Statements and opinions expressed are those of the author and not necessarily those of the American Academy of Pediatrics.

Products are mentioned for informational purposes only. Inclusion in this publication does not imply endorsement by the American Academy of Pediatrics. The American Academy of Pediatrics is not responsible for the content of the resources mentioned in this publication. Web sites are as current as possible, but may change at any time.

Every effort is made to keep *CyberSafe* consistent with the most recent advice and information possible.

CB0063
9-267

1 2 3 4 5 6 7 8 9 10

What People Are Saying

My most beloved treasures are my twins. To keep our children safe in the world in which they live, we must understand that world! O'Keeffe's book is a must for every parent who cares!

Nancy Grace
Anchor, CNN HLN

Finally we have a trained and licensed professional who can talk to parents about the real kid cyber-health issues. Got a cyber-wellness question? Ask Dr Gwenn. I do.

Parry Aftab, Esq
Executive Director, WiredSafety.org

The facts of modern life now include social media, cyberbullying, texting, and constant electronic connections. Dr Gwenn makes the call on what parents need to know to help their kids navigate the wired (and wireless) world we now live in. *CyberSafe: Protecting and Empowering Kids in the Digital World of Texting, Gaming, and Social Media* is an invaluable guide for me at home as a mom and at the office as a pediatrician. It should be on everyone's bookshelf!

Jennifer Shu, MD, FAAP
Coauthor of the award-winning books *Heading Home With Your Newborn: From Birth to Reality* and *Food Fights: Winning the Nutritional Challenges of Parenthood Armed With Insight, Humor, and a Bottle of Ketchup;* medical editor in chief, HealthyChildren.org; medical expert on CNNhealth.com; and editor in chief, *Baby & Child Health: The Essential Guide From Birth to 11 Years*

Online safety is still a basic parenting issue, even if our kids are the "digital natives." Dr O'Keeffe's entertaining and wise insights on the Internet, kids, and their changing interests will help you to be confident and guide your children to Internet safety.

Marian Merritt
Norton Internet Safety Advocate, Symantec Corporation

Kids, technology, and hormones. A heady mixture! Good thing we have Dr Gwenn to help us navigate this challenging yet ultimately rewarding digital landscape.

Stephen Balkam
CEO, Family Online Safety Institute

Dr Gwenn combines common sense with quality research to help parents delve into the murky (and, for some parents, intimidating) area of kids and technology. If your child has—or is about to get—a cell phone and/or Internet access, read this book for the download on all things technology before it's too late.

Jen Singer
Author, *Stop Second-Guessing Yourself* guides to parenting, and editor in chief, MommaSaid.net

CyberSafe: Protecting and Empowering Kids in the Digital World of Texting, Gaming, and Social Media is an eye-opening guide for parents who want to learn how to best navigate the digital world. Whether you're preparing for your toddler's television journey or trying to keep up with your texting teen, Dr Gwenn O'Keeffe explains clearly and effectively how you and your family can surf, survive, and live in harmony on the Internet and beyond.

Tanya Remer Altmann, MD, FAAP
Mother of 2 boys, pediatrician, parenting expert, and author, *Mommy Calls: Dr. Tanya Answers Parents' Top 101 Questions About Babies and Toddlers*

Dr Gwenn allows parent readers to not only truly understand what is going on in a teen's digital world, but also how to communicate with youth about it. Her use of personal stories, facts, and conversation starters make broaching this topic with kids infinitely easier and more relevant. I particularly loved the sample e-mails and colorful examples for parents. Every parent must buy this book!

Vanessa Van Petten
Youthologist and teen author for Radicalparenting.com

In today and tomorrow's digital world, becoming cyber-aware and understanding why and how to teach cyber-safety with your children is an essential skill. Dr Gwenn's book is a necessary read and a great start!

Donald Shifrin, MD, FAAP
Former Chair, American Academy of Pediatrics Council on Communications and Media

To my parents, Stan and Judy, digital immigrants by birth but digital natives at heart, for setting me on my own cyber-exploration the day they convinced me to trade in my beloved typewriter for my first laptop.

To my daughters, Caitlin and Megan, my digital natives, for always amazing me with online and off-line abilities I couldn't predict if I tried.

To my husband, Will, for taking this crazy ride with me, providing the best tech and parenting support in the world, and reminding me that life's best moments are the unplugged ones.

To all the cyber-savvy families of today and tomorrow, remember that connecting daily, online and off, is the true secret to cyber-safety. You taught me that; I'm just here as a friendly reminder!

Table of Contents

Appendixes

Acknowledgments

Hillary Rodham Clinton was wise to pick the old African proverb, "It takes a village to raise a child," as the theme for her book, *It Takes a Village*. As I have found with any project involving the growth, development, and well-being of children, "village" becomes an understatement for the amount of people required for the success of such a project, including a book such as this one.

I am truly indebted to my own village of technical experts, medical colleagues, parents, kids, and teens for their time, support, and generosity of experiences, advice, and input as I embarked on the earliest days of this book and as I fine-tuned the chapters leading to its ultimate publication. The overwhelming support as I slogged through the reams of data and ideas to complete a project that, in truth, began 5 years ago has been truly humbling.

My biggest source of inspiration for writing this book has been the myriad of people I've met online as I started my own online adventure. From parents, to editors, to producers, to experts in everything from technology, to law, to writing, to child health and pediatrics, knowing you has shaped my path, my dreams, my ideas, and how I parent my own children online and off. Without meeting you, I wouldn't have been able to understand the unique safety issues of the online world. Thank you for opening my eyes.

This book would still be a dream if it were not for the wonderful staff of the American Academy of Pediatrics Department of Marketing and Publications. To Mark Grimes, Carolyn Kolbaba, and Kathy Juhl, thank you for believing in my dream and helping shape it into a reality.

To not become tangled in my own book's details, I'm endlessly grateful to an amazing group of colleagues and experts who gave their time for chapter reviews, interviews, and advice on concepts.

To Vic Strasburger, MD, FAAP; Brian Vartbedian, MD, FAAP; Gil Fuld, MD, FAAP; Dimitri Christakis, MD, FAAP; Mike Brody, MD; danah boyd; and Parry Aftab, Esq, thank you for your sage advice on chapter concepts, charts, and diagrams.

To Jennifer Shu, MD, FAAP; Don Shifrin, MD, FAAP; Kathleen Clark-Pearson, MD, FAAP; Marian Merritt; Gina Steiner; and Will O'Keeffe, thank you for taking the time to read, read, and read some more. Your input and editing made this book what it is today.

To the following individuals and their groups for their time, quotes, screen shots, and technical advice on the many complex topics covered throughout the book:

AT&T: Andrea Brands, Brent Olson

Bully Coach: Joel Haber, PhD

Digital Nation: Rachel Dretzin

Disney Club Penguin: Karen Mason

Edutopia: Ken Ellis

Entertainment Software Rating Board (ESRB): Eliot Mizrachi, Pat Vance

GetNetWise: Tim Lordon

Google: Scott Rubin

iBrain Author: Gary Small

K9: Laurie Coffin

Love Our Children USA: Ross Ellis

Microsoft: Kenny Gold

My Body Belongs to Me Author: Jill Starishevsky

Optenet: Karyn Martin

PCMag Digital Network: Neil Rubenking

Safe Eyes: Forrest Collier, Stanley Holditch

Spector Soft: Doug Taylor

Sprint: Jennifer Schuler

Symantec/Norton Online Family: Marian Merritt

Verizon: Jessica Lee

WiredSafety: Parry Aftab, Esq

To the following groups and families who contributed their stories and time, a huge thanks:

- Anastasia Goodstein from Ypulse for contacting me with her digital teens: Bernadette, Mike, Sarah, and their parents
- Ken Ellis from Edutopia and his digital teens: Cam, Dylan, and their parents
- Marian Merritt and her daughter Maddy

Finally, no project like this would be possible without the endless love and support of family.

My parents get a special shout-out for talking me into my first computer. That was not an easy sell. I loved my typewriter and was just as happy to stick with it! Who would have known that my reluctant dip of a toe into the computer pond would lead to where I am today?

I also have to thank my parents for staying with the digital wave and not running from it. The day my oldest daughter exclaimed, "Wait…Nana can text?" is a day I'll never forget and is proof that today's digital divide is closing fast (if it still exists at all).

To my own daughters, Caitlin and Megan, I wish I could bottle what you both have. Your energy for life and ability to unplug is contagious. Thank you for seeing that there is a world beyond screens and for reminding me and Daddy of that when we forget. I love you both endlessly!

To my husband, Will, thank you for always rallying behind me regardless of how many "paths less traveled" I seem to take in life…and for reading this book cover to cover in one sitting. That dedication is what makes riding through life with you so sweet and why I love you beyond words.

Introduction: Parents, Start Your Digital Engines!

We live in remarkable times. Remarkable and very high-tech times, if the truth be told.

It's remarkable to think how our lives are today as parents compared with the lives we had as children, carefree and unplugged. It's even more remarkable to think of our children's lives today compared with our lives when we were children, arguably less carefree and most definitely not unplugged.

Today's kids are all digital at home and on the go. Today's kids are the first generation of kids to be raised all digital. We're the last generation of parents to remember what it's like to live life without something digital, something plugged in. Future generations of parents will only know life as digital parents.

This means we are in a unique position to offer guidance that is truly now or never. The onus is on us to instill in our children seeds of the non-digital world and make sure they embrace aspects of life we came to value from that world so future generations will have that to enjoy and value.

At the same time, we have to come to understand the digital world ourselves. Not being born into a digital world, we are learning as we go and doing a commendable job adapting. Where we are not doing so well is keeping pace with parenting in the digital world; our forte is off-line. That's as we'd expect because that's how we were raised—that's our frame of reference.

It is truly daunting to think about how quickly our digital world is evolving. Just preparing for this book was a constant reminder of how difficult it is today to keep pace and stay up to date!

To give you some perspective, when I first put down the early seeds of this book in 2005, the social networking Web site Facebook was a blip on the Internet and limited to people enrolled in one of the schools or organizations registered with it. It was also ranked number 2 behind MySpace, the other popular social networking Web site. Similarly, Twitter (another service) had just launched and few had even figured out what a "tweet" was.

By the time I submitted my book proposal in 2008, Facebook had become the number 1 site, open to everyone wishing to have a profile. Within the next year, with my first draft barely complete, Facebook and Twitter popularity were off the charts, with Twitter increasing in users 1,444% since the prior year!

Of course, no rise in stardom comes without a price.

With the dramatic rise in popularity and use of social media sites, we now have new issues to contend with, complete with new lingo like cyberbullying, Internet addiction, extreme texting, sexting, and Facebook depression.

This has become such an important part of our lives that it's now captured as part of our pop culture on TV and in the movies. During a 2008 episode of *The Simpsons* ("Mapple My-Bill," www.youtube.com/watch?v=iof1qw7cr2c&feature=related), we saw usually brainy and thoughtful Lisa completely consumed by a newly acquired "Mapple" MP3 audio player (pronounced to rhyme with Apple) This is art imitating life down to the teeniest detail. We see an impulsive teen go completely out of character and become more impulsive than ever. She then learns a tough lesson that nothing is free and has to face the music to pay off her account. (Incidentally, one of the best scenes is when Lisa buys fake earbuds so her friends will think she has a MyPod. Just goes to show how important having the latest technology is to today's digital youth—in cartoon towns and every town USA.)

These issues may seem surprising but really are not. Just as kids push limits off-line, they do just the same online—it's just a bit harder to detect. At the core, though, kids and teens are true to themselves. What we have to learn is to be true to ourselves and parent in this new digital world as we so adeptly do in the non-digital world. This book will show you how and help you apply what you already know how to do off-line to the online and digital worlds.

Birth of the Computer Age: A Double-edged Sword

How in the world did we get here? Today, we're grappling with kids so computer savvy that they're onto the latest and greatest new thing before we've even learned the old. Even more daunting than the progress of technology is the fact that none of this was around when we were kids in a usable way. It was all very advanced and so surreal, none of us could imagine any of it becoming even remotely close to the digital era we are experiencing with our kids right now.

I'm certain that when the first computers emerged on the scene, my parents and the parents of my friends were not remotely interested in their effect on our developing minds. By the time we were exposed to computers in a learning environment, we were in middle school. I still recall vividly my seventh-grade math teacher dragging this gigantic cart down the hall to show us the school's new computer. It was enormous; must have been the size of a 24-inch TV with the weight of about 3 combined. It ran off of a disk operating system (DOS) and had a very gray screen. It didn't leave us with the impression that it was worth paying attention to.

Flash forward 5 years and computers were now user-friendly and more than big boxes with gray screens that required very advanced computer skills to operate. Not only were they smaller, but they could actually do things that were useful, like word processing. As I graduated high school and entered college, desktop and simple laptop computers were emerging and revolutionized our ability to do schoolwork. Keep in mind, the Internet was still years away, but at least we could type, save, and print without going through drafts and drafts on a typewriter!

The computer age seemed to move quickly back then but not as quickly as it's moving today. Now the technology has become so advanced, modifications and new applications seem to emerge at the blink of an eye, are more portable, and are much more user-friendly.

Computers today replace many things we used to have to leave our homes to do. Growing up, not that long ago, movies were an outing. Now, they are a click away. We used to have to go the music store to get the newest record from our favorite artist and hope it wasn't sold out. No need to worry about that today—all music is available online by download and on the day of release to anyone interested. Not too long ago, cell phones were a novelty and landlines were our main focus. Now, landlines are becoming extinct and cell phones are becoming the way we communicate by voice, Internet, or text. We can even shop online and have just about everything delivered to our front door, even on weekends. Long gone are the days of unique stores where only certain merchandise could be found.

Beyond practicalities and our social lives, the rise of the digital age has had a profound effect on our kids. When we were kids, computers were a novelty and didn't affect our childhoods one bit. Our childhoods were essentially "low-tech"—we had time just to play and enjoy life after school. For our kids, however, computers are a staple and they are actually more expert users of them most of the time than we are. Our kids' lives are very connected with their peers and family and very "fast" all around, in school, online, and after school. Experts in the pediatric and child psychiatry worlds agree that this pace of childhood is concerning and needs to be curtailed. We do have to ask if the "hurried child" phenomenon David Elkind wrote about more than a decade ago is now uber-amplified by all the extra watts, plugs, radio waves, Web sites, chat rooms, and the myriad of other high-tech influences on our kids. Frankly, TV is the least of their worries.

New Media and Child Health

While Lisa Simpson provided us a wonderful make-believe example of our teens' digital lives, the issues our tweens and teens are grappling with and our inability to parent effectively in that space are captured daily in headlines. These headlines are flares as well as beacons.

To give you a sense of the type of headlines occurring daily, here's a sampling of a search I did in the summer of 2009 using the phrases "MySpace and teens" and "Facebook and teens."

- "Teens hang out at MySpace": Yesterday's street corner has gone online.[1]
- "Doc Reaches Out to Misbehaving Teens on MySpace": One doctor utilizes a popular online site to change risky online posting behavior with success![2]
- "MySpace Bug Leaks 'Private' Teen Photo to Voyeurs": A MySpace glitch creates a backdoor into private settings, allowing people to see private photos on profiles.[3]
- "Teens Ambushed, Beaten Over MySpace Posting": One teen's MySpace posting resulted in a calculated beating that was videotaped and posted on YouTube.[4]
- "Family Sues MySpace After Teen Commits Suicide": Sad reports of 2 teens who committed suicide after contact with people they met via MySpace.[5]

Not the ideal image of our teenagers, but realistic. If you read through these headlines, you'll also notice that they cross through all cultures and socioeconomic groups.

Digging a bit deeper into the online world, other headlines reveal some unsettling information about not only the teen culture but the parenting culture.

- "Teens use Internet to share drug stories": One of many online stories about how teens use the Internet to feed their drug habits.[6] Your teens could be using drugs without you knowing. With a bit of insight into what to look for, you could be a step ahead of them—online and at home.
- "Parents: Cyber Bullying Led to Teen's Suicide": This is a story we all likely have heard about and should not forget because it helps us understand the dangers of anonymity online and how powerful that unseen persona can be.[7] Beyond bullying, Megan's untimely death raises many questions about the online safety of our kids that we need to understand. I hope if nothing else, making more people aware of this issue will help more kids be safe online.
- "Police say MySpace page had nude photos and videos of middle school students": Pornography or teen wildness gone awry?[8] Regardless, nude photos of underage minors online can never be allowed. This is a good example of the dangers of Web sites where teens can have profiles parents are not aware of and how necessary it is that parents know where our kids have profiles and check them often.
- "Parents Often Unaware of Cyber Bullying": This article summarizes the results of a study that concludes that 70% of kids are cyberbullied, yet only 1 in 10 kids tell their parents about it.[9] Bullying vehicles included instant messaging (IMing), e-mail, MySpace, and Facebook. Two-thirds of the victims knew their cyberbullies and half of the bullies were known to the victims from school. Knowing what signs to look for and how to monitor your kids' online habits is one way to intervene and help your kids stay safe.
- "Learn how to get drunk - on You Tube": A study from the US Office of National Drug Control Policy (ONDCP) conducted in June 2008 revealed that 5% of teens are using the Internet to view drug-related videos.[10] It concluded that parents need to monitor their teens' online lives by checking browser histories, cell phone logs, and IM chat logs. John Waters, ONDCP director, said this wasn't "censorship" but "parental supervision." That's it in a nutshell—it's all a matter of knowing what to look for under the hood of the World Wide Web in your homes.

It's time we faced 3 important facts.

1. Kids and teens are online more than any generation before them, and savvy and facile with today's many technologies and online venues. But the ability to use does not correlate with the ability to understand how the technology should be used.
2. Technology is changing very quickly, with new applications on the scene each year that may not be on the radar the year before, and with new ways for our kids and teens to find good and not-so-good uses for those technologies.
3. The biggest reason our kids and teens get into trouble online with any technology or venue is not because they are evil, malicious, or taken over by aliens but because they are kids—still developing and not quite grasping the greater world around them.

We were all young once and have had at least one moment where we demonstrated poor judgment. Over time, we've softened our internal criticism of ourselves because we've come to understand that being so young, it was unlikely we could have made a more sound decision—the ways of youth and innocence are not always protective. In fact, they can sometimes put even the smartest of kids in harm's way.

When we were young we may have done a great many things we wish we could take back, from defying our parents, to dabbling with drugs and alcohol, to dating the "wrong" type of person, to pushing the boundaries of what to wear. The technologies we had were TV, radio, and automobiles, so we'd push those limits when we could.

Today's kids pull the same stunts but with more sophisticated technology, such as the MP3 audio player and the computer. Kids are so bonded with these technologies and crave them so much that these themes have become fodder for some of the more popular sophisticated cartoons, such as *The Simpsons*.

So the questions remain: How do we keep our kids safe online? How do we reach our kids? Let's not try and race them with today's technology. We'll lose. But we still have an edge in brain power, and collectively that's how we keep our kids safe when venturing into any area of the cyber-world.

This book will be your universal translator for answering these questions by sorting out the online world of kids, tweens, and teens. We'll walk together through the various aspects of what is happening today on the World Wide Web. If all goes well, you'll soon not only be as savvy as your kids but also a step ahead. You will know when to put your hand up and say, "Not so fast!" Technology is fast and sometimes being hurried can be very dangerous—once you hit that "send" or "enter" button online, there is no turning back. We know that, but do our kids?

We have to understand these technologies better to know how they should and should not be used. We have to recognize where the real world begins and ends and help our kids develop boundaries around those worlds. And we have to be willing to step into the online world of our kids to help them negotiate the tricky waters, learn the rules, learn from our adult experience, and be safe.

Becoming Untangled

It's not surprising that our kids have trouble negotiating the online world at times—they stumble in their off-line world too. That's to be expected; they are still growing and developing, still trying to process the ins and outs of what's expected of them in the world. Off-line life is challenging enough in this age group with their impulsivity and quick judgment calls. Add to that the anonymity and facelessness of the online world and we can start to see why issues begin to creep in.

Just as with their off-line lives, though, they have a safety net that we can enable for them: us.

Before we get to that, it's important to understand just how tangled our kids really are online. Think about the amount of technology they use a day, all involving the World Wide Web and instant communication. Between cell phones and computers, our kids are instantly connected to the world in a myriad of ways for a gigantic proportion of the day, sometimes using technologies we haven't even heard of and many times using those technologies simultaneously and at lightning speeds. My 14-year-old will often be IMing one friend while chatting on her phone and video conferencing with another. It's truly a sight to behold. I have enough trouble with just the phone and computer one at a time and am mocked mercilessly for that "archaic" use of technology. While my kids will sometimes reluctantly admit pride that I can edit a Web site, they will toss in that they are sure they could do it faster if they knew code. They are a card-holding member of today's high-tech kid culture, so I will plead the fifth and not even attempt to argue with them on this point!

I will, however, argue that they may know how to use technology faster than their "old" mom, but that doesn't make them smarter or a pro. And I'll further point out that being able to click keys at the speed of light and multitask with more gadgets than an octopus could juggle doesn't replace common sense or ensure their safety. Enter the eye roll, which increases in magnitude by age of tween and teen.

The Reality

Parry Aftab, Esq, executive director of WiredSafety.org and one of the world's premier cyber-safety experts and Internet safety lawyers, summarized the situation the best during a phone call: "Kids know more about technology. Parents know more about life."

We have to start embracing our ability to parent independent of technology and be less daunted by our kids' technologic prowess and even our own technologic deficiencies. In the end, those issues matter less than our ability to be consistent parents online and off!

As you'll see, the "digital divide" that you're heard tossed about isn't a gap in technology between us and our kids; it's a gap in our ability to parent and keep our kids safe in all realms with technology in the mix.

Many who came to America from across the ocean in the late 1800s or early 1900s spoke little or no English. Did that stop them from parenting? Of course not. As Ms Aftab noted in our conversation, parents back then never once abdicated their parenting despite communication issues, and children responded. Parents learned what they needed to communicate with those around them, sometimes with the help of their kids, to get through their day.

We need to do the same today. It's time we reclaim our parenting roles in all realms. This book will show you why it's so important with the online world and how you can begin to reclaim that important role back with your kids, whether they are very young or already teens. This book will also show you that technology need not be feared but embraced for all ages, and that the goal is achieving a healthy media diet as opposed to imposing restrictions or banning it altogether.

We're all slightly tangled in the Web. Becoming untangled is a matter of embracing our inner parent. You already do that so well off-line—let's start the journey to doing that online!

References

1. Kornblum J. Teens hang out at MySpace. *USA Today* Tech Web site. Available at: http://www.usatoday.com/tech/news/2006-01-08-myspace-teens_x.htm. Published January 8, 2006. Updated January 9, 2006. Accessed March 2, 2010

2. Brownstein J. Doc reaches out to misbehaving teens on MySpace. ABC News/ Health Web site. Available at: http://www.abcnews.go.com/Health/ story?id=6581085&page=1. Published January 6, 2009. Accessed March 2, 2010

3. Poulsen K. MySpace bug leaks 'private' teen photos to voyeurs. *Wired* Web site. Available at: http://www.wired.com/politics/security/news/2008/01/myspace. Published January 17, 2008. Accessed March 2, 2010

4. Teen ambushed, beaten over MySpace posting. WOAI Web site. Available at: http://www.woai.com/news/local/story/Teen-Ambushed-Beaten-Over-MySpace-Posting/lW9q1QDf2k6e6N52MsHGPw.cspx. Published April 8, 2008. Accessed March 2, 2010

5. Hansson W. Family sues MySpace after teen commits suicide. DailyTech Web site. Available at: http://www.dailytech.com/Family+Sues+MySpace+After+Teen+Com mits+Suicide/article10013.htm. Published December 13, 2007. Accessed March 2, 2010

6. Leinwand D. Teens use Internet to share drug stories. *USA Today* News Web site. Available at: http://www.usatoday.com/news/nation/2007-06-18-online_N.htm. Published June 18, 2007. Updated June 19, 2007. Accessed March 2, 2010

7. Parents: cyber bullying led to teen's suicide. *Good Morning America* Web site. Available at: http://abcnews.go.com/GMA/Story?id=3882520. Published November 19, 2007. Accessed March 2, 2010

8. Meenan K. Police say MySpace page had nude photos and video of middle school students. First Coast News Web site. Available at: http://www.firstcoastnews.com/ news/news-article.aspx?storyid=100128. Accessed May 6, 2010

9. Parker-Pope T. Parents often unaware of cyber bullying. *New York Times* Health [blog]. Available at: http://well.blogs.nytimes.com/2008/10/03/parents-often-unaware-of-cyber-bullying. Published October 3, 2008. Accessed March 2, 2010

10. Reuters. Learn how to get drunk - on YouTube. Available at: http://www.stuff. co.nz/4720222a28.html. Published August 10, 2008. Accessed March 2, 2010

Part 1

The Internet Unplugged

Chapter 1

Old Versus New Media

It's the ultimate irony that I'm using an old media venue, a book, to talk about the consummate new media forms that our kids use in today's society. I have no doubt we'll always have books but can't help but wonder if the days of the true print industry are numbered as the digital world slowly stakes its claim in all aspects of our lives.

People are still reading, just online. According to a Pew Research Center for the People and the Press survey conducted in December 2008, the amount of adults now using the Internet for news has increased to 40%, up from 24% in 2007. Print newspapers, meanwhile, are holding steady at 35% readership. Interestingly, for adults, the under-30 crowd prefers the Internet for news, while the primary news source for the over-30 crowd is still TV.[1]

Depending on your own digital habits, this may or may not come as a surprise to you; given what you see around you in your own community, it should not. More people are adopting the Internet as their primary source of information for just about everything. Over time, you may find yourself struggling with this issue as you opt in for more digital subscriptions and opt out of more print subscriptions. Even books are becoming more digital as technologies such as the Amazon Kindle become more advanced and sophisticated.

With the book and publication industry changing dramatically, it's anyone's guess what it will look like by the time you read this chapter. Will everyone still be reading books? Will e-book readers be all the rage? What about newspapers? Will they even still be around for you to read book reviews, or will you be getting all those online?

The changes we can visibly see in the publishing world are a reflection of the greater battle of old versus new media that has been building in strength, intensity, and impact throughout the past decade. If this conflict were a baseball game, we'd be in the bottom of the ninth inning with the bases loaded, a full count, and 2 outs. New media is in the field with its closer on the mound. Old media's power hitter is at bat, down to her last strike. The pitcher accepts his signs, winds up, and woosh! A 98 mile per hour fast ball goes flying toward the old media batter who, with a determined swing, goes for it…but misses. The power of new media just proved too much. Old media leaves the field, determined to return with a new focus.

Will the focus be online? Off-line? A combination? That's where we are today, and the signs where the path will lead are mixed. Will the teams even look the same, or will they blend more? Will old media even be back for another season? This is an industry in transition with its players uncertain of their future. There are some early scouting reports, though, to give us an idea of where this may be heading. Fans love the new media team. It has a fancy park with amazing designs on the wall and easy-to-use kiosks that give you anything you want at the touch of a button. You don't even need any money. The entire park is automated. The team uniforms are incredibly slick and colorful and sometimes change during the game for extra flare. But some fans find the bells and whistles too much. Some still prefer the old media team.

The old media ballpark is basic but usable. It has everything you need but not many frills. It is friendly and clean and gets the job done. It definitely heralds back to a different time, and you can sense the history as you walk the halls, which are warm and filled with charm. The old media uniforms are mostly black and white and never change but are incredibly classy and classic. Fans love the old styling and look to them for comfort in times of trouble. Not having those around seems unthinkable to many faithful followers. Everything within its walls is well vetted before taking the field but operates incredibly slowly compared with the new media team, and that is frustrating to many fans.

Many people find the distinction between old and new media confusing, but it's really quite straightforward. Hot-button issues are keeping up with the new media and keeping pace with our kids, who are beyond capable of using the stuff.

Understanding new versus old is essential because new media is what our kids are all about. New media is what they are interested in and what pulls them online and gets their fingers clicking on keyboards large and small. In a nutshell,

- **Old media:** This group includes all pre-Internet media and communications venues and technologies. Under this umbrella you'll find all non-digital TV (including cable), radio, all print products (eg, books, magazines, comics), movies, and non-digital music. Content creation and publication of content are not user generated in the old media world but controlled by the parent company. Turnaround time for old media is typically slow because of production time. Sharing is typically via the traditional business model of purchasing the right to use, such as buying a newspaper to read an article or buying the CD to listen to music.

- **New media:** This group includes everything that has evolved since the creation of the Internet, including the Internet itself and any device that can receive electronic information. So the Internet, podcasting, video casting, Web sites, blogs, MP3 players, and all user-generated content sites including social networking sites fall under this umbrella. Old media venues that include new media frills such as videos, DVD, and Internet content are also included in this category. Content creation and publication are not only user generated but user controlled and available almost instantaneously, with zero lead time to the public if that is what the publisher desires. Sharing is the philosophy of new media, and the more eyeballs and ears on a venue, the better.

Evolving from old to new media has affected our online experiences, how we use digital applications, and the business of the media world at large. While outside the scope of this book, I will note that the definition of *journalist* has changed as new media has taken root in our society. Once something you needed a degree in and housed in a specific media group (print, radio, or TV), today's journalist includes anyone who blogs, video blogs (vlogs), tweets, or runs a Web site. This was clear during the 2008 presidential campaign, during which bloggers were part of the official press corps and were "live blogging" the events and interviews. We see this at conferences and events where being a blogger is enough to get a press pass. At the 2009 Health 2.0 conference, I was at one of at least a dozen tables of new media journalists covering the event, sitting among "old" media journalists. The press room was nonexistent because we could do our job from our iPhone or laptop, compliments of the Wi-Fi at the event.

What may be helping the old media print world at the moment is the fact that many of us still value those venues because we grew up with them. We so-called "digital immigrants" remember the days of 100% old media and still often prefer flipping through the pages of a book or magazine. Reading online still sometimes feels foreign to us, and downloading music from an online store just doesn't feel the same to many of us as the monthly trek to the hometown record store to get the new releases of our favorite artists. We also value how well edited and vetted traditional publishing materials are compared with new media content produced today.

But those were our lives, not our children's lives; they are "digital natives," born into an all-digital world. With a few remnants of old media tossed in, they really don't know anything but what they are living—the digital age. Sure, they read books and magazines, but they are equally comfortable reading online. In fact, many prefer it.

We don't need to look at more studies and reports to confirm that Internet use is on the rise. We can see it in all aspects of our lives, from commerce to education to health care. But it does help to see data to gain a perspective of just how plugged in and digital our world has become, especially since 2007. It's as if the new media took a sudden gulp of an energy drink and overtook old media with no signs of slowing down. In November 2008, Harris Interactive reported that 4 out of 5 adults were online and were spending 14 hours a week online, up from 11 hours in 2007.[2]

In October 2008 eMarketer.com reported 2 important trends. First, some old media venues, such as local and national newspapers, are still alive and are holding their own, while other old media venues, such as overall TV, are steadily declining. Second, some new media venues, such as shopping Web sites, social networking sites, blogs, and videocasts, are clearly on the rise.[3]

These data are almost identical to the Pew Internet and American Life Project Generations Online, a study that summarizes each generation's online use.[4]

However, Pew and Harris point out something that parents have to be realistic about—there are generational differences in online use. For example, while most generations are using social networking sites more than in the past, they are the most popular among teens and Generation Y (18–34 years) and begin to decline with the Generation X population (34–44 years) and the baby boomers. So the people parenting the kids most online are not online where the kids are—they are doing other things online! This discrepancy has been referred to as the *digital divide*.

Just like with online use itself, we didn't need these data to know there was an issue with how we use digital media compared with our kids, especially our tweens (8–12 years) and teens (13–18 years). In public places where families gather, the differences become very obvious. Parents often have some digital hardware, perhaps a phone, but also a book or newspaper. Kids will be all digital. Just walk along a beach or by the chairs at your public pool on a summer's day and this will pop right out at you. The blankets or chairs of a digital native will be covered with cell phones and MP3 players, next to the sunblock and towel. Parents' chairs, however, will likely have a cell phone but also something in paper to read, a book or magazine.

In many ways, new and old media are an evolution from one generation of technology to another. Once thought of as 2 sides of a coin, new and old media are more like 2 closely related flavors of ice cream that, when mixed just the right way, can create an entirely new flavor to propel the media industry in a new and more robust direction.

There's a natural momentum taking us in that new direction. There's something about new media that is attractive to all people because of how powerfully it can define us and connect us at the same time. *TIME* magazine, in fact, named the 2006 person of the year *you* for this very reason.[5]

If nothing else, we are curious at all ages and in different ways. It's age-old knowledge that teens have their own language that parents never seem to understand, so we shouldn't be surprised that our kids have adapted to the digital world with a language suited for that space. Our job is to be curious enough and care enough about what they are doing in that space to understand and speak that language, so we can speak to and understand our kids. At the same time, we have to remember a sobering fact—many of us are from the last generation that will be able to recall a pre-digital life. Our kids are the first generation to truly live all digital. The further we go without catching up to our digital kids, the more upstream we will end up without a paddle to get back.

In the end, we have to provide our kids with a road map to have a healthy digital diet and show them there is a world full of activities that are unplugged. In just a few chapters, you'll see that helping our kids do that really isn't so difficult, even when dealing with teens.

Part of this road map is helping our kids understand the rules of the road; to do that, we need to know the rules too. We need to have a healthy perspective of what and what not to worry about. We need to know the pit stops of the roads and the controls to avoid flying out of control. I'll cover all of these issues in the coming pages.

If you look at the big picture of Internet safety and the digital world, parenting around those issues is no different that parenting any other issue. Think of it like this: would you just toss your kids the keys to your car and let them drive if they were not the right age and did not have the right practice and training? Of course not! Well, we've basically done that online. Now we have to backpedal and quickly learn to drive the online world ourselves so we can toss the keys to them when it is the right time and in the right way.

Where do we start? Understanding the Internet and the search engine Google helps to keep our kids stay safe online. We'll begin our journey with a quick tour of the Internet and Google. Then you'll be ready for the fun stuff—a tour of the new media world your kids are living in right now, whether you know it or not!

References

1. Internet overtakes newspapers as news outlet. Pew Research Center for the People and the Press Web site. Available at: http://people-press.org/report/479/internet-overtakes-newspapers-as-news-outlet. Published December 23, 2008. Accessed March 2, 2010
2. Four out of five adults now use the Internet. Harris Interactive Web site. Available at: http://www.harrisinteractive.com/harris_poll/index.asp?PID=973. Published November 17, 2008. Accessed March 2, 2010
3. Traditional media use stabilizes as online rises. emarketer Web site. Available at: http://www.emarketer.com/Article.aspx?R=1006892. Published January 29, 2009. Accessed March 2, 2010
4. Jones S, Fox S. Generations online in 2009. PewResearchCenter Publications Web site. Available at: http://pewresearch.org/pubs/1093/generations-online. Published January 28, 2009. Accessed March 2, 2010
5. Grossman L. Time's person of the year: you. TIME magazine Web site. Available at: http://www.time.com/time/magazine/article/0,9171,1569514,00.html. Published December 13, 2006. Accessed March 2, 2010

Chapter 2

The World of Google

Who's on Google, and Why Should We Care?

One fall day in the Midwest when my oldest daughter was a toddler, we were experiencing what we had come to know and love as a "basic" Midwestern thunderstorm. These things would roll in without much warning and pack quite a punch. Typically, they'd occur during nap time, bedtime, or quiet time, just to add fun to a busy parent's day.

This particular day, the storm occurred mid-morning when I was attempting to quiet her down. I had promised her a few minutes of *Sesame Street* and then a book. Just my luck—as the show came on, crack! The power went out instantly and I heard the sizzle of the transformer down the street, having just been struck by a bolt of lightening.

She was used to reading books before a nap, so I figured we'd just move that familiar low-tech plan to the forefront and move on with our day until the transformer was juiced back up.

My daughter was not quite as cooperative as I expected. Even at her young age, she was quite upset by the power being out. In her mind, the beeper not talking to the TV was quite a blow to her morning. "Elmo?" she kept asking. Luckily, at her young age, she was still quite distractible, but that morning left quite an impression on me. Even for the very young, the power of technology was gigantic and trumped anything low tech I could offer for a bit of time.

Flash forward a decade; with the Internet in our homes, we often take for granted that we'll have instant access to anything our hearts desire 24/7, especially when we wake up and get our day going. We count on that Googling fix as we do our morning cup o' joe; if something happens to disrupt our Internet connection, a down server or cable outage, our days become frozen and off-kilter for more time than any of us want to admit.

I often wonder if Google had any clue that the world of search would have such power over our lives when it launched its first search engine in 1998. I wonder even more if any of us had any clue the power the Internet would have on our lives when we wired up our homes with broadband over the past decade. According to the Pew Research Center Internet & American Life Project, teens with broadband access have increased from 50% to approximately 65%, while their parents have increased their broadband access from approximately 35% to 40% to 65% between 2005 and 2008. By 2009, nearly 80% of teens and 90% of adults had broadband access.[1]

If you take a step back, it's amazing to think just how connected we've become in just a short amount of time in our life span. At the same time, this amount of connectivity is all our kids have ever known. It's amazing to think of the effect the Internet has had on our lives given how little it's been around in our lives!

As adults, the Internet has transformed how we live our lives, from shopping, to hunting for information, to reading books. It has also revolutionized the concept of socializing now that social networking has come of age.

We have to have a healthy perspective that our kids are not the only ones spending huge amounts of time with digital technology. In fact, adults are actually leading the way in that arena. If you believe the adage "the apple doesn't fall far from the tree," perhaps our kids are not just hooked on digital technology solely because of its allure but also because we are too, and they are learning some of their habits of use from us.

In 2009, Nielsen documented that Internet use among teens is very similar to their parents but not nearly as lengthy as any of us had predicted. In the first quarter of 2009, Nielsen showed that teens were online for an average of only 11 hours a month, compared with the adult average of 29 hours a month for all adult generations.[2] That same year, Pew documented that we have much in common with our kids in our Internet habits but differ in some important ways. For example, all generations go online to use e-mail, search and do research, and get news. Teens dominate the digital world in gaming, video watching, music downloads, instant messaging, virtual world creation, social networking, and blogs, while we dominate in health information hunting, online shopping, going to government Web sites, religious information hunting, and online banking. There is a bit of overlap in small groups, but by and large we are not where our kids and teens are online![3]

Despite our generational difference, all generations search the 'net. Launched in 1998, Google has become not just a search engine but a state of being and an action itself. If you tell a friend you spent the morning

"Googling," your friend will know exactly what you were up to. If your child needs to find some information online, you are likely to say "try a Google search," even if your family happens to have a different search engine installed on your computers! Web searching, Googling, is truly one of the few shared Web experiences that spans all generations.

What's interesting is that we spend so much time learning the features of our TV sets, dishwashers, and vacuum cleaners, yet we don't pay much attention to our Internet searches. Similarly, we put our knives up high, cover our outlets from small fingers, and put gates up so toddling children don't go where they don't belong, yet we don't spend much time learning how to help our kids learn safe Web searching.

We truly turn on and Google things every day and allow kids of all ages to do so without so much as a second thought compared with just about everything else we do in our lives. It's time we changed that thinking.

The world of the Internet is not something we should take for granted or drive without understanding the user's manual. We don't have to become Internet experts or even know how to create Web pages; all we have to do is understand the basics of what we use each day so we can keep ourselves and our kids safe and sound.

Our journey begins with the one activity we share with our kids, the one activity many of us do every day and take for granted that is responsible for not only our digital footprints but for getting us into the most trouble when we click first and think second—Web searching (or Googling to refer to Web searching in a more general sense).

The Game of Search

Googling takes some finesse to pull off well. The World Wide Web has an amazing amount of information, and if you don't know what you are looking for, you can find yourself spending huge amounts of time searching without finding what you are seeking. You can also find a great deal of content that is distasteful and unwelcome, content you don't want your kids seeing at any age without some significant discussions.

This is where age, experience, and skill come into play and why we need to build up our own online skills and not just rely on our kids. Right now we are talking about Web searching, but our kids do a lot more online and all at once! They are multitaskers who may be searching, sending out electronic invitations (also known as evites), and socially connecting with friends via Facebook or MySpace all at the same time. The best way to help our kids make competent decisions online is to know the online world like we know the off-line world, so we can parent both. That way we will have confidence that when they search they will know when not to click on a Web address or when to get some help.

There is a big difference between being able to use technologies and understanding how to use technologies. We can't misconstrue being born digital with having the judgment to understand how to negotiate that world.

The Search Is On

The online world is really one big treasure hunt. The map is written in invisible ink and your "X marks the spot" won't come to light until you figure out what your treasure truly is. Our online treasures have a way of molting as we go and sometimes change altogether, so we have to stay very focused. There are also times when we have no clue at all what we are looking for, just a vague concept; Web searches are geared up for that kind of hunt too.

Searching is based on the concept of *key words* that allow search engines to match up what you type with Web sites. The more specific you are with your key words, the better your search results will be. These days, Web people have figured out how to label Web sites with commonly searched key words to help make your search more successful; that helps you minimize time and not worry so much about being too vague. The bigger issue is sorting out which site to click on once the results pop up after you've done your search.

For example, say you are looking for information on the flu, a commonly searched-for term during the 2009 flu season with seasonal flu and H1N1 issues. When the results appear, would you know the difference between a Web site and a blog? Would you be able to tell if the material were generated by a true expert or an interested individual? If you are unsure how to verify a Web site's content, imagine how your kids feel!

To add insult to injury, did you know that search results are one big game? That's right—the sites listed at the top of a search page may not actually be the most reliable and "best" site for that result. All the top sites indicate is that those sites are well optimized. *Search engine optimization* is the technical term for how Web developers tag the content of sites with key words so that search engines such as Google and Yahoo! will notice them above all others and rank them higher in the group.

Google is number 1 by a wide margin, but there are many other search engines online today that will get us where we want to go. However, Google is the only one whose name happens to be synonymous with the common act of Internet searching, and that gives it a special place online. No other Internet company has had its name generalized in the online Web language quite that way, and by all cultures and ages worldwide.

For the longest time, the top 5 Internet search sites were relatively constant—Google, Yahoo!, MSN, AOL, and Ask.com. By mid-2009, that began to change, as people's search habits began to change and as new search engines started to enter the scene. The spot in hot contention seems to be the number 2 spot, for the longest time held by Yahoo! YouTube, now owned by Google, is now surpassing Yahoo! as the number 2 site used for search, as is Bing, Microsoft's newest player to the search scene.[4,5] These trends tell us where the online action is and give us a place to start our hunts when we start talking about things like digital footprints (a concept I'll cover in Chapter 17).

Search engines also help us get a sense of where our kids likely are. While we may not be spending a great deal of time on YouTube, given the nature of the site, it's a safe bet our tweens and teens are, even if they don't admit to it. These trends matter, and it's clear that "to Google" could refer to any one of a variety of popular search engines.

What matters more than popularity of search engines is sheer numbers of use. Google alone reports 2 billion visits with 140 million unique visitors a month, just to give you a sense of the magnitude of total Internet searches. What about individual use? According to an August 2008 Pew Internet and American Life Project report, nearly half of all Internet users now search the Internet (up from only one-third in 2002) and do so more often than other online activities such as checking the news or weather (but still not quite as much as the number one online activity—checking e-mail, which 60% of users do per day).[6]

Searching: Kids' Style

The Internet is an invaluable tool for parents and kids of all ages. However, "Parents and kids use the Internet differently," notes Parry Aftab, Esq, of WiredSafety.org. "Parents tend to use it for booking airline travel, work, research, pictures, and communication. For them it's a tool. Kids use it as an environment."

Ms Aftab's observation is confirmed by recent data from Pew Internet Generations Online. In that report, a health search was the fourth most common online activity for parents, whereas for teens health search fell to number 14 out of 17![1] Interestingly, other than news in general, health information was the only specific topic teens tended to search for. The Pew report didn't show search as an important activity for the teens but did for parents. What was the important activity for teens? Interactive and social networking activities, confirming Ms Aftab's comment that our children use the Internet as an extension of their environment.

Successful Internet search requires not just academic skills but life experience as well. Depending on our kids' ages, there will be hurdles with being successful with a search that we have to recognize out of the gate. In addition to the logistics, interpreting the results will be a challenge to many.

Consider this experience like going to a restaurant. By the time our kids go to their first one with us, they are very familiar with the food on the menu and in front of them on their plates. As they get older, their experience with different foods allows them to extrapolate when the food gets a bit fancier and is presented a bit differently from what they may be used to. They also learn to tell the difference between food that is well prepared and food that is not so well prepared. Not so with 2 of the most important aspects of the Internet, searching and understanding Web sites. While children have familiarity with features that they enjoy, they uniformly lack experiences to assess the "menu" presented to them on a search, meaning the interpretation of the search results may elude them!

Tweens and teens think differently than adults and that will make searching challenging. Searching requires identifying the needle in a haystack sometimes. Kids may not be able to do that. Kids also may have issues with spelling and may think more in phrases than words. All these variables will make a search challenging for them.

To add insult to injury, searching on unfiltered, mainstream search engines opens the door to online places that our kids are not ready to be exposed to—some are too adult, and there are pornographic areas online that are simply not appropriate for anyone under 18.

The Web world has stepped up to help us with kid-oriented searches just as restaurants have created kid- and teen-friendly menus. There are some fantastic kid-safe search engines online that contain preapproved and pre-previewed content so our kids will have a safe search experience. Many of these sites have home pages akin to our adult home pages with kid-friendly news and facts, too. According to Ms Aftab, Yahoo! Kids and KidZui are the best online search sites for kids younger than 10.

If your child needs a more robust search engine, you can use Google, Yahoo!, MSN, Bing, or whatever your search engine of choice is and set the filters to whatever level you feel most comfortable with for your child's age and stage. This will allow your child to have access to more of the World Wide Web, but just know that the filters are not 100% and your child may still end up on some undesirable sites. This is an acceptable trade-off if your child is mature and you have a pact in place to inform you when this occurs.

By the time our kids are tweens and certainly teens, they are ready for "real" search engines. By this time, they should understand safe searching and you will have instilled some great Internet safety concepts in them to keep them out of trouble. Experts agree this is the appropriate age for kids to be on unfiltered search engines, and homework and development interests make that decision appropriate as well.

Beyond basic search for terms and ideas, some kids do well with focusing on specific Web sites they learn about from friends, teachers, and librarians. You can "collect" these Web sites for your kids in their bookmark folder on your computer or on a "bookmark and share" account so your child can access favorite sites from any computer that has an Internet connection. (Incidentally, this is a great way to organize information that can be accessed virtually; I'll address this more fully in Chapter 16.)

You'll find that your kids' librarians and teachers are some of your best sources for Web information, especially searching. Encourage children of all ages to ask them for help with Web searches, then discuss the results of their quest at dinner!

The final option for assisting our kids with their Web searches is to function as their search tech support. Instead of doing the search for your kids, ask them to provide you key words for the search. The best way to get at this is to have them describe the search to you and to start typing in their terms and see what the search engine churns out. Use the opportunity to point out that strong key worlds yield good results; weaker ones, not so great results.

For example, if your child is hunting for information on the history of chocolate, he or she will get more useful information hunting for specific candies as opposed to "chocolate," which is generic.

The one area that stumps kids and adults is searching for health information. This is a different cup of tea than searching for any other information online given the consequences of finding inaccurate information and the plethora of poor information. But it's important for your kids to be able to ask questions and get answers. The key to health searches is to help them understand what I like to call "the Dr Google effect," which is covered more in Chapter 4.

Search: The Beginning, Not the End

Web searching is the bread and butter of just about every aspect of the Internet, including sites such as Facebook, MySpace, and Twitter. If we all learn to master searching and help our kids understand it, we've gone a long way in making our time online not only more efficient but a lot more safe.

References

1. Jones S, Fox S. Broadband access has increased for many age groups. In: Generations online in 2009. Pew Internet and American Life Project Web site. Available at: http://www.pewinternet.org/Reports/2009/Generations-Online-in-2009/Part-2-Broadband-access.aspx?r=1. Published January 28, 2009. Accessed March 2, 2010

2. Covey N. Breaking teen myths. NielsenWire Web site. Available at: http://blog.nielsen.com/nielsenwire/online_mobile/breaking-teen-myths. Published August 3, 2009. Accessed March 2, 2010

3. Jones S, Fox, S. Generational differences in online activities. In: Generations online in 2009. Pew Internet and American Life Project Web site. Available at: http://www.pewinternet.org/Reports/2009/Generations-Online-in-2009/Generational-Differences-in-Online-Activities/5-Video-downloadsare-now-enjoyed-more-

equally-by-young-and-old.aspx?r=1. Published January 28, 2009. Accessed March 2, 2010

4. Hill J. YouTube surpasses Yahoo as world's #2 search engine. TGDaily Web site. Available at: http://www.tgdaily.com/content/view/39777/113. Published October 16, 2008. Accessed March 2, 2010

5. Wauters R. Did Bing just leapfrog Yahoo search? TechCrunch Web site. Available at: http://www.techcrunch.com/2009/06/05/did-bing-just-leapfrog-yahoo-search. Published June 5, 2009. Accessed March 2, 2010

6. Fallows D. Search engine use [memo]. Pew Internet and American Life Project Web site. Available at: http://www.pewinternet.org/~/media/Files/Reports/2008/PIP_Search_Aug08.pdf.pdf. Published August 6, 2008. Accessed March 2, 2010

Chapter 3

An Internet Tour

During an interview in 1999, Al Gore told CNN's Wolf Blitzer that while he was in Congress he "took the initiative in creating the Internet." There has been a great deal of debate since then over what Gore actually meant. While initially some took Gore at face value to mean he literally invented the Internet, Gore later clarified that he was referring to the legislation he helped put in place that made the Internet we know today possible. In fact, Gore had been involved with the concept of computer-based communications since the 1970s and much of his work led to the formation of the current Internet. Gore himself actually coined the term *information superhighway,* and the "Gore bill," or the High Performance Computing and Communications Act of 1991, did indeed lay the groundwork of what would become today's Internet. So while he didn't invent the technology itself (the creation of the Internet dates back to the early 1960s), Al Gore was instrumental in moving the technologic infrastructure forward.[1,2]

In the case of the Internet and the World Wide Web, there was actually a cascade of events that paved the way for what we take for granted every day online. Having a sense of how this all came about is important to help us know where the technologic landscape is heading, how we are using the technology, and how kids and teens are using the technology.

Dawning of the Digital Native Generation

I was at a meeting recently about transitioning to high school. As I was listening to the presentation I was struck by how much education had changed since I first stepped foot in that very same school 30 years earlier. Presentation after presentation emphasized computers and the Internet. I had flashes of my experience in each subject with only books, reel movies, and audiotapes to guide my learning and research. Yet my daughter will have the complete 360-degree experience of any subject imaginable and any area around the globe. What a snapshot of the world she will leave high school with compared with the small still images I had.

As we search the Web each and every day, connecting with people and places near and far and finding resources that in our youth could only be housed in a library or found by librarians with the magic touch for finding obscure literature and research annals, it's easy to take for granted the Web's power and abilities, as well as to become intimidated by it, especially when we hit a technologic hiccup. Deconstructing the Internet will help you realize that you don't have to be a computer expert to understand this technology or become incredibly savvy in its applications. The best place to start is at the beginning, in its creation.

Using Technology: A Lesson From a Quest

My initial Google search of "history of the world wide web" turned up no less than 44,000,000 results. A search for "history of the internet" yielded 118,000,000 results. "World wide web history" yielded 31,200,000 results. "Internet and world wide web history" dropped the numbers down to 10,100,000.

The reliability of the search results was difficult to determine. The sources seemed all over the map, from computer companies to sites that were obviously popular. The only site that seemed to be on the top that had any semblance of potential accuracy was Wikipedia, an online, user-generated encyclopedia whose accuracy has been questioned. (As a side note, this exercise shows that search results are variable. You have to be careful when checking the validity of sources because sites are clever with *search engine optimization,* a Web method that allows site authors and developers to get their sites listed at the top of searches. Finding a site near the top does not necessarily mean it is the best. It just means that the site is well optimized.)

The Internet started off as a project for the Department of Defense as part of the Advanced Research Projects Agency (ARPA) in 1958 as a response to the Soviet Union launching Sputnik.[3] The early roots began in 1962 when the world had all of 10,000 computers; ARPA took steps to develop what would be the first rudimentary computer networking system that would later become today's Internet. The 1960s were all about planning for this system and involved many groups, from MIT to IBM to NASA. They all had a concept of networking via computers but no definitive technology. Key computer code and log-in systems we use today were all developed during this decade. In 1974 ARPA attempted to network together the many ARPA sites. The term *inter-networking* was coined, or Internet for short.

While early computers were large and not user-friendly, by the 1970s they started to become smaller and less expensive; they had operating systems that would give rise to home computing. Many of the inner workings of our modern home computers such as file transfer protocols (FTPs), e-mail with @ signs, and Internet protocols (IPs) were born during this period. By the end of the decade, computers were linked all over the globe, planting the seeds for our modern Internet.

The earliest Internet was a system for universities and the Department of Defense, but that began to change by the early 1980s as computers became smaller and faster thanks to the rise of the IBM and Apple personal computers and the domain name system (DNS). Common DNSs that we know, love, and still use today were developed at this time—.com, .net, .gov, and .edu.

What allowed us to finally have computers in our homes, however, was the 1991 Gore bill. This bill allowed the Internet to move from government and university use into commercial and private use. So in a way, Al Gore did invent the Internet—he paved the way for it to exist in the form that has revolutionized our lives and been the only lives our kids know. Without the Gore bill, Facebook, Twitter, Web sites, blogs, eBay, and the many other online destinations we know and love would never have been able to evolve.

Fast-forward to today, when there's an even greater evolution of technology that allows users to have more control in their online experience. The initial wave of static, traditional Web sites has been labeled Web 1.0, with subsequent, user-friendly Web sites referred to as Web 2.0. Actually, most of what's online today is Web 2.0 and the technologies called new media.

You are very familiar with the Web 2.0 world. This is the world of Facebook, MySpace, texting, instant messaging (IMing), Twitter, YouTube, Hulu, iTunes and other MP3 music sites, and blogs.

The shift in technology reflects a shift in focus of online use philosophy. Web 1.0 sites were about showcasing information and getting people, businesses, and groups online so people could just see what they were all about. Web 2.0 venues emerged out of a need to connect people and make the online experience not only more real for people but more user-friendly and personal. The goal shifted from the big business and group to the individual. The message shifted from the corporate mission statement and group philosophy to individual opinions.

Interestingly, the adaptation of our most popular Web 2.0 technologies may be relatively new, but the introduction of these venues is already some years old.

- **Blogs:** This is short for Web log and was first introduced in 1997 by Jorn Barger when he posted, in reverse chronologic order, a daily log of what he was reading and working on. The first popular blogging platforms emerged around 1998 and 1999. (Twitter CEO Evan Williams was one of the pioneers of Blogger, by the way.) Today there are more than 12 million blogs and counting, on multiple platforms.
- **Audio (MP3) downloads:** The first true online venue was Napster, which was online from 1999 to 2001. It was eventually shut down due to massive copyright violations of recording artists and is now a pay-for-downloaded music site.
- **Audio (MP3) devices:** First emerged around 1998. File sharing technologies started to evolve at this time as well, which is the foundation of our current download system in general.
- **iTunes:** A digital media playing application launched by Apple in 2001.
- **MySpace:** A social networking site founded in 2003 by eUniverse employees.
- **Facebook:** One of today's most popular social networking sites online, it was founded by 3 Harvard students in 2004.
- **Flickr:** A photo and video hosting company launched in 2004 by Ludicorp that includes social networking features.
- **YouTube:** A video sharing Web site created in 2005.
- **Twitter:** Created in 2006, this is a popular social networking and microblogging (very brief postings) site.

Cell phones have their own history, but newer features correlate with demand to have everything at your fingertips and be as connected to your networks as possible.

- **Cell phones with cameras:** The first digital camera phone entered the scene in 1997.
- **Cell phones with Web access:** Mobile telecommunications, or 3G, first emerged in Japan in 2001 and started to spread to other countries in 2003. Today, 3G is the network most people use and what allows

multimedia access from a cell phone, such as going online and accessing social networks. These phones are really handheld computers.

- **Cell phones with texting:** First on the scene in 1993, their popularity
  and global adoption started in 2003.

What This All Means

It's amazing to think that the Internet, part of the ebb and flow of our daily
lives that still feels so new in so many ways, is already a half-century old.
What's even more amazing is that most of the technology that has made
the Internet accessible is only a decade old, if that!

The hallmark of all the scientists and engineers involved in the Web 1.0
and Web 2.0 evolutions is that they are all visionaries and pioneers, especially the folks who figured out how to get us online from a completely
off-line world. Web 2.0 is amazing but they have technology to build from.
The original Internet developers didn't have any preexisting technology.
They had to model their ideas from their imaginations. That is perhaps
the most remarkable aspect of the entire enterprise.

Our kids reap the benefits of this overall genesis, but they still have to
grapple with the implications of how to use the technology. As digital
natives, technology is second nature to our kids. That's not the issue. What
is the issue is helping them see beyond their technologic savvy and understand that actions have consequences and that impulse sometimes needs
to be tempered with moderation and restraint. Those are tough traits for
kids of any age to exhibit, especially teens! Thankfully, as parents we can
help. We can be their voice of reason and superego as they work out their
consequences.

What you'll learn as you read on is that our kids are online pioneers. Their
ability to create and use new media is astounding. They are true superusers
who never seem to need tech support, a help line, or the user's guide. On
the other hand, parents are often a step behind. For that digital divide not
to become huge, we need to join their journey and learn what they learn.

Every time we go online, we are writing more of our own online history.
The more you go online, the more you'll be writing your own online history, too—also called your *digital footprint*. You have to remember that what
you and your kids do online is a form of history and will be preserved for a
long while, if not forever. How that information is archived and played

back is up to your ability to close the digital divide and speak your kids' language. By the end of this book, I'm confident you'll be there!

Resources

Internet history. Computer History Museum Web site. Available At: http://www.computerhistory.org/internet_history/index.html. Accessed March 2, 2010

Howe W. A brief history of the Internet. Walt Howe's Internet Learning Center Web site. Available at: http://www.walthowe.com/navnet/history. html. Updated September 1, 2009. Accessed March 2, 2010

History of the Internet. Wikipedia: The Free Encyclopedia Web site. Available at: http://en.wikipedia.org/wiki/History_of_the_Internet. Modified March 2, 2010. Accessed March 2, 2010

World Wide Web. Wikipedia: The Free Encyclopedia Web site. Available at: http://en.wikipedia.org/wiki/World_Wide_Web. Modified March 2, 2010. Accessed March 2, 2010

References

1. Al Gore and information technology. Wikipedia: The Free Encyclopedia Web site. Available at: http://en.wikipedia.org/wiki/Al_Gore_and_information_technology. Modified March 1, 2010. Accessed March 2, 2010
2. Al Gore. Wikipedia: The Free Encyclopedia Web site. Available at: http://en.wikipedia.org/wiki/Al_gore. Modified March 1, 2010. Accessed March 2, 2010
3. History. Defense Advanced Research Projects Agency Web site. Available at: http://www.darpa.mil/history.html. Accessed March 2, 2010

Chapter 4

Calling Dr Google

Health Literacy: The Basics

It's natural for kids and teens to have questions about their developing bodies and health in general, especially as their teen years arrive and sexuality kicks in. So it shouldn't be a surprise that the Internet is one of the major resources our kids and teens turn to for answers, especially when problems or concerns arise.

If adults have trouble finding information online, you can imagine how challenging this is for our kids. This is where online health literacy comes into play—understanding not just how to search but how to locate appropriate health information.

Hunting online for health information is a consumer task, similar to shopping for any other good or service we need for our home or family. At times, the health product we seek is very tangible and we truly do shop online, but most other times what we seek is more elusive and hard to define, and falls square in cyber-information land. That form of virtual shopping is much more challenging, even for savvy consumers and online power shoppers.

In the winter of 2009, our fancy furnace, powered by a high-tech system and computer, died—not the best timing given we live in the heart of New England! Our hometown plumber already had the situation well in hand but because it was a weekend, as all such events tend to land, we had to hit the Web to do a little homework to prepare for what was ahead. Would it be warm enough outside to heat our home with just a fireplace, or would we need to pack up for the evening and head to a hotel? What about the missing part—could we find an emergency on-call group that happened to have what our plumber needed? We were able to find the weather information we needed to realize it was in the best interests of all of us to head to a hotel but struck out in finding that missing part on a Sunday!

I'm sure you have similar stories of hunting online for home goods and services, whether it be for a new car, home appliance, new paint color for a room, summer camp for your kids, or even grocery shopping. All can be done from the comfort of our homes and with peace of mind—we have a sense of the validity of the information we are finding.

Not so with health information. The many different forms of health information today make the process of finding good, reliable information about as easy as finding a shiny needle in a haystack, unless you really know what you are seeking and have a sense of what you are looking for already.

You would think that the more educated and sophisticated a computer user is, the more health literate he or she would be. Yes and no. Higher education and computer skills do make it easier to read and understand the health information you are given, and make your online experience of searching and navigating relatively effortless, but that doesn't mean you have any more luck teasing through the many sites that initially come up in a search than someone who has slightly less education, especially if you are pushed out of your comfort zone, such as on a weekend or in an emergency.

I have a highly educated family member whose lips would swell up randomly for a few minutes, then subside. One weekend, his face became puffy after dinner out with friends. He wondered if he had developed a food allergy, even though it had never been an issue for him in the past, and he had dined at this particular restaurant before.

His symptoms got worse, but instead of alerting his wife or calling a doctor, he Googled "swollen tongue" and wondered if he was allergic to one of his medications. Two hours later he ended up in a local emergency department (ED) where it was confirmed he had developed an allergy to a blood pressure medication that he had been on for quite a while but was known to pull such nonsense over time.

When I heard this story, I couldn't help wonder that if this educated man had trouble sorting through the issue of when to call for help and when to Google, others must have trouble as well.

Once he was out of the ED and the reaction subsided, I had a chance to ask him what he ended up finding online. He told me it was very, very challenging: "Many blogs and Web sites. It was hard to know what to read."

That is the million-dollar question with health information searches— what do you read online and how do you figure out the source?

These are the key issues in online health literacy. Luckily, there are a few telltale signs a Web site is reliable and worth perusing and not a more opinionated sites that may be fun and interesting to read but won't give you the reliable, valid health information about you, a family member, or your child when you need it the most.

Web Speak: Knowing What You Are Reading

When you buy a new car or appliance, you have reviews and ratings to go by, as well as lists of recalls and warnings to alert you to products that may not be the best to pursue. This can be of enormous help in deciding where to put your money and avoiding lemons!

For online health information, caveat emptor, let the buyer beware, should be your driving principle. Why? Simple! Even well-written, sleek-appearing Web sites and blogs can be the master of deception in a number of ways.

1. **Authors and experts:** The site may have generic authors and not true experts, so the information you are reading may be secondhand or even thirdhand from the source. This doesn't mean the information isn't reliable, but it's always helpful to know the author so you can verify the accuracy of the information.

   A word about experts. Experts don't need to explain their expertise. You can quickly discern that from their biography and background. Experts in a field often have MDs, PhDs, or master's-level degrees with education and experience in that area. Writing a book on a topic does not make a person an expert; it makes that person an author. Those people will, however, interview the experts in their fields to bring you the information.

2. **Sponsorship:** Some sites are sponsored by corporations and pharmaceutical companies, which may drive some of the content, digital and text. A credible site will highlight sponsored material, but not-so-credible sites will bury links to sponsors so that it is difficult to discern the connection.

3. **Intent:** Some sites have reasonable material, but their intent is not true health promotion and information—it is actually the sale of a product. You can usually sort this out after clicking through a few pages. Sites of this nature will have the product noted at every turn.

4. **Stamp of approval:** Is there a stamp of approval on the site? For health sites, most have what's called Health On the Net certification. For blogs, there's a Healthcare Blogger Code of Ethics that you'll see on many health blogs. Both seals accomplish the same goal of having a list of

standards that the sites must follow to post the code. My blog and Web site have these stamps, and it is reassuring to my readers. Many other Web sites, such as WebMD, do too, as well as many of my health blogger colleagues.

5. **Financial interest:** Does the site have any financial interest and if so, what is it? Many sites have advertisements. Those should be well labeled. There also needs to be a clear statement of how a site makes its revenue, if it is a revenue-based site and not nonprofit. Does the site offer professional services? Is the owner of the site a spokesperson for a product or involved with the sponsors on any level? These issues need to be stated in a transparent way for your comfort level and for the validity of the site.

With so many sites to choose from, those with experts/authors are the most reliable. This eliminates the "telephone game" effect. Look at it like this. As a parent, do you want to read about ear infections from a health writer who talked with a physician, or a physician-writer? There are so many physician-writers and editors online today that at the very least, you want to be sure the information you are reading has been reviewed by a medical expert. Those sites will have the author's name followed by "reviewed by Dr X" and the date.

The date of the review is very important, more so than the initial draft. The "reviewed by" date tells you a number of important facts about the site and the people operating it. The date represents how current the information is. Many large health sites have an editorial policy that outlines how they update their information. Smaller sites and blogs may not make this so obvious; however, all reputable, reliable health sites will have the "last update" date for the site, if not the material itself, well marked. This is a sign that the site is constantly being reviewed for accuracy.

One of the most important issues to consider when choosing a site to read is whether the site is a Web site or a blog. A Web site tends to have more article-based information, while a blog is, by definition, opinionated. Both sites can have reliable information, but you have to be sure to look closely at the source.

For Web sites, make sure the site isn't sponsored by a large group promoting a product or cause that may create bias in the information. Where health information is concerned, you are better off with unbiased sites. For this reason, health sites or hospital-affiliated sites are sometimes the most reliable to start with. Medical organization and government sites are also great sources of information.

For blogs, the author and author's credentials and intent are important. All blogs are opinionated. Blogs are really an online op-ed column or letter to the editor. Blogs can contain some wonderful information and have the advantage of being easy to read in a short amount of time. Many are also great fun, which has value in and of itself at times. But authorship is important. Just as with Web sites, be sure you know the blog's author so you can verify the accuracy of the information. It's also helpful with blogs to know the blog's purpose. Some blogs are just for fun, while others strive for information. When seeking out authors on Web sites and blogs, look for the "about" or "about me" button on the navigation bar itself, the sub-navigation bar, or the sidebar. Web sites tend to place the "about" button on the navigation bar and blogs, the sidebar.

Once you start hunting for signs of reliability on Web sites and blogs you are reading, you'll quickly start to notice a difference between good and "other" sites. But what about our kids and teens? Do they know the difference? Unlikely. Moreover, they are more than likely to believe the opinion-based, emotionally charged material because that is how they think. Kids are often less likely to do a thorough hunt and check out the source of the material and more likely to go for a site they know from their friends, teachers, and parents.

The other issue with kids and teens online is that they can be highly influenced by what they read about their own health online. They don't yet have the life and health experience to know how to interpret the information they seek online and don't have the health literacy skills to problem solve to determine if what they are reading makes sense.

For example, take an average teen girl worried about acne. She's likely to search "my face is oily," read advice in one of her teen magazines, or ask her friend. A Google search will produce a bunch of community boards and few health Web sites on the first page. Not exactly where you want your teen daughter obtaining skin advice! You may catch her doing a hunt on YouTube for a video on skin care—that's another popular place for teens to obtain health advice today. Or, the epitome of teen health advice, she'll text a friend.

Being the observant parent that you are, you'll have picked up on the flurry of high-tech scanning for "oily face" and ask her about it before harm is done, but sometimes these searches fall under the radar. Sometimes the searches happen in code. To be health literate on our kids' behalf, we have to be where they are, which isn't necessarily Web sites and blogs. Teens and kids tend to be on the more social Web venues—Facebook, MySpace, texting, instant messages (IMs). Learn to decipher these sites and you'll be more attuned to where your kids are with their hunts for anything, from the innocent "diaper rash" to "how to get high."

The Good, the Bad, and Everything In-between

Health literacy embodies all the skills we need to search for, identify, open, read, and process health information online. Anything online that involves health involves health literacy skills for us to really be able to interpret the content. This could be a text we receive from a friend or a Web site address, blog post, or tweet.

Unlike buying a car or household appliance, where we have many choices, the consequences of choosing the wrong online information could be harmful to our health and well-being. For example, reading a Web site that we don't understand because the material is written in jargon or above our literacy level can make us nervous and either act rashly in decision-making or freeze altogether. Reading a site with faulty information can lead us to make the wrong decision or become apprehensive about calling our health care providers for advice. And reading a site sponsored by a pharmaceutical company or other product could sway us to believe that that product could help us when there may be better options had we consulted our doctor.

The goal of gathering health information online is not to help you be a surrogate physician for your own health or the health of your family; it should be to gather information so you can be more informed when sorting through issues with your own physicians. Denise Basow, MD, is the editor in chief of the Web site UpToDate and calls this "shared decision making." UpToDate, incidentally, is a great online resource. However, its content may not be as approachable as HealthyChildren.org or KidsHealth. org for kids, or American Academy of Family Physicians or MedlinePlus for adults.

Literacy Doesn't Happen Overnight

The other issue with the online world is that there are hidden health pitfalls, especially for kids. Kids can be easily swayed by what they read and are typically driven by emotion and friends over reason. They often don't have the world and life experience to use as a litmus test against what they are reading to determine the accuracy of the material. And they don't always check with adults to confirm the validity of what they have found online.

Problem solving is difficult online where the players are often not easily identified. If this task is arduous for adults, think what it is like for kids at various ages of development. For young kids who are very concrete, they may not be able to sort out the slight differences in accuracy of online information and can easily be misled. For older kids, their emotions can blind them from reason, making decisions challenging at times.

When we were kids, we may have privately written our innermost thoughts and ideas with a pen and paper in a journal. Sure, sometimes a sibling would grab hold of a page and torment us with it, but by and large it was out of public view.

Our kids' and teens' inner thoughts are very often written online via Facebook, texts to friends, and IMs. Kids may not understand that those online logs are not as private as they realize and can be sent to many people at any time. This is how more serious issues like sexting (sending sexually explicit messages or photos electronically) and cyberbullying occur. As parents, we need to lay the groundwork for online health literacy when our kids are young, well before they even know what technology is. We have to start by empowering our kids to be part of their own health care and understand their bodies in the off-line world before we can expect them to be competent and literate online.

When our children are born, we love watching them learn about their bodies. We delight in asking them question such as, "Where's your nose?" and seeing their adorable fingers try and point to the right spot on their faces. We spend a great deal of time when our kids are infants and toddlers helping them learn about the outside of their bodies. The inside, however, we only cover remotely and on topics that are safe. Most of what our kids learn about their bodies and sex education comes from school. But they could get this information from their friends or online from their own hunts. This is how misinformation and misperceptions develop.

While school is a wonderful resource , home is a better place to help kids process the tough topics of their bodies and health issues. If we don't open the door to these conversations, they will turn to their friends and the Internet. While these may be OK for reassurance and gathering basic information, ultimately we want our kids turning to us to have discussions that involving problem solving and health consequences. Those are not results that can occur via a Web search.

In addition to fostering open conversations about health topics, another way to plant the seeds for health literacy is to allow our kids to be more involved in their own health care. When they go to the doctor, who usually answers the questions asked by the health care provider? If you answered "me" or "my spouse/partner," you are in good company. More times than not, parents answer for their kids, but our kids are the patients and the owners of their bodies. They should be the ones giving their own health histories, at least at first.

As a pediatrician, I find kids amazingly reliable about their own bodies, even at very young ages. It's important to encourage them to talk about their bodies and empower them to feel comfortable about it. There isn't a right or wrong answer. Mom and dad can fill in the gaps with important information when the kids are done, if needed. The advantages of encouraging our kids to answer their own questions in the examination room are numerous. First, it reinforces to our kids that they are in charge of their own bodies. This is important for them to learn early. It's important for kids to learn that it's important to take an interest in their bodies and be comfortable with being able to discuss them.

Second, it's important for children to learn to talk to adults, and they can do that most effectively if we get out of the way. That's one of the best literacy lessons there is—to learn to talk about the issues.

Third, if they are able to engage with experts, they will learn proper health care terms.

So what's our role as parents? To be there to encourage our kids to be part of their own health care and support them by filling in the gaps. Off-line, we help fill in the gaps by learning to talk with our kids about health. We can use headlines, books, and topics they bring up to sort through what needs to be discussed. At the doctor's office, we need to balance being a fly on the wall and allowing our kids to interact with health care providers, and knowing when to step in and interject. At all costs, we need to be sure our kids are part of the conversation and not a bystander of their own health.

If we talk to our kids off-line, online they will know the issues well enough to at least know if what they are reading doesn't make sense. And perhaps they will not go online at all but go to you first.

But what if they do go online? Where will they go and how should you prepare them? The issues are similar once you know what they are, but it helps to understand where kids are going and what they like to do on those sites, and how quickly they can forget the commonsense rules they know off-line.

Chapter 5

The Tangled Web We Weave

Taking the Temperature of Our Concern for Our Kids

What's your response when you hear a poll's results? We are talking about opinions, so a great deal has to do with the mood of the people taking the poll. That's why the best polls gather information from a huge amount of people. And the best polls have a prior data point for us to compare them against—perhaps a past similar poll.

In 2007, C.S. Mott Children's Hospital in Michigan released its first annual National Poll on Children's Health (NPCH). Beyond just being informative, this top 10 list helps us redefine our priorities as a parenting community by taking the temperature of the actual issues on the minds of real parents in real time. This list provides a useful cornerstone for a variety of purposes, including the foundation of legal and educational programs for kids of all ages, and the development of better public awareness campaigns targeting adults and kids. Beyond legal, educational, and awareness programs, the NPCH increases the volume of the sometimes hard-to-hear voices of our children. After all, these concerns didn't pop into our collective minds out of the blue. These concerns came to us from our children vocalizing where they need us, individually and as a society, to pay a bit more attention.[1]

In 2009, the top 10 child health concerns of the 2,000-plus adults surveyed was essentially a mirror image of the 2008 list and included childhood obesity, drug abuse, smoking, bullying, Internet safety, child abuse and neglect, alcohol abuse, stress, not enough physical activity, and teen pregnancy.

Serendipity? I don't think so.

The reason the issues on these lists have been so stable over the last few years is that they are the major health issues of the day for kids and are on everyone's minds—parents, pediatricians, legislators, educators, law enforcement…everyone touched by and who cares for the well-being of kids. It's important that everyone, including parents, is on the same page with these issues because that's the only way to help our children become more healthy with regard to all of these items. Agreeing on the core issues also allows us to have a solid foundation to discuss and build better policy, educational plans, and community programs that help our kids tackle these often-challenging issues. If we do this right, we'll be able to support our kids in all the settings they meander through in a given day—home, school, and community. A true team approach!

The Effect of Media: An Important Part of the Team Often Left on the Sidelines

These issues are also very closely related to each other in a way you may not be aware of. Each and every one has been directly or indirectly linked to childhood exposure to the myriad of forms of media in our children's lives.

Don't worry, I'm not going to break into a gloom-and-doom diatribe about the horror of media and how we're all frying our kids' brains, souls, and development. I love the media and feel it can, and usually does, do a lot of good for our kids and for us—I wouldn't be writing this book if I didn't believe the media was, at its core, good!

Let's face it—under the umbrella of digital lives, our children are experiencing a very different childhood than we did as kids. We'd be foolish to ignore the explosion of childhood problems like those named in the NPCH that have occurred since we were kids and since the digital age began.

Think about kids we used to play with when we were our kids' ages. How many of them were really overweight or obese? Not too many, by my recollection, and I'm sure yours, too. And that's just what statistics confirm. According to the Centers for Disease Control and Prevention, only 7% of 6- to 11-year-olds and 5% of 12- to 18-year-olds were obese between 1976 and 1980. That rate doubled for the younger group and tripled for the older group by 2000, when the digital age was taking off. Recent studies have shown these trends have plateaued, but we have not made any headway in reducing the numbers at all.[2,3]

Trends in free play and playtime are equally disturbing. Since the 1970s, kids have lost 12 hours in their week of total free time, with a 50% reduction in outdoor time and a 25% decrease in generalized play.[4] This particular trend parallels increased homework, increased after-school activities and time away from family, as well as an increase in media time.

Teenage pregnancy rates, risk-taking behavior, bullying (online and off), and childhood stress have also shown increases since today's parents were kids. As with childhood obesity, each of these issues is tightly woven into the fabric of our kids' digital lives. In other words, all of the top trends in childhood today are tangled together with media acting as an amplifier or an igniter of the trend.

Whether it be pollen, paint fumes, lead, video games, music, or what we see on TV or computer screens, our bodies are affected by what they are exposed to in the environment. It's important that we recognize the spectrum of those factors as parents, try to mitigate what we can control and be on the lookout for what we can't control directly, and include media on the list of factors we monitor.

Think of it like this. If you are investigating nutrition choices for your family, you research the foods, look into portion control, and determine recipes. You try to make some sense of the variables that nutritionally impact your family members' lives. Should they have more tomatoes and more fish? Should you cut out all processed food or just reduce it? You work hard to help your family eat better by focusing on the nutritional areas that you perceive they need help with.

With media, however, all too often we take it for granted and fail to investigate what we allow our kids to have access to, whether it be a TV show, a DVD, a Web site, or even music. We can identify that we should be concerned and note that on surveys such as NPCH, but we fail to take the necessary steps to monitor our kids' use and help them understand the health and safety issues with media as we do with other issues, such as nutrition, learning to drive, or learning to cross the street. There's a bit of a disconnect with how we think of media compared with other health and safety areas in our kids lives because we don't think of media as a health and safety area—yet. There's hope, though. Media is the hot button of today's culture. Every generation of parents has its hot-button topics to focus on with its kids. The effect of media and the digital world is among the hottest for us—not just hot but volcanically hot. This is the type of topic that explosions are made of. And in fact, these issues do have that potential with our individual kids and for this generation.

We know media and digital technologies can be beneficial in our lives and our kids' lives. Technologic progress in a society is always good and we don't want to sell those advances short or downplay their effect on our lives. None of that is in dispute.

The hard-to-accept reality is that for all the good media and the digital age can do, there is some harm that can come for adults and kids. The element we have yet to sort out is how to exercise caution with its use and how to create balance in our digital lives so we don't go on complete digital overload.

In a recent *JAMA: The Journal of the American Medical Association* article, pediatrician Victor Strasburger, MD, FAAP, wrote, "The media are not the leading cause of any pediatric health problem in the United States, but they do make a substantial contribution to many health problems...."[5]

Would we turn a blind eye to our child if he or she had a fever or strep throat? Of course not. Would we turn a blind eye if our child developed a horribly itchy rash? No. How about nightmares or anxiety that prevented our child from getting through the day? Again, no—we'd seek help.

So we have to stop turning a blind eye to media and the issues it can potentially create. Our job is not to vilify media venues we are all using but to understand them, demystify and uncloak them, so we can find ourselves on a path better suited for balance between our off-line and online lives, and help our kids lead full, fun, productive lives with a fantastic and seamless mix of digital and non-digital worlds.

Preserving a Touch of Yesterday While Moving Into Tomorrow

If you're feeling a bit anxious about this, you're in great company. At a recent conference, Rachel Dretzin from Frontline's digital_nation said she sensed that anxiety is overwhelming for most parents she's talked to. Whether in a room of parents, educators, or health care industry leaders, there is a unified sense of uncertainty, almost as if we collectively have been on a merry-go-round operating at warp speed and still haven't found our footing or our bearing.

What allows us to regain our footing is experience with digital technologies themselves, not running away from them. While the digital world keeps marching forward with new technologies and advances, all we really have to focus on is what we're comfortable with and what our kids are using—it really is that simple.

At the same time, that merry-go-round feeling can make us want to shelter our kids from technology when they are young and just hit the pause button for a while. While it can be tempting, we live in a digital world. Sheltering doesn't help our kids learn to live in the world at all; in fact it hampers their ability to grow.

We have to temper our adult concerns about new media and technology and strike a balance. That's the key, really—balance. We have to recognize that even the most sheltered child will eventually grow up, become an adult, and enter a world loaded with a 24/7 digital capacity. If we don't allow our kids access to that world, they will not only be behind in skills but behind in understanding the world. That is a heck of a burden to place on an individual at any age.

The data are clear about the good and the bad of technology and the effect of digital life on our kids. Some experts understate the risks, but they are real. Without becoming doom-and-gloomy we can become realistic. We can understand the risk our kids face with digital stimulation and understand that there is a lot we still don't know about the impact of digital life on kids, and even on us. In fact, there is a great deal of evidence that when media is used correctly, it can have a profoundly positive effect on learning, health, and socialization.

The best we can do is try and understand the digital lives of kids so we can understand how to help them have a healthy digital diet. We don't need to become cyber-police and heavy-handed to do that. All we need to do is peek into their world a bit, get to know it better than we do today.

It isn't a question of if our kids will go online, but when. Our job is to attempt to keep up and to do our best to keep our kids safe by coupling communication with our kids with tools we can enable on our computers and cell phones that put age-appropriate limits in place (see Chapter 18).

You know what this is really about, don't you? Being able to connect with your kids and talk with them. Have them show you what they are doing online and on their cell phones. Knowing where they are and how they think, we can better relate to them and connect with them. Given how digitally connected tweens and teens are, we have to get with the program and get a bit more connected too. That's how we'll achieve a healthy media diet.

If all goes well, we'll learn more about technology and move into the future with our kids while teaching them to live with a bit less technology and feel comfortable living a bit more unplugged. We have to help our kids recognize that it's not old-fashioned to be unplugged and actually talk to people—it's just part of living and having a healthy media diet.

Disney/Pixar's *WALL•E* is a great movie to remind us what could happen if we fail to pay attention to our media diets and the power of the human touch once we regain control of our media lives. That's the lesson we want our kids to understand, well before they are grown-ups!

References

1. C.S. Mott Children's Hospital National Poll on Children's Health. Available at: http://www.med.umich.edu/mott/npch/about/index.htm. Accessed March 3, 2010
2. Childhood obesity: prevalence and identification. American Obesity Association Web site. Available at: http://obesity1.tempdomainname.com/subs/childhood/prevalence.shtml. Published May 2, 2005. Accessed March 3, 2010
3. Odgen CL, Carroll MD, Flegal KM. High body mass index for age among US children and adolescents, 2003-2006 . *JAMA*. 2008;299:2401–2405. Available at: http://jama.ama-assn.org/cgi/content/short/299/20/2401. Accessed March 3, 2010
4. Albert Einstein College of Medicine. Daily school recess improves classroom behavior. e! Science News Web site. Available at: http://esciencenews.com/articles/2009/01/27/daily.school.recess.improves.classroom.behavior. Published January 27, 2009. Accessed March 3, 2010
5. Strasburger V. Media and children: what needs to happen now? *JAMA*. 2009;301:2265–2266. Available at: http://jama.ama-assn.org/cgi/content/extract/301/21/2265. Accessed March 3, 2010

Chapter 6

Internet Safety: Myths Versus Reality

Digital Myths and Citizenship

Because the Internet never sleeps or shuts down, we can travel through its corridors anytime we wish. It's very easy to lose sense of time and place online, and small problems and issues can take on bigger meanings than they should. We may have an easier time gathering information online, but discerning its accuracy and gaining perspective about scope is much more challenging. As a result, we tend to have trouble sorting out what to believe in the online world, and much of what we think is true ends up being more myth than reality.

Two of the biggest generators of myths is the disconnect in how parents and kids use digital technology, and how kids use digital technology compared with how their parents think they do. This includes not just the Internet but video games, music, cell phones…the entire digital world!

Good, old-fashioned myth busting will allow us to better understand how our kids are using the digital world and what we can do to help them be better digital and global citizens.

Myth Busting the Digital Way!

To get a sense of digital myths, I turned to 2 colleagues for guidance—Victor Strasburger, MD, FAAP, from the University of New Mexico, and Parry Aftab, Esq, executive director of WiredSafety.org.

Dr Strasburger, an expert on adolescent health and a member of the American Academy of Pediatrics Council on Communications and Media, viewed the situation from a global, societal perspective. He felt that parents misinterpret the digital world in 3 important ways. "[First,] I suspect that parents overestimate the importance of new technology and underestimate the importance of old technology. [Second,] too many people still believe in the catharsis theory. [Third,] third-person effect—ie, too many people think it's other people's kids who are affected by media, not their kids."

There is a great deal of evidence to support Dr Strasburger's comments. We know from Pew, Kaiser, and similar groups who have looked at trends in digital use in teens that they do use old as well as new media and are using media more today than in the past with a trend that seems on the rise. From the same research, we also know that parents don't always know what their kids are using and that there is a digital divide.

I've been struck by how savvy parents, especially of tweens and young teens, are so caught up in their kids' abilities to produce videos and complicated digital projects for school, including Web sites, that they fail to recognize some of the well-documented issues with these age groups online such as content exposure, too much screen time, issues with kids younger than 13 being involved with social networking sites such as Facebook and MySpace, and lack of family time. Dr Strasburger's second point is an intriguing one and I've seen this play out with TV arguments. Parents are often bystanders to what their children are doing, like watching a play. With so many other kids being online, it's easy for parents to wash away their own anxieties within a broader group of society.

Finally, the "not my kid" line will always get a parent into trouble! Parents have difficulties seeing how their children are affected by the same data and trends as other kids.

For a more specific digital myth perspective, Parry Aftab shared a list that includes issues many parents take for granted as "safe" or acceptable but are, in reality, not what any of us are doing. Let's run down Parry's list and follow each with a myth-busting commentary.

1. **Parry's Myth:** Social networking is dangerous.
   Dr Gwenn's Myth Bust: Social networking can be safe and often is, if done thoughtfully, age appropriately, and with a conscious following of stated age limits and privacy rules. Social networking becomes unsafe when parents allow tweens on sites not meant for tweens, such as Facebook or MySpace, and when parents are so uninvolved that young teens do not know how to manage their privacy settings or digital footprint.

2. **Parry's Myth:** Predators track down kids in real life from their addresses online.
   Dr Gwenn's Myth Bust: Studies have shown that predators are not only not where are kids tend to be online but don't have the technologic

capabilities to find our kids from their online addresses. In fact, our views about how predators use the Internet in general have been found to be myths (see Chapter 20).[1]

3. **Parry's Myth:** All online "friending" is dangerous.
   Dr Gwenn's Myth Bust: What we have to emphasize to our kids and teens is that rules of friendship off-line extend to the online world, including the act of friending. The best guideline is to only friend people you know and have a connection with off-line. Friending only becomes iffy when we add people to our lists who we don't know well or at all, and when we fail to set our privacy to "friends only" so that only our friends can see our posts, pictures, videos, and comments. In addition to these simple measures, it's important for digital youth to understand that what goes online, stays online. Appropriate posting etiquette needs to be reinforced, as well as reminders not to post information that is too personal. For example, kids need to understand not to shoot from the hip with texts and e-mails, and not to write things in e-mails and texts they would not say face-to-face off-line.

4. **Parry's Myth:** All online discussions with strangers are dangerous.
   Dr Gwenn's Myth Bust: Think about all the strangers we meet each and every day. We chat with and accept help from bank tellers, grocery clerks, police officers, firefighters, office administrators, department store clerks, doctors, nurses, medical assistants, landscapers, appliance repair folks, and postal workers, to name a few! By observing our behavior with these people, our children learn that it's OK to interact with these types of strangers, and when they become more independent they'll understand how to negotiate these social norms, whether in person, by phone, or online. So let's not panic when our kids have the occasional innocent conversation with a peer they don't know too well. Likely the purpose is innocent, such as homework help, and the contact is someone they actually know, at least by icon, which is no different than our own buddy list!

The key is helping our kids understand how to build a safe buddy list, to keep their information private, to not meet their online friends off-line, and to help them have appropriate limits with their online time.

The same predator study that proved that predators are not where we think they are also debunked the myth that predators lie about their age, so we don't have to worry that a predator is hiding his or her age.

If your child is interacting with someone claiming to be 14 years old, studies are reassuring that you can believe the stated age!

5. **Parry's Myth:** Online games are safe if they use cute cartoon characters.
Dr Gwenn's Myth Bust: Cute doesn't mean safe by any stretch of the imagination. The world of gaming is very complex because of the effect of graphics and issues with multiplayer involvement.

It's important to check out all the games your kids are playing. Ratings and descriptions are useful for this purpose, as well has having your child show you the game he or she is interested in so you can thoroughly check to be sure it's appropriate for your child's age and development.

If you have a young gamer at home, look past the character and first check the rating. If the rating is not appropriate for your child's age, that's your first red flag. Second, check the content of the game yourself to see if it is appropriate for your child. Third, are there other players with whom your child will be interacting? If so, those players may be adults, and the game just took on a worldwide meaning that isn't something to enter into without thought.

6. **Parry's Myth:** Updates for antivirus software don't need to be purchased.
Dr Gwenn's Myth Bust: There are many free antivirus programs available online and through major protection companies such as Norton and McAfee, but those are very basic programs. To get a full and comprehensive protection plan against more sophisticated threats such as worms and Trojan horses, and to have some anti-spyware protection, you need a subscription service (often called a "professional plan" depending on which company you are using). Having had my computer attacked by a threat before, it's money well spent! An explanation of the differences between "free" and subscription plans in general can be found at www.isoftwarereviews.com/professional-antivirus-vs-free-antivirus-software.

7. **Parry's Myth:** Parents know their kids.
Dr Gwenn's Myth Bust: This is one of the most commonly expressed phrases from every parent I know, but the honest truth is we have to admit we're getting to know our kids as they grow up! In truth, we really don't know our kids well as teens, and that is one of the reasons we find them so frustrating at times.

We know their history. We know their prior likes and dislikes. Our teens won't know who they are for some time yet. They are just learning to be comfortable in their teenaged skins. Our job is to help them learn to wear those new independent coats comfortably, to give them limits when needed but in the rubric of independent living. I know, tall order! But it's what teens need.

So the best we can admit is that we're aware of the people our teens want to be and help them with that process. But to say we know our kids is just asking for all sorts of trouble!

In truth, we know what our kids want us to know about them. In reality, our kids will behave just like all the other kids their age eventually, in one way or another, even if in a small way. We're kidding ourselves if we think our kids will be above it all or somehow forge a different path.

This is actually a timeless situation. My mother told me that when she was a teenager, her father was adamant that she and her sisters wear skirts to school every day. Well, they wanted to wear jeans. So they would leave home with the skirt but with jeans in their bags. They'd wave to my Grandpa—and then change behind a bush around the corner! One day, they were nabbed when my Grandpa was out early doing something in the yard!

A family told me recently that they allowed their 12-year-old to go on Facebook because he's "mature" (I'll cover this more in Chapter 21). Dad had a rule dictating that no games or quizzes were to be played. In his first month or so online, this 12-year-old played a quiz. Given his age, I'm not surprised; this is the age of games, so the temptation is going to be there. Plus, the 12-year-old may be "mature," but he is acting just like every other kid on Facebook!

8. **Parry's Myth:** The other kid is the bad guy.
   Dr Gwenn's Myth Bust: If you have a head-butting moment in your adult life, do you own it? Do you try and see your role in the moment and accept your responsibility for your contribution? Most adults recognize it takes 2 to tango regardless of who instigates the situation.

   However, when it comes to their kids, defenses go up immediately and most parents quickly take aim at the other child and family. Usually I find few parents are interested in the facts and just want to protect their child's honor. But we have to be willing to recognize that our child isn't innocent all the time. Where cyber-situations are concerned, your child or teen is as likely as others to be part of the issue, from cyberbullying, to sending inappropriate texts and e-mails, to not handing the receiving of a sext correctly.

The best way for us to help our kids learn from any issue, especially online misunderstandings, is to help our kids be realistic about their own behaviors and to own their role in a situation that doesn't turn out well. The one exception to this rule is in the case of dangerous, destructive, and illegal situations; these must always be handled quickly and decisively for the safety of those involved. As you'll see in chapters 20 and 21, that can be done without freaking out or pointing fingers.

9. **Parry's Myth:** Handheld gaming devices don't connect to the Internet.
   Dr Gwenn's Myth Bust: One of the first expressions I learned in my tween years was omnes viae Romam ducunt, or all roads lead to Rome. For today's digital natives, a better expression would be, all devices lead to the Internet.

   The vast majority of today's handheld gaming systems connect to the Internet, most by Wi-Fi. This means that our kids can connect to the 'net and communicate with others by chats set up through the games. Once on the Internet via any channel, our kids have access to the entire World Wide Web!

10. **Parry's Myth:** Cell phones are fine for young kids.
    Dr Gwenn's Myth Bust: When considering a first cell phone for any child, purpose is essential. Are you considering the phone because every other child has the phone, or is there a greater need such as a medical condition?

    The cell phone landscape is complicated today by cyberbullying and sexting. If you do not feel your child is old enough to discuss these issues and understand them, your child is not old enough for a cell phone.

    Cell phones come with many bells and whistles, so try and match the phone with the needs of your child. You can still get phones that just call, which is very appropriate for younger kids. And there are phones tailored for young kids that you can program with just a few numbers.

    You are in control of the features you enable, so use that control to tailor the cell phone plan and choice of phone for the intent you are hoping to achieve. Keep in mind that most cell phone carriers now have parent control features so you can restrict your child from accessing content and features that the phone may come with, such as the Internet or video and music downloads.

Moreover, young children never "need" a cell phone. They are always supervised after school and transportation is provided, by car or bus or by parents walking them.

I sometimes hear parents tell me they want to be able to reach their child at a playdate. That's what parent-to-parent contact is for—call the home of the other family.

What's the appropriate age to being to consider a cell phone? Older middle school or high school, when kids become independent and are home alone.

11. **Parry's Myth:** Everything kids are storing is stored off-line.
   Dr Gwenn's Myth Bust: What happens online, stays online! In fact, material is actually stored online and is called our *digital footprint*. The management of our digital footprint is the key to all of our online reputations, and mismanagement can ruin lives. There have been many cases of missed opportunities from parents and kids not understanding how to handle one's digital footprint, including lost jobs and college placement.

12. **Parry's Myth:** Kids would never pose in the nude for a picture.
   Dr Gwenn's Myth Bust: There are 2 things that parents should never underestimate in teens—the power of the peer group and the power of hormonal teens trying to attract love interests. Teens, include good teens, straight-A-student sort of teens, lose all sense of reasonable thought in both situations and will do things like pose nude. Think back on your own teen years and the sort of things you found alluring. Your teens are no different.

13. **Parry's Myth:** Kids will not use their webcam for any stupid things.
   Dr Gwenn's Myth Bust: See number 12. The same conditions that lead teens to pose nude cause them to do dumb things with webcams. If you saw the movie *American Pie,* that's not a Hollywood fictional situation but truly art imitating life!

14. **Parry's Myth:** Kids don't hack other kids.
   Dr Gwenn's Myth Bust: Just like nice kids sometimes say mean things to kids online, nice kids sometimes hack other kids' computers.

However, another reason kids hack computers is because they know that no one is looking. The thrill of not getting caught is a high for many, coupled with the skill they have to pull it off. Given our over-achieving society, kids may have many motives to hack other kids and play all sorts of games. In some ways, this is no different than seeing parents violate the Facebook terms of service (TOS) and allowing 11-year-olds to go online, even though the TOS is for 13 years and older.[2]

15. **Parry's Myth:** The reason kids use headsets and microphones when playing games is to listen to game sound effects without disturbing the family.

   Dr Gwenn's Myth Bust: The best way to learn what your kids are listening to is to listen with them! You'll be surprised by the lyrics of songs and phrases in games. Many times when kids look like they are "listening" to a game, they have a very different soundtrack running, so pop an earbud in once in a while.

16. **Parry's Myth:** Xbox is a game device.

   Dr Gwenn's Myth Bust: Xbox is a game device, but that's just the tip of the high-tech iceberg! If you tease out all the features, Xbox, PlayStation 3, and Wii are multimedia entertainment units that can run everything from games to DVDs to music. And with the convergence of content into devices, future devices will likely have many more applications than today's "game" and digital devices.

Myths Reexamined

As you can see, the chasm between our understanding of the online world and reality is gigantic. So what's the solution? Learn to drive the Internet, its components, and the issues yourself. That will narrow the digital divide between you and your digital native and send a clear message that you know how to use and understand technology and are there for your kids online as well as off.

References

1. Wolak J, Finkelhor D, Mitchell KJ, Ybarra ML. Online "predators" and their victims: myths, realities, and implications for prevention and treatment. *Am Psychol.* 2008;63:111–128. Available at: http://psycnet.apa.org/journals/amp/63/2/111. Accessed March 3, 2010

2. Callow R. Kids under 13 using Facebook. Available at: http://www.sync-blog.com/sync/2009/09/kids-under-13-using-facebook.html. Published September 10, 2009. Accessed May 6, 2010

Part 2

The Teen/Tween-O-Sphere Uncensored

Section 1
Snapshot of Daily Life

Chapter 7

Screen Time and Childhood

Have you ever tried to go "screen-less"? I often tell the story of taking my girls to New York City on an April vacation, looking forward to Turnoff Week. This is a semiannual event that encourages families to flip off the screens and bond more in the unplugged real world with books, board games, and outdoor fun. Being a member of the American Academy of Pediatrics (AAP) and its Council on Communications and Media, this cause had particular meaning for me because this is *the* issue we try to help parents practice. So I blogged about it and told all my friends at the AAP and in my life that I was going to do this.

As soon as we arrived, I knew this would be more of a challenge than I was ready for. Back home in Massachusetts (not exactly what I'd call remote living!), screens were in homes and places we opted to put them, including cars and even refrigerators. Our home only has basic screens—TVs, computers, and cell phones. We're very old-fashioned that way!

Well, our first cab ride—a screen. Times Square—thousands of screens. The hotel elevator—more screens. The hotel lobby—many more screens.

I had 2 choices: blindfold my girls as we explored New York City, or simply keep them so busy our focus would not be on the screens but on our tasks at hand—the shows, the museums, and hitting every deli and diner we could find. By the time we were back in the hotel room each evening, my girls passed out from happy exhaustion so quickly, no extra screens were required. That was the best I could do, so I did it.

They were both tweens at the time, so we could talk about my dilemma. They understood my passion for this cause and why I'm concerned about small children, as well as older children, being exposed to too many screens so young. Of all the kids viewing screens, it's the smallest of children I'm concerned about the most. I can't help worry that they have too many screens in their lives at the expense of what matters most in childhood—playtime.

Are Young Kids Online?

We don't need studies to know that the very youngest members of our society are online. The images are everywhere.

- Toddlers and preschoolers using their parent's smartphones and digital devices to watch videos and play with the text screens
- Small kids playing with gaming devices in and out of home and playing games on their parents' and older siblings' phones
- TV games that are essentially small computers that glue our small children to all sorts of devices under the excuse of "education" or "fitness"
- And of course, some young children with phones of their own at a variety of very young ages

What's interesting in the world of parenting is that while there are some milestones that we take for granted our kids will do when they are ready or at a similar age as other kids, there are other issues we worry about and go to great lengths to sort out the "right" path to take. Sometimes we develop a strong gut opinion and just go with it. Other times we poll friends and relatives to get a sense of past precedent that we may not be aware of. And other moments we'll turn to experts by contacting a trusted community figure by phone and e-mail or by doing Internet research.

We tend to do best when we have a past path to follow from other generations of parents. For hot-button topics such as sex, driving, first dates, and clothing appropriateness, we may feel less lost than we do on some of the newer high-tech issues, where the path is partially blazed or not blazed at all.

At the same time, can we really blame technology entirely? If you think back through the past few generations, they all have had similar issues with increasing technology, struggles with parents about wardrobe, and growing independence of teens. The Internet and digital world is acting as a gigantic amplifier for these issues and adds a layer of daunting complexity with its 24/7 availability, but the core issues are the same.

Instead of being blinded by the bells and whistles of technology and thinking of it as glorified toys, it's better to discuss issues about technology with our kids as soon as they are able to use it (which means at much earlier ages than we currently do)! We already do this by helping our kids negotiate the world they explore, from safety around the house to safety beyond the house, and mold our discussions depending on our kids' ages. In fact, we grow these discussions as our kids grow. Now that their world involves technology, we have to include those topics too. As with all important issues in life, the younger children are, the more impressionable they are, and this is no less true with technology. For young children, including tweens, the goal is to empower them to use technology to the best of their abilities and have fun with it, but learn when to hit the off switch and change to unplugged childhood activities. Especially for our youngest kids, a balance of screen and non-screen time is what helps them thrive best, with a big skew toward non-screen activities!

Early Childhood: Kids, Computers, and the Boxes They Arrive In

How many times have you hunted high and low for a toy for your toddler or preschooler, only to have your child more interested in the ribbon on the package or the box itself? We've all had that experience and have the pictures to prove it! So before you rush out and buy your preschooler or toddler a computer or digital device, be realistic that the box may win out over the gadget. Why? Because this age group is all about creativity, imagination, and hiding! The digital whatever that so intrigues you likely won't keep their attention span for more than a few minutes, and at some point they will use it for something you likely never thought it could be used for, such as a javelin or even a doll. This is just the reality of small kids.

The other issue we have with young children is not thinking long term. We often think of the high-tech world in terms of a game or toy or as "just entertainment." What we have to do is start recognizing that the high-tech world involves screens, content, and an experience that affects our kids directly as well as indirectly, even at young ages. So before we hit the on switch to anything high tech, we should take a moment to ask ourselves if the time spent on that activity is worth the time put into that activity.

We expend this sort of reasoning with every decision we make for our kids, from crossing the street, to playdates, to attending camp (day or overnight?), to sleepovers with friends, to nutritional issues, to name a few. Now we need to go a step further and apply that same sound reasoning to everything high tech, from using the computer, to which TV show or movie to watch, to cell phone issues.

Deciding to Turn the Switch On

Do you stick to your guns or enter into negotiations? Like most parents, you've likely found it's a balancing act. Some issues you can give in on, while others you more or less stick to your guns.

Most of us find, though, that sticking to our position blindly backfires once our children are old enough to problem solve and directly ask something by name, especially if that something has a reference point in the peer group. Are we going to be the one parent to say "no" or do we cave? These are not straightforward issues and we have to balance our own values with what others are doing. Peer pressure runs in parenting groups too, and we've all experienced it.

With decisions relating to our children, we often end up using a few tried-and-true references points to help guide us.

1. **Is there a norm?** This can be helpful in guiding us because if there seems to be a societal norm for kids for a particular issue, it can give us perspective on our own views. Are we just out of our comfort zone? Is this an issue pushing our moral compass beyond what we have considered? Keep in mind that having the norm doesn't mean that the issue is right for our family or kids, but it is helpful to be mindful of what is considered "standard" in society. If we are going to buck that, we have to do so thoughtfully because it will be our kids who may pay the price in their peer groups, not we parents. Many parents don't consider this point of view, so it is worth noting.

2. **What's our child's position?** If our child is old enough to ask for something, we have to at least be thoughtful in our response and problem solve a bit to see if our child is mature enough for what is being asked. I met some parents not long back who once told me they would "never" allow their daughter to have a cell phone before the end of middle school (sixth through eighth grade.) By the end of sixth grade, however, all their daughter's friends had cell phones and their daughter was able to prove to them that she knew how to use it and was willing to follow their rules. They were also working parents and started to recognize that having a cell phone could be helpful within their family. As a family, they worked through the issue and entering seventh grade, surprised their daughter with a cell phone for her birthday.

3. **Should price or payment matter?** I hear a lot of parents say that kids should not have technology such as cell phones or e-mail until that child can "pay" for the gizmo. I understand the life lesson and agree. In my family, my girls do chores and we have family rules that have to be followed for proper use of the cell phone. However, can we expect our kids to really hold down a job? We have to be careful about what we expect of our kids because a great deal is expected of them already and the extra burden may not be fair to them.

4. **Don't judge others until you are in their shoes.** It can be tempting to think you'll know what you'll do with technology before your kids are at that point or to think you have it all figured out, but the honest truth is you don't know more than you did for any other parenting issue you thought you had sorted out better than any parent before you. That's a lesson we all learn quickly. Until we walk in the shoes of parenting a child at a particular age and stage, we have no clue what we'll do! We have to recognize that early on and not add to our burden with rules and ideas we'll never be able to follow.

5. **What's your style?** Our kids are already using technology and gravitating toward it. Instead of being fearful of it, a better path is to allow our kids to engage in technology at normative ages for each venue and to learn about those venues so we can keep an eye out for issues and be part of our kids' digital lives. When our kids are young, we can control a great deal if we want to. As they get older, they will naturally break away and we need to let them do that. Part of this process will involve our kids becoming more digital and us needing to allow that to occur. Parents who are relaxed with a more "go with the flow" style will handle this better than parents who tend to become anxious when they don't know what their kids are up to or who need to control or plan their kids' entire lives (the so-called helicopter parents).

Stepping Into the Digital Pond

There really is no "right" age to allow our kids to dip a toe into the digital pond, but if we pay attention to the issues, we'll be able to decide what makes sense for our kids without getting in the way of a process that will occur whether we like it or not. At the same time, there is no rush. We can keep the pace reasonable and developmentally appropriate and allow our kids to use technologies that make sense without granting them access to technologies that don't make sense for their age.

For example, cell phone use seems to be trickling to younger ages. Studies and reports show that middle school is the time that adoption for cell phones and technology really takes off. Before then, kids who have cell phones don't use them as expected. Why do they have them? Families I know who give their elementary schoolkids cell phones do so mostly for safety issues.

1. **Medical:** Some children have emergency issues for which every second counts. For these kids, having access to a cell phone matters because landlines are not as easy to find as when we were kids, even in after-school programs (although the adults supervising those programs usually carry cell phones, or should). Some families whose children have medical issues feel more secure knowing their child can reach them if symptoms start to flare. Assuming these kids are supervised, this may not be needed but does give families peace of mind.

2. **Emergencies:** With both parents often working out of the home, many feel more secure if kids of all ages have a way to reach them and vice versa. This is an issue every family needs to sort out independently, but if elementary schoolkids are supervised after school, a personal cell phone for the child may not be needed.

Our Pre-tween Screen Viewers and Their Digital Lives—the Good, the Bad, and the Ugly

We live in a screen-laden world and it's no surprise that screen use starts young (infancy in some homes). For our very young children—infants, toddlers, and preschoolers—there are 2 issues to consider.

1. Is there an age younger than which we shouldn't allow any screen time for the sake of growth and development?

2. For kids older than that no-screen age, what is an appropriate amount of screen time for early childhood, if any at all?

In 2009, startling data emerged that proved that toddlers are watching much more TV and are online. Think about that—toddlers online!

Nielsen Wired reported in October 2009 that kids are watching more TV than in the prior 8 years, especially in the 2- to 5-year age group. That age group was reportedly watching 32 hours a week, with the 6- to 11-year age group close behind at 28 hours a week. Interestingly, Nielsen found that the younger kids are viewing their TV shows mostly via playback—DVD, DVR, and video—and they are watching more commercials.[1]

Some parents will counter these data with the fact that the time on the Internet or games is "educational," but we have to remember we are discussing very small children who are still learning basic developmental skills in all areas. The early childhood years are the formative years for developing language, social skills, and the building blocks of motor skills for sports that will help a child later on as they hone those skills for more complex activities.

In all realms of child development, children learn best with direct off-line interaction and the ability to explore their environments. Computer programs and TV shows can be fun and educational but need to be used thoughtfully and judiciously.

This is the reasoning behind the AAP screen time statement, which advocates zero screen time for children younger than 2 years and 2 hours of screen time for older children, with a strong encouragement of off-line activities for the 2- to 4-year age group.[2]

Where media is concerned, we often forget that what seems cute has content that has a huge impact. I'll never forget taking my youngest daughter to *The Adventures of Elmo in Grouchland* when she was 3 years old and almost having to leave because she couldn't stand the fact that Elmo's blanket was missing. At that age she had a much-loved blanket and the thought that Elmo might not get his blanket back was almost more than she could handle.

The early days of our kids are the building blocks of their future. The online world affects them greatly, so we should not ignore its ability to mold, shape, and redirect.

Tweens Online

Tweens have wonderful abilities to use technology. They begin to create and delve into technology in interesting ways and can have an endless thirst to learn how to master the intricacies. Their growing maturity and ability to please adults makes them a pleasure to be around, and it can be easy to get lulled into thinking they are ready for more than they are. As tweens approach the teen mark, this issue becomes very challenging to negotiate.

While most digital issues are applicable to all age groups, the tween group's unique place in childhood—no longer a child and not quite a teen—also creates some unique challenges in the digital world. This is why we have to be very careful to not open the door to teen concepts in the tween years. This group can talk the talk, but they are not ready to walk the walk!

Do We Have a Norm for Tweens?

For better or worse, we do have a new norm being established today which studies and reports are confirming. YouthBeat: The Syndicated Report by C&R Research is the most recent to the landscape that not only confirms what today's digital youth are using but how families seem to be adjusting.[3]

Similar to other reports on the use of digital devices by today's kids and teens, YouthBeat confirms that today's kids are starting very young, as young as first grade, and gravitate to TV, DVD, video, the computer, cameras, music, and cell phones. Use increases with age and parents provide the majority of purchasing power. Despite views that kids "need" cell phones when they are young, cell phones use among younger kids is markedly lower than tweens and teens—22% of kids reported using cell phones, compared with 60% of tweens and 84% of teens. The percentages of use were not as wide for other digital technologies.

The reasons for this are likely developmental. Cell phones play a huge social role that doesn't become interesting in a child's life until the tween and teen years. Before that, show watching and gaming are the prominent interests and are reflected in the digital activities the younger kids gravitate toward.

E-mail and Shooting From the Hip

Most kids have their first digital experience with e-mail. There isn't an accepted "right" age for a first e-mail account, and there are many variables to consider.

For young kids, e-mail accounts can be tricky because they don't always understand the ins and outs of their use. By a twist of fate, an e-mail intended for my 11-year-old daughter came to my in-box recently. The overall e-mail exchange was rather innocent, mostly about potential new puppies, movies recently seen, and who likes who. Then I noticed this small exchange:

```
From: my daughter's friend
To: my daughter
Subject:

I was there today jerk :)

-------------- Original message -----------------

From: my daughter
To: my daughter's friend
Subject:

Will you be in school tomorrow?
```

I was a bit taken aback to see my daughter's friend call her "jerk." My daughter claims it was meant as a joke, but was it? At the very least, it was not appropriate. I sat my daughter down and explained to her that it is never OK to call a friend names and especially not OK in an e-mail.

The anonymity of the online world is where the danger begins and keeps on going. As adults, we usually recognize the dangers of being separated by a computer even when the person on the other end is known to us. At the same time, how tempting it can be to shoot from the hip and just rattle off an unedited, uncensored e-mail! That does occur, doesn't it? If we as adults recognize how tempting it can be to send those sorts of communications and how difficult it can be to tap into the restraint to not respond when we receive an inflammatory communication, imagine how difficult it is for a developing child at any age.

If kids are truly spending as much time online as studies are telling us, what is this doing to their social development? It isn't helping, that's for sure. Think about kids today compared with kids of our generation. Being comfortable around adults isn't something kids are born with. None of us loved those uncomfortable moments as kids and neither do our children. They learn to become accustomed to those situations by being in them. Being online too much will only make it more difficult to recognize an e-mail that is inappropriate, as had occurred with my daughter.

Beyond inappropriate e-mails, the next step is true bullying, always dangerous and destructive. But do we have to get to bullying to say a behavior is unacceptable? Should there be acceptable manners for use for all online venues as there are for social manners? I certainly think so.

Think about basic real-world etiquette a moment. Here are some scenarios to ponder.

1. Would you ever let your daughter call another child "jerk," "dummy," or "idiot" to that child's face?
2. If your son didn't like a friend's new sweater, would it be OK for him to yell at his friend, calling him names like "idiot" and saying, "Where does your mom shop?" or "You call that a sweater?"
3. If your teen was upset with a clerk at a store, would it be OK to start yelling at the clerk, telling the clerk he or she was an idiot?

These are 3 examples of the type of e-mails or forum posts you can see online a great deal. People, often young people, do not censor themselves at all online, yet in the real world we would never allow any of these encounters to occur.

It's time we used real-world etiquette online and reminded ourselves of the manners we use in life that we want our kids to use. Here are the rules I try to get my kids to follow with their friends in all settings.

Dr Gwenn's Online and Off-line Guide to Social Conduct

1. Treat people as you'd have them treat you.
2. Don't write anything online you would feel uncomfortable saying to a person live or over the phone.
3. Shooting from the hip never produces good results. Count to 10 and then think before you write or speak.
4. Calling people names is a form of bullying.
5. Gossiping is a form of slander. For kids, this means that it's not a good thing to do and can get you into a lot of trouble. For adults, people have to realize that gossip can have a significant kickback that goes beyond public embarrassment. You never know who is around, so be careful who you talk about and the setting you are talking in.
6. Don't use code online—use real words and full sentences. Code can be difficult to interpret and sometimes has meanings beyond what you intend.
7. Never give out personal information online or off.
8. Don't e-mail or post inappropriate pictures or videos.
9. Never keep secrets from your parents, online or off, and let your parents know if someone asks you to do so. Nice people don't want kids to keep secrets from their parents.
10. If you are ever in a dangerous, destructive, or unsafe situation online or off, find a grown-up right away.
11. Adults are not the enemy—they have judgment you don't yet have. Don't be mad if a grown-up in your life tries to get you to talk about something you are doing online or off. The grown-up's job is to keep you safe, which is also one of the best ways the grown-up can show you he or she cares.

Viewer Beware: Tweens and Content

Content is an important issue for all kids but especially for tweens, who tend to try and uprate the types of movies and TV shows they rally to see because they feel so mature and look so mature at times. What we have to remember is that 12 may be almost 13, but it's not there yet!

Our kids have only one childhood. What's the rush in being exposed to content they are too young to see such as violence, drinking, and sexuality?

In addition to these topics being too mature for their ages, they also cause development issues, especially violence.

As the 2009 AAP "Media Violence" policy noted, "Research has associated exposure to media violence with a variety of physical and mental health problems for children and adolescents, including aggressive and violent behavior, bullying, desensitization to violence, fear, depression, nightmares, and sleep disturbances."[4]

The AAP policy further states the media violence is not isolated to just TV and movies but also video games: "Video games also are filled with violence. A recent analysis of the Entertainment Software Ratings Board (ESRB) ratings of video games revealed that more than half of all games are rated as containing violence, including more than 90% of games rated as appropriate for children 10 years or older (E10+ and T ratings)."[4]

The end result of exposure to emotionally charged content in the media such as violence is our children becoming desensitized and accepting violence as a normal aspect of everyday life. As Victor Strasburger, MD, FAAP, reminded me recently, "First-person shooting games are the most dangerous media today. The military uses them to desensitize new recruits. Most E10 [games] have violence in them."

References

1. McDonough P. TV viewing among kids at an eight-year high. NielsonWire Web site. Available at: http://blog.nielsen.com/nielsenwire/media_entertainment/tv-viewing-among-kids-at-an-eight-year-high. Published October 26, 2009. Accessed March 3, 2010
2. American Academy of Pediatrics Committee on Public Education. Children, adolescents, and television. *Pediatrics.* 2001;107:423–426. Available at: http://aappolicy.aappublications.org/cgi/content/full/pediatrics;107/2/423. Accessed March 3, 2010
3. YouthBeat: the syndicated report. C&R Research. Available at: http://viewer.zmags.com/publication/2be698e9#/2be698e9/2. Published 2009. Accessed March 3, 2010
4. American Academy of Pediatrics Council on Communications and Media. Media violence. *Pediatrics.* 2009;124:1495–1503. Available at: http://aappolicy.aappublications.org/cgi/content/full/pediatrics;124/5/1495. Accessed March 3, 2010

Chapter 8

Digital Life: Real Kids, Real Families, Real Issues

As parents, we have to recognize that our view of our kids' digital lives is biased from their experiences or perceptions of their experiences. What can help us gain perspective on whether our kid's digital inclinations and passions are normal is to have a sense of what other kids are doing online, as well as how other parents tackle digital issues.

Through social media channels, I met 5 amazing families who graciously shared interesting snapshots of their own digital lives. The parents were knowledgeable and aware of the digital world and the kids were technologically savvy. I was curious if their online confidence made them any more or less aware of the broader safety issues most of us struggle with.

Each family was sent 2 questionnaires to fill out, one specific for the parents (digital immigrants) and one for the kids (digital natives). I have no doubt you'll find the results of these interviews very intriguing.

Meet the Families

Family 1: Cam, 12-year-old middle school student, and dad Kevin
Family 2: Dylan, 13-year-old middle school student, and mom Krithi
Family 3: Sarah, 15-year-old high school student, and dad Tom
Family 4: Mike, 19-year-old college student, and mom Barbara
Family 5: Bernadette, 19-year-old college student (Parents did not fill out questionnaire.)

From Data to Reality

The stories of these digital families provide interesting perspectives on some of the issues we need to think about when we give keys to the online world to our digital natives, whether at approved ages of use or a bit earlier.

It was interesting that the younger digital natives seemed to have parents who were a bit more attuned to the digital world, whereas the older teens were already out of reach in many ways from their parent's grasp. If you think about it, the 9 years from our youngest digital native to the oldest is almost an entire decade. That's a gigantic amount of learning and growing in the child years, spanning almost the entire tween and teen experience. It's no wonder that the teen's experiences were very different from the tweens'. It's also no wonder their parents had very different perspectives and expectations.

The one amazing characteristic they all shared, however, was a unique prowess for the digital realm and a similarly adept ability to negotiate within it. Whether for learning, entertainment, communication, social connection, or just the old-fashioned fun of it, all the digital natives had an almost innate ability to walk the walk of the digital life.

Similarly shared was not only their parents' inability to always be caught up to their digitally savvy kids in technologic skill but how easily blinded their parents often were to any danger because of how competent their kids seemed. The question to ask is whether being digitally competent at ages 11, 13, 15, or 19 years makes these kids any more mature or safer than their online peers. Should it matter to a parent how digitally savvy a child is when rendering an opinion about, for example, whether to allow that tween or teen to be on Facebook? Or do we need to strictly follow the age guidelines set by Facebook, similar sites, and the law?

Before we get to know our digital natives, I'd like you to ponder 2 questions that I'll revisit later in the book.

- **Question 1:** Would you allow your 11- or 13-year-old to attend a weekend party with 16- or 18-year-old kids? (Forget the small details such as if you know the family or whether the parents will be home, and focus on the peer-to-peer concept only.)
- **Question 2:** Would you let your teen operate a car without a valid driver's license?

Once you've met our digital natives (and a few of the digital immigrants) and had a chance to get acquainted with the online world a bit more, I'll come back to these questions.

Cam's Story, Age 12

Cam is a very inventive tween who at 12 years of age is wowing his teachers and members of Edutopia.org with his ability to create videos and projects for an educational purpose. What's impressive about Cam is not just his technical abilities but his passion for creating his projects and for his off-line life. He's far from the techno-wiz who only wants to play with digital toys. You honestly wouldn't know Cam from any other 12-year-old boy in a school yard, but when you flipped on his projects, you'd know something was different!

Cam has been online with his very involved parents since the age of 2. Daily he uses a few of the following: TV, computer, HD camera, cell phone, Wii, Nintendo DS, iPod, and occasionally his parents' iPhone. Of these, he always has his cell phone because texting and staying connected with his friends is important to him. "I can talk, text, IM, and watch TV from my cell phone." Cam's father, Kevin, shared with me that Cam was 10 when first allowed to have a cell phone and one of the reasons for that decision was his travel hockey team and being away from home.

Cam is online 4 to 7 hours a day but spends a great deal of time off-line too. His off-line activities include hockey, piano, guitar, student council, lacrosse, and reading.

His parents have never had steadfast rules of when he could or couldn't explore the digital world; instead they have tried to go by his cues and wait until he seemed "mature" and "ready." To that end, they actively discuss safety issues such as sexting, Internet safety, and social media issues including the "digital imprint" (which I'll discuss more in Chapter 18).

Cam's father tries to help Cam be responsible for his behavior online by explaining the importance of the digital imprint and the need to act responsibly. In our initial interviews, Kevin felt this was enough because Cam acted so mature. By the time of my final touch point with Kevin, he wasn't as confident. He had heard an Internet safety talk at Cam's school and began to realize that being 12 years old and online was fraught with more issues than he realized; Kevin was starting to recognize the need for a more organized plan.

Here's how Kevin's turnaround came about.

Kevin, Cam's Father

As online as Cam is, Kevin said Cam is equally off-line: "Being non-digital, he does sports, student council, has a 'girlfriend,' plays hockey, lacrosse, bikes, scooter, reads tons of sci-fi, video projects, and commercials. Has taken pictures and video of weddings and gotten paid."

Cam is the oldest of 3 (he has younger sisters aged 5 and 8 years), so his parents are feeling their way through the digital world with him. At 12 years of age, Kevin finds Cam an easygoing tween who's reliable and follows rules. "Cam is so responsible—we'd love for him to get into trouble!" he joked with me. The first issue to test Kevin and his wife Debbie's faith in Cam online was addressing whether to allow Cam to go on Facebook when only age 12. While they recognized he was "too young" by the stated age, they felt he was ready. Kevin explained to me: "Cam and his mom got on Facebook at the same time." They discussed with Cam some simple family rules—no posting of pictures, he and Debbie have to approve everything, privacy is locked down, only friends they know are allowed. And no games. Kevin told Cam clearly that if he finds out that he tried games or quizzes, he'd consider it a violation of trust. Cam did try one quiz once and did tell Kevin. Kevin handled it by discussing why it was not safe and that doing it again would result in having Facebook shut down.

As for other online venues, Kevin assesses the greater risk to his kids and the ability to manage the "digital imprint" when deciding what to allow online. Kevin's motto is "Trust by verify," meaning that we have to allow our kids to be online but be with them and check, check, and check some more, with the kids knowing they are being checked on and also sometimes with them not knowing. For a while, he and Debbie were checking Cam's browser to see where he was hunting while surfing.

For his daughters, he notes that they gravitate to Webkinz and chat, Barbie. com, and PBS.

They have each computer set up on "mobile me" so that they can all be synchronized and bookmarked. In fact, he found that bookmarking sites helped all his kids know where to go when they were younger.

One big issue he's had to monitor, especially for his daughters, is printing. "They would print everything!" (I can vouch for this in my home too!)

Of concern: "Chatting worries us. Not monitored. But that's like texting. I'm concerned about instant messaging with too many creeps trying to get in."

For family communication, Kevin made a fascinating point about e-mail: "We use our e-mail—not Cam's—for friends, etc. He uses our e-mail like a house phone," referring to a general use public phone one may find in a hotel or even a landline phone for general use for a family. Kevin is a very big texting fan and hasn't seen any issues with Cam so far: "Texting is like our walkie-talkie without the stating. He can reply without letting friends know mom and dad are checking."

Ditto on the cell phone: "During travel hockey while in the hotel, we used the phone to know where he was. Phone helps with contact. He was 10 to 11 years old."

Finally, as with Facebook, Cam is on Twitter via Kevin's accounts: "Cam doesn't see followers. [Direct message] component expands his brand. I manage followers and he only uses if I'm there. Helps with his growing educational needs 'cause he's beyond the basics and has big passion."

Instead of a hard, fast, printed set of house rules, Kevin and Debbie try to tailor their use rules via conversation and address issues as they occur, dictated by their kids' ages. Kevin shared with me that one of the biggest issues he discusses with his kids is the digital imprint. He explains that "Google crawls the Web and takes pictures and those pictures don't go away!" He uses relatives as examples and shows Facebook profiles and examples of job hunts to illustrate how what a person does today can affect the future. His goal is to facilitate discussion and empower use and creativity, but he and Debbie have no problem taking away privileges if needed.

Kevin feels strongly that parents have to be involved until kids are old enough to really understand the digital world. "We have to manage digital imprint as parents until he is ready to take it over. The goal is to find the middle of road before he does and test it out like driving."

Kevin finds that not all parents do this and worries about that. "Many parents abdicate responsibility to kids and don't want to know."

For their daughters, they find they used the same approach they have used with Cam but have to tailor their approach to each child's needs. Kevin notes: "We introduce technology when young and add as they get older by each personality. Right now our 8-year-old is into laptop and video diary. That will change again and we'll change with her."

Finally, I asked Kevin what advice he has for parents, and he notes: "Never say never…last year I said 'no' to Facebook and now he's on it!"

Kevin doesn't view Cam as a typical tween and has rationalized that as one of the reasons it's OK for Cam to be on Facebook and Twitter at age 12. But what's right for Cam? And once Cam is a teen, will this tween-age maturity remain or will he become a bit less reliable, as teens tend to do? Many families grapple with these issues, and they are not as straightforward as you may think. I've asked experts to weigh in on this important issue in Chapter 11.

Dylan's Story, Age 13

I first "met" Dylan online, on Edutopia.org (www.edutopia.org/digital-generation-profile-dylan-video) and on Twitter through his nonprofit, Lil' MDGs (www.lilmdgs.org). I didn't realize initially that @lilmdgs was Dylan! He is your typical 13-year-old teen boy in so many ways—he has endless energy and an unmatched ability to use the latest technology of the day.

Unlike most 13-year-olds, though, Dylan pushed the adults around him to go past basic school projects that introduced him to global issues such as hunger, poverty, and natural disasters (eg, tsunami, hurricanes), and he set out to do something about them.

Via social networking and the creation of Web sites, Dylan now runs a nonprofit, Lil' MDGs (Lil' Millennium Development Goals), with the mission to "leverage the power of the Internet to educate, engage, and empower youth to work together to meet the UN Millennium Development Goals." To date, Lil' MDGs has raised more than three quarters of a million dollars toward tsunami relief from kids in 31 states and 34 countries. It has raised funds to build a dorm for a school in Tibet.

Dylan loves making movies that empower people and also uses technology for fun. At the moment, Dylan uses 7 digital pieces of technology a day: digital camera, iPhone, Flip video phone, DVD camcorder, digital calculator, computer, and gaming/TV system. Of these, he always has his iPhone, digital camera, and Flip video camera with him. With these technologies he makes videos, shares music, bookmarks sites he visits, and texts.

I learned that he has not talked about sexting formally with his parents, but they have discussed Internet and social networking safety. They've addressed specific issues such as friending, making online purchases, maintaining privacy, and protecting passwords.

Dylan first went online with a computer his parents set up for him at 10 months of age! And his mom, Krithi, told me she first gave Dylan a cell phone when he was 7. They don't have a formal family computer plan, but she is very involved with what he uses.

What I found interesting is that while Dylan told me his parents didn't talk to him about sexting, his mom told me she didn't have to because he talked to her about it! Krithi also noted that she doesn't have many worries about her kids' online use given their nonprofit experience.

Krithi feels the same about cellphones; her only concern is the possibility of going over the minutes and running up a huge bill. Nonetheless, Dylan is aware of the plan and how to use it.

She finds many benefits to the digital age with kids: "Using the power of the Internet and digital media, Dylan has engaged several thousand children from almost 40 countries. It is through the power of the Internet that he chats and runs his meeting regularly. Besides, he has raised funds for the nonprofit using the Internet."

Dylan is online 5 to 6 hours a day at times but has a full off-line life with karate, snowboarding, music, swimming, and tennis.

The family has used parent controls in the past and found them to be helpful. The biggest benefit was keeping control of playdates, so when friends were over the content was appropriate.

Sometimes there were overload issues, so Dylan's parents pulled the plug on an activity that he seemed to be spending too much time on.

Krithi thinks Dylan's favorite digital activity is social networking. He's involved with a few, including Facebook, Twitter, Eventful, Flickr, You-Tube, and iTunes. She did allow him to go onto Facebook under her name at age 11 because of his nonprofit work.

I asked her to tell me about a digital memory, good or bad, and this is what she shared: "The most important and meaningful story in Dylan's case relate to his nonprofit, Lil' MDGs. He founded that to leverage the power of the Internet to educate, engage, inspire, and empower children in all corners of the world to meet the UN MDGs. This started in 2004 and has gradually turned out to be a model organization that is recognized by the UN as #1 when it comes to tackling poverty using the power of the Internet.

"To date, they have mobilized children from 31 states in America and almost 40 countries and raised $780,000 million for tsunami relief and over $10 million for hurricane relief, all via the Internet and social networking sites. You can see more here: www.lilmdgs.org/accomplishments.php.

"There are pros and cons for children to consider while using the Internet and the services available online; nonetheless, if they have the right approach, are receptive to directions and guidance, and show that they understand how to stay safe while capitalizing on what the Internet has to offer, it is one of the greatest opportunities available for anyone and everyone."

Dylan and his family illustrate a few concepts I'm going to address later in the book about Internet safety and social networking called the 2Cs, 3 Es, and TECH.

Sarah's Story, Age 15

Sarah is a tech-savvy teen and represents the "in-house tech expert" that many families have. Sarah can't actually recall a time she hasn't been online. She represents the all-digital generation in that way. This is really the only life she has known and remembers.

Sarah uses 4 to 5 digital devices daily, typically her desktop computer (an iMac), her cell phone, iPod, and cable TV. Of these, only her phone is portable and goes with her daily.

Her parents may not be as technologically advanced as Sarah, but they are aware of her online life and are up on the issues—they have discussed sexting, Internet safety, and social media safety with her.

As with many kids her age, she is a busy texter and shares pictures and music with her friends digitally. She also uses social bookmarking.

Sarah describes herself as in-house tech support and a bit of a sponge for technology: "Since I have been using technology for as long as I can remember, it has never been 'the new thing' for my sisters and me. I'm no Mac genius, but I know a lot about the brand and how the technology works. My parents are constantly asking for help with tasks that I find super simple. I take the skill I have for granted because there was no training involved. Everything I learned was through experience or online blogs. I watch TV occasionally, not nearly as much as some of my classmates, because I would much rather go to bed early over staying up very late to watch 'my shows.'"

Mike's Story, Age 19

Mike is a 19-year-old who loves technology but doesn't go overboard with its use. He is also frugally minded. Tech savvy since the age of 3 and a Web surfer since the age of 6, it's no surprise that gaming is among his top favorite digital activities. His laptop and Xbox 360 are the 2 digital devices he frequents daily, although his cell phone is the one he carries all the time. Unlike many of his friends, however, Mike doesn't text because he and his family do not have an unlimited text plan and he has decided not to text until he can pay for it.

His parents are very up to date on what Mike does online, but he doesn't discuss things with them like sexting, Internet safety, and social media, mostly due to his age, according to his mother Barbara.

For Mike, digital life is about sharing, and music tops the list. About the digital world, Mike says being online has "made getting music much easier, it's totally opened my horizons to new bands. The hype machine (ie, PR and advertising industry) used to be a big part of that, but now I don't visit it as much because there's just too many new bands to listen to at once. I still find new good music—it's just not as huge now. There is a dark side to the Internet, as today, one of my favorite Web sites got partially blocked by my ISP and I'm very mad at them for it. But…the Internet enables me to get most anything I want at any time, and that's what makes it so special."

Barbara weighed in with some interesting comments. She noted that they didn't give Mike a cell phone until he was 15 because before then it just wasn't needed. I asked about house rules and learned that her husband monitored Mike's Internet time for a while but when they realized he was being responsible, he just backed off and decided to go with the flow. The best house rules she has found have been emphasizing the importance of good grades and priorities, especially once social networking sites such as Facebook and MySpace entered the picture, and staying grounded off-line. Barbara feels that the digital world can blunt the world around kids today.

Even for Mike, who isn't online as much as other kids, she finds this to be true. She shared this story: "A young person in the 21st century has so much to say to friends that they constantly have a phone in their hand if not up to their ear. They use a phone to keep in touch, gossip, take pictures, let friends know what they are doing every minute of the day. Take away a cell phone and most young people are lost.

"I am a product of the '60s. We enjoyed our music, but nothing compares to the kids today. They have an MP3 they can carry in a pocket and listen to a wide variety of different types of music.

"I am not sure they are actually aware of what is going on in the world around them, as they are plugged into their favorite music, and telephone calls to friends. When do they listen to the news or read a newspaper? Unless it is something that everyone is talking about, I am not sure they are aware [of] what is going on.

"For years, my son went with me most everywhere. At least once a month we went past an apartment complex near us. One day when he was learning how to drive, he was actually paying attention to what was around him, he asked, 'When did they build those apartments?' I told him, 'Before you were born.' Now, 4 years later, he still doesn't know his way around the area of suburbia that we live in."

Bernadette's Story, Age 19

Bernadette is also 19. She typifies what happens when teen life dips a toe into the young adult world and experiences independence from parents. Unlike our younger digital natives, Bernadette is in college and on her own. And unlike many of our other families, Bernadette found she was living a digital world her family knew little about until well after she was on to the next thing.

Bernadette recalls being in sixth grade, around 11 years old, when her digital life began. Of all her digital devices, her laptop and cell phone are the 2 she relies on the most and the ones that go with her almost everywhere.

When asked if her parents discussed safety issues with her, Bernadette told me that her parents didn't talk to her about sexting because "they'd have no idea what it was." They did discuss Internet safety with her, but she felt "it was too late; way past the horrors" she had already experienced online. As for social networking, they did discuss that with her too, but she had already sorted it all out by the time that conversation occurred. Interestingly, her mother is trying to get onto Facebook now, but Bernadette is unsure about whether to friend her.

As a college student, sharing is important to Bernadette, but she's reluctant to share music "because of the Napster/copyright scare."

Bernadette is living the digital life. In her words, this is what it is for her: "Digital media IS my life. Or, at least, that's what I *should* be saying as a member of Generation Y. It's been strange for me, to grow up completely dependent on digital media like everyone else my age, yet as I get older, increasingly skeptical of its effect on healthy, human lives. I'm in awe and in denial about the weight of social media on my generation.

"A few weeks ago, I took on Tim Ferriss' 'media diet' in his book *The 4-Hour Workweek*. The diet challenged me to dramatically reduce my daily digital media intake for about 4 days. This meant no news TV channels, no news Web sites, no news radio, no Web surfing unless it's for a *specific* task that takes no more than 5 minutes, no more than an hour of pleasure TV, and very, very limited e-mail time. I was only able to check my e-mail once at 12:00 pm and at 4:00 pm, for 5 minutes each. This gave me a mental heart attack, considering that laptops are a college student's extra arm and we're used to thinking that we are each, indeed, important enough to be checking our e-mail 70 times a day.

"But I did it, all 5 days of it, and it completely changed my outlook on digital media. I realized how self-centered I was to think the world would collapse had I not checked my e-mail every 10 minutes. I realized how much useless information clogs up my Google Reader and Twitter feed. I realized how much useless information I put out, via what-I'm-eating-right-now tweets. Most importantly, I realized how incredibly productive I was when I used the Internet like a useful but optional tool, as opposed to…an oxygen tank. Or a candy jar. Not only did I feel productive, I felt rested—days seemed twice as long; I sat in the sun and planned out big business or project ideas I never gave my full attention to; I reconnected with abandoned hobbies such as knitting and interacting with humans in the flesh; and when I was tired, I actually slept.

"Maybe it's 19-year-old narcissism. I know it isn't good Gen-Y form to be biting the hands that have RSS-fed me. Without a doubt, digital media has changed the dynamics and volume levels of major conversations—business to consumer, revolutionary leaders to supporters. Digital media has flipped the way humans interact upside down. It has given unprecedented access, control, and overall empowerment to anyone who can type and frankly, I'm frightened to see what the next generation will be able to do with it.

"Also, I'm basically building my PR career by deep diving into digital/ social media. Digital media is my sword. Digital media will be my paycheck. I'm connected, curious, and I love to talk about it. I really should not be denying it.

"But I also think digital media has eaten up a lot that is valuable and simple in life. I think it is incredibly addictive and deceptive in that you can spend hours believing you're 'improving your social media skills' or 'catching up with friends' but go to bed that night restless and empty-minded. I think it perpetuates terrible ideas in young people, such as the tendency to connect over a screen than over lunch, total neglect of physical health and nature, exhibitionism, narcissism, and endless-endless-endless image and body issues. And I fear it's producing humans who will, down the line, be less like tall, intelligent Amazonians and more like antisocial Quasimodos who melt in the sunlight but can write a witty tweet."

Bernadette's honesty and openness is refreshing and reveals some important messages about the digital world. Are our kids going to be much different from Bernadette someday? I'll come back to this in a bit, but keep her comments in mind for now and how the snapshots of the younger kids look in a life!

A Note of Caution

It would be foolhardy not to acknowledge that these are self-selected families and that some of the answers may be candy coated. What's interesting about the families I talked with, however, is there were no outliers or answers that were not consistent with other authors who have talked with digital families. So it was reassuring that I had found families who represented a nice cross section of the digital world—and that was my goal.

Chapter 9

The Parent-O-Sphere: The Digital Divide

Do Good Things Come in Small Packages?

Understanding the online life of our teens is our best ally for keeping them safe. By knowing how they spend their time online and what that time may involve, we can better prepare ourselves for the conversations we need to have as well as the problems our children may be having at any age.

Don't let the eye roll fool you—your teens want (and need) you to be involved. But to do this, you need to start recognizing that you are not parenting in 2 different worlds, online and off, but one world—just the world. The technology and lingo of today's youth culture is overwhelming and can be intimidating, but does that mean we abdicate our parenting role? Of course not. Parry Aftab, Esq, of WiredSafety.org points out that we don't view the kitchen in our home differently from the bathroom in terms of safety issues. "We may not know a lot about tools," she told me, "but we know they are dangerous."

She notes that parents today are mentally drawing a line between real life and the virtual world of the Internet, and that's what's making it hard for many of us to parent when our kids are visiting that virtual world. "We can't draw that line," she notes. "We have to be involved in life, period. And we don't need to know a lot to do it."

The Parent-O-Sphere

Your kids may be able to edit a movie and put music to a photo montage at age 10, but that doesn't mean they know the intricacies of social networking or understand the ins and outs of e-mail. It bears repeating that technologic skill has nothing to do with a child's ability to understand how to use that technology in a social setting! Kids are going to do dumb things with technology; hence the evolution of sexting, cyberbullying, and sending "shoot from the hip" e-mails and inappropriate pictures and videos. Does this mean we take an extreme view of the digital world and ban it or restrict our kids? No.

It's the lack of understanding that creates fear of technology and a tendency to avoid it and keep our kids away from it. If we learn to understand technology better, we'll embrace it more and be less fearful. If we help our kids to understand the digital world as soon as they go online, we can empower them to be safe and responsible and make good digital use decisions. That alone will be an improvement over where some kids are today.

Consider this. We know driving can be dangerous and kids sometimes get into accidents and fender benders. Do we ban our kids from driving when they are the proper age? No. We have them take driver's education classes. We educate them about the rules of the road and make sure they understand how to drive safely. Society has now also stepped up by having the graduated driver's license program.

Let's not forget that history has taught us that new technologies are healthy for society in the long run, provided we understand their uses, appropriate applications, and pitfalls. It's only when technology is used for unintended purposes or to extremes that issues arise. Where kids are concerned, those extremes can occur right before our eyes and often well before our kids show any outward signs of trouble. Sometimes we may not even know there is trouble brewing until something shows up on YouTube, Facebook, MySpace, or a similar site!

As parents, our job is to be a step ahead of our kids—to know what they are doing and show them how to do it appropriately; to know the limits of kids at different ages and be realistic that despite our kids' mature moments, they are still kids; and to parent online as we do off-line so if they are crossing a line, we can intervene.

Developmental differences factor into our kids' online lives in tangible ways. Just because our kids may look and act maturely, that doesn't absolve us of our license to parent any more than it gives our kids a license to freely use these applications. As you'll see in the next couple of chapters, it's all about development, especially of our kids' brains!

That being said, there are actually many ways we can talk with our kids using technology.

Using Technology to Talk With Our Kids

Technology	Uses in Talking With Kids and Teens
E-mail	Advantages: great for letter-like communication, updates, sending pictures, attachments, references, humor, and staying in touch
	Disadvantages: not great for "instant" communication or for having a significant conversation that is better off-line
Text	Advantages: updates such as plan changes
	Disadvantages: not great if requires immediate reply; not perfect for full, long conversation; may hinder writing and social abilities in teens because of shorthand used
Social networking post	Advantages: great way to stay connected and let kids know you are involved; good for humor and just being involved
	Disadvantages: privacy concerns—entire network can view post; not appropriate for private conversation but often used that way
Cell phone call	Advantages: allows direct communication
	Disadvantages: limited by cell coverage
Instant messaging	Advantages: instant communications like texting
	Disadvantages: must be online and logged on to the service to communicate with the person of interest; not great for full conversation
Video chat	Advantages: visual conversation in real time; can see body language and facial expressions to gauge emotional responses
	Disadvantages: connection issues; interference issues if music or other ambient noise on either side; need to be online and logged in

The Digitally Connected Kid: Now and Then

Brightly colored earbuds connected to various MP3 devices, along with the constant thumb clicking on cell phones, are telltale signs of how digitally connected this generation is. Even their fashion and accessories are wired to go for their digital lives. Backpacks, purses, jackets, pillows…you name it and it likely comes in all colors of the rainbow and with cleverly located headphone exit locations.

The addition of digital connections may be relatively new, but the need to connect among teens is ages old. Strolling through art about teens, such as images captured by Normal Rockwell, to Broadway shows such as *West Side Story* or movies like *High School Musical,* we see consistent pictures of teens as very social beings needing to connect, hang, and converse.

One of the best depictions of teens that stands the test of time comes from *Bye Bye Birdie.* In "The Telephone Hour," teens sing a "who's dating who" song; by the end, the entire town is shown talking to someone. While the scene is set in the 1950s, it could easily have been in the 1960s, '70s, '80s, '90s, or today. Replace the 1950s fashion with today's and the old Bell phone with cell phones, computers, and teens on social networking sites, and you'll have modern life today. What won't change? The topics discussed! Teens today will still be discussing dating, gossip, fashion, and parties. Some of the details may change, but the general themes will always be timeless!

If we do a quick "then and now" snapshot, there are some staggering similarities between pre- and post-Internet observations of our kids that are worth noting, proving the old adage, "The more things change, the more they stay the same."

It All Starts at Home

In 1943, *Nature* published "Sociological Value of Family Meals." The abstract reads: "Family table talk plays a vital part in rearing children. During mealtime, the time when the whole family is likely to be together, children learn moral values, absorb family culture, and develop as individuals…."[1]

This was published decades before the Internet was in any American home, decades before we had digital lives. Yet today in our digital world, the concept of the family meal is not only very much alive but being heralded as one of our best allies in helping our kids negotiate the digital word.

In his book *iBrain,* Gary Small, MD, noted that University of Minnesota research found a positive effect of family meals on kids: "Adolescents from homes having fewer family dinners were more likely to exhibit high-risk behaviors, including substance abuse, sexual activity, suicide attempts, violence, and academic problems." The family meal "not only strengthens our neural circuitry for human contact…but also helps ease the stress we experience in our daily lives…."[2]

Politicians and academicians alike have reiterated the importance of the family meal. Ronald Reagan once said: "All great change in America begins at the dinner table."

Miriam Weinstein confirms this in her book, *The Surprising Power of Family Meals:* "The things we are likely to discuss at the supper table anchor our children more firmly in the world…. When families prepare meals together, kids learn real-life skills…become better team members…. Sharing meals helps cement family relationships, no matter how you define *family.* The world *companion,* which dates back to ancient Rome, means 'one who breaks bread with you.'"[3]

We are global citizens and that citizenship starts at home. If we reinforce that important lesson by having meaningful conversations off-line at home, our kids will learn that those human-to-human connections are important and work toward achieving them in their own lives. We won't get anywhere with our attempt at crossing the digital bridge with our kids if we can't communicate with them, and the way to start is likely around our own dinner tables!

Proclamations and Progress

President and First Lady Clinton were big supporters of not only the promotion of the Internet and the good it could do for our children and communities but of families and kids in general. In May 2000, First Lady Hillary Rodham Clinton hosted the White House Conference on Teenagers. During that event, an interesting YMCA survey was discussed. It confirmed that teens want to talk with their parents—3 out of 4 teens, in fact. Yet a huge disconnect was found between parents' and teens' perceptions of conversations happening at home. While 64% of parents reported that they talked with their kids frequently about important topics, only 41% of the teens felt their parents did so. Similarly, 62% of parents felt that their kids shared their values, whereas only 46% of teens reported that to be the case. The vast majority of teens reported turning to their friends for help and advice over their parents.

Interestingly, while most parents reported that their biggest concern for their kids was threats outside the home, teens reported that their biggest concern was not spending enough time with mom and dad.

The message from this survey was clear: teens wanted a more heartfelt connection with their parents.

In 2009, Norton came out with a Norton Online Living Report that gives a reassuring glimpse of today's digital world.[4]

- We're connected in a way that matters more. Seven out of 10 adults report that technologies like e-mail and instant message (IM) have made relationships better. Imagine if we help our kids learn to harness the power of those tools with a bit more finesse?
- The Internet has improved family ties. Fourteen percent of online relationships are family groups, now called e-families. These families report that using technology has improved their bonds. In this group, 9 out of 10 report that their kids follow their online use rules, compared with 8 out of 10 people who are not in e-families. E-families tend to be more digitally savvy than their non–e-family friends.
- Kids online: "The Internet is kids' new backyard, where they spend an average of 39 hours a month, nearly twice as much time as their parents think they spend."
  - TV is still used more than Internet and cell phones.
  - Eighty-six percent of kids text, 73% e-mail from cell phones, and 23% Twitter.
  - Ninety-two percent socialize online with family and friends.
- More kids are being caught when not acting appropriately online.
- More kids are opening up to their relatives, parents, and grandparents about what they are doing online (1 in 4 are friending their parents).
- The majority of kids are acting "graciously" online, yet many parents worldwide continue to monitor them for behavior issues.

So, is there still a digital divide? Clearly not by the numbers. The issue is in how we think of ourselves online, and that may be the last hurdle to preventing us from uniting with our kids.

Becoming United Online

Digital divide sounds ominous. And in truth, there are slices of our society struggling with this. Thankfully, there are resources to close that technologic gap, from programs at the local libraries, to adult education programs, to online programs such as Enough is Enough.

For most of us, though, the only divide remaining is in our minds. We see ourselves as far away from our kids, so we parent them differently when they are online or involved in a digital venue. In the end, the divide may be less technologic and more ideologic within ourselves. To fix that, we have to start parenting in 1 world, not 2, and just close the divide! If we tune in to what our kids are doing differently and recognize that we have to parent more consistently with whatever they do and be more technologically independent of how we think about what they are doing, the divide in our minds and with our kids will close.

We can also look at this from what our teens want of us. We know they want to spend more time with us and talk more with us; that should be easy to accomplish with a bit of unplugged time and undivided attention.

We can also review data on the online world of teens to better understand their values and activities so we can determine our starting point and focus.

The Cox Communications 2009 Teen Online & Wireless Safety Survery[5] confirms what other reports have stated—teens are online a lot and are socially connected. One concerning finding is that while teens are aware of safety issues, 3 out of 5 post photos of themselves and half post photos of their friends online. Another concerning finding is that one-third of teens reported cyberbullying and 1 in 5 sexting. And even though three-fourths of teens said that their parents talked with them about safety, there was no enforcing of rules online and zero enforcing of their behavior with cell phones. (In the 2008 survey of tweens, 90% reported being online by age 9.)

The number of tweens that tell their parents what they do online drops with age. "Only 69% of 11-12 year-olds tell Mom and Dad a lot/everything versus 86% percent of 8-10 year-olds."[5]

With regard to social networking,

- Thirty-four percent of 11- and 12-year-olds have a profile on a social networking site.

- Tweens with social networking profiles post more online and face greater exposure to unknown contacts and online bullying.
- More than 1 in 5 tweens post information about themselves online, including pictures, the city they live in, and how old they are.
- Thirty-seven percent of tweens aged 11 to 12 admit to posting a fake age online.

When it comes to contacts from strangers,

- Twenty-eight percent of tweens have been contacted over the Internet by someone they don't know.
- Twenty-nine percent of tweens have been contacted online by someone they don't know; 18% of them keep the messages to themselves, and 11% have chatted.

It's time we recognize that our tweens and teens are not always clueing us in to their whereabouts online! They are actually signaling us to be with them and want us to be involved. Now how cool is that?

Forging a Bridge Across the Digital Divide

Sometimes the best way to ward off trouble is to have a handy checklist of symptoms to be on the watch for. Here's a quick list to help you determine if you and your digital native are where you want to be in building a better communication bridge.

Possible Signs of Trouble

1. Contacts, followers, friends, IM chats from folks you don't know
2. Unusual behavior such as turning off the computer screen when you walk in or acting overly jumpy
3. Instant message or text code that is alarming, such as references to parents in room or drugs
4. Alarming clues in Web browser or on Facebook or MySpace profile or wall of interests your child may have that are causing him or her harm
5. Something unusual emerging in cell phone records/logs (Is your child being bullied by someone? Are there names, numbers you are not familiar with? Do any messages alarm you?)

Positive Ways to Use Technology With Kids of All Ages

1. Off-line family time
2. Changes in plans
3. Checking in
4. Just staying connected

When Not to Use Technology With Your Kids

1. Confrontation—wait until your child is home.
2. Having a fight.
3. Making accusations.
4. Pretending to be someone you are not.
5. Dangerous and destructive behaviors—these boil down to anything that puts someone in harm's way physically or emotionally.

References

1. Sociologic value of family meals. *Nature.* 1943;152:271. Available at: http://www. nature.com/nature/journal/v152/n3853/abs/152271c0.html. Accessed March 3, 2010
2. Small G, Vorgan G. *iBrain: Surviving the Technological Alteration of the Modern Mind.* New York, NY: HarperCollins; 2008
3. Weinstein M. *The Surprising Power of Family Meals: How Eating Together Makes Us Smarter, Stronger, Healthier, and Happier.* Hanover, NH: Steerforth Press; 2005
4. Norton Online Living Report 09. Norton From Symantec Web site. Available at: http://www.nortononlineliving.com/documents/NOLR_Report_09.pdf. Accessed March 3, 2010
5. Cox Communications Teen Online and Wireless Safety Survey. Available at: http:// www.cox.com/takecharge/safe_teens_2009/media/2009_teen_survey_internet_and_ wireless_safety.pdf. Accessed March 3, 2010

Chapter 10

How and When Kids Get Online

If the online world were a fairy tale, would the Internet be the big bad wolf?

That's what many parents still worry about, but the reality is that the Internet is more akin to Goldilocks being ultra-curious about which bed to sleep in and porridge to eat.

In truth, we fear what we don't know, which is why when it comes to allowing our kids to go online, we tend to pull the plug quickly one moment and blame it for everything at another. If we took the time to learn how to drive it, we'd find that it wasn't so intimidating at all and much safer than even our worst fears.

Think about the words of wisdom you tell your child when learning something new such as driving: "Relax. It seems hard and overwhelming at first, but once you learn the steps and how to use the car and have some practice, it's really easy and you'll do great! There are a few things you do need to know to be safe, and that's what driver's education and practice are for."

When a young driver learns to driver a car, there are 4 basic steps.

Step 1: Once proper age, register for a learner's permit at your local registry.
Step 2: Take driver's education to
  • Learn the rules of the road and how the roadways work.
  • Learn the parts of the car and how they work.
  • Practice!
Step 3: Take the driver's test.
Step 4: Congratulations! You're a licensed driver and now can explore the roadways, following the laws in your state.

Learning to drive the Internet has similar principles.

1. **Age parameters:** Many sites now have minimum ages, especially social networking sites. This isn't just to keep the site to a more mature audience but to protect our kids. Social networking looks easy, but it is actually a bit more complicated in the hands of a young teen. Similar to

driving, young teens can be impulsive and a bit reckless. Pushing the age of use older allows teens to mature so when they do start using the sites, they are ready for the experience.

2. **Technical assistance and tutorials:** Learning to use popular Web venues is easy. There are manuals, books, courses, and online tutorials. The popular sites are all very user-friendly and designed to be intuitive and similar to many of our other online experiences. Once you understand how to use one area of today's Internet, it becomes much easier to adapt to another. As a parent, learning the technology becomes not only essential so you can understand what your kids are doing but quite easy.

3. **Fundamentals:** Cars have parts and are run by keys. Web sites have sections and are usually run by passwords. Your job as a parent is to be familiar enough with the online areas your kids frequent to
   - Know the on and off switch.
   - Understand the navigation of the site.
   - Understand the privacy and safety features of the site.
   - Know the purpose of the site.
   If you know these 4 things, you'll be able to get around a site enough to see what your child is experiencing, and learn enough to have a conversation with your child about the site.

4. **Know the roadways:** The Internet doesn't have a handy map system; it is interconnected via searching. If you understand just enough about how searching works, how to Google, you'll be able to find your way around the Web and find out where your child is hopping to and from. You'll also become more efficient in your own searches, which is an added plus.

5. **Follow the rules and make sure your kids follow the rules:** Just like there are rules to driving and laws, there are online rules, including
   - Etiquette
   - Age of use for sites
   - Age-appropriate content

One of the best lessons you can teach your kids is to follow the rules. If a site isn't appropriate, don't fudge the rule—it's simply not worth it. For example, Facebook's minimum age is 13. What lesson are you teaching your child if you allow him or her on younger?

6. **The real world is off-line:** Ideally, our online time will help us learn something about life to make our off-line time more fulfilling. To do so, we need to help our kids balance their media diets so that their off-line life still matters and isn't completely consumed by their online worlds.

Getting Online: Where to Begin

At some point, all of our kids will need to learn how to use a computer and the Internet. There are actually no established guidelines for when these tasks need to be achieved, except that it's clear that by the time our kids are in middle and high school, being online is part of the culture and important socially. And by the time a child has progressed to middle school, the Internet and computer skills have usually been introduced in most school curricula.

Families have different values of technology and its role in childhood. To help as you sort out when your kids should first be introduced to the computer and Internet, have some idea of what a child can do at each age and what the experts say is appropriate.

Because computers are a screen, as are cell phones and handheld smartphones such as iPhones and BlackBerries, it's important to consider overall screen time and age as an initial consideration. As a general rule of thumb, kids younger than 2 years should not be on any screen, computer, TV, or otherwise. This is the recommendation of the American Academy of Pediatrics, and it is supported by other psychiatric experts because infants and toddlers develop best in their early days with off-line play and human-to-human contact. Reading, music, floor time, dancing, time outside… these are the activities that small children younger than 2 need and thrive with.

For children older than 2 years, the consensus is 1 to 2 hours of screen time maximum. This always causes a bit of a stir because we include TV and computers in this mix. I consider this guideline to apply to recreational screen time and not homework for older kids. We have to recognize that as with their adult parents, tweens and teens may have additional screen time for schoolwork that will fall outside this 1 to 2 hours. The concept is to be thoughtful and mindful of the screen time our kids have so the numbers don't keep escalating, as they do for many kids. Right now, by the way, the average 8- to 18-year-old is still watching close to 4 hours of TV and using a computer for 1 hour, with video games for 1 more hour. What's clearly on the rise, however, is mobile media, cell phone, and MP3 player use. If you tally up the old players with these new contributors, our kids are on screens nearly 7½ hours a day according to the 2010 Kaiser Generation M^2 report![1] If multitasking is included in the tally, that number increases to nearly 11 hours of total screen use each day.

For children older than 2, the way to think about Internet and computer use is similar to how they approach riding a bike, their first exposure to the freedom obtained from a moving vehicle.

- Two to 4 years: land rovers
- Five to 6 years: pedal pushers
- Seven to 8 years: training wheelers
- Nine to 12 years: training wheels optional
- Thirteen to 18 years: look, mom, no hands!

Our kids progress through the states of computer skill mastery and Internet competency in a similar way.

Two to 4 Years: Land Rovers

Not having had a reason to use a computer before this point in life, this age group is just becoming exposed to the world of computers and the Internet. They've seen their parents and older siblings use computers and cell phones, may have played with toy versions, and now have their first true exposure to not only touching the real thing "with permission" but getting to use it with age-appropriate games and online sites.

This age group is not independent initially with the computer or the Internet, but rather is either sitting on someone's lap or in a seat next to a parent or an older sibling.

Computer time is just an introduction to the venue. Keeping the time personal will help kids understand one of the main functions, staying in touch with relatives and friends. This age group may enjoy seeing pictures and videos of relatives, using a webcam to see a relative on the other end, or placing a Skype call to someone they know. They will also enjoy Web sites that focus on characters they are familiar with and that have songs and activities they can get involved with. Read-aloud story programs are another fantastic way to introduce this age group to the computer while they are still learning skills to participate on their own. Many of these programs are CD-ROM–based or Web-based and include different levels to allow a child to progress to the next level as their reading skills and computer skills advance.

Five to 6 Years: Pedal Pushers

This age group becomes fascinated by the online world and their ability to become involved with it. This is likely the youngest that kids can start to use a mouse enough to control any aspect of the computer more independently. With emerging reading skills, kids will begin to become independent online and with the computer to a greater degree during this phase, but not all will do so at the same time.

What this group can do with a computer and the Internet is skill dependent. Those who have emerging reading skills and learn to use a mouse will be able to tackle more, while others may need some assistance. Overall, though, this group needs supervision to be sure they are not on the computer too long and don't click to places they should not.

For kids who have more interest and skills, consider kid-specific browsers and setting up your toolbar so they can click on Web sites you approve. There are products that help make getting online streamlined, such as the Fisher-Price Easy Link Internet Launch Pad, which allows a child to launch child-friendly Web sites from a designated character-labeled console.

Many families put on some sort of parent control or only allow their children to use the computer when an adult is nearby to provide an extra safety net for this age group.

Once kids go online, it's important to discuss Internet safety with them and have a family plan (see Chapter 18).

Seven to 8 Years: Training Wheelers

Training wheelers are true big kids but not quite tweens. They are bursting with reading, writing, and computer skills, and growing independence. They are also very naïve and very social, have little understanding of how the online world works, and are only just figuring out how the off-line world works.

Virtual worlds, multiplayer gaming, and even e-mail may start becoming interesting to these kids as well as their friends. What's important is to find a few sites you trust that their friends are involved with and talk to your kids about appropriate rules of the road (see Chapter 18).

For kids interested in exploring their hobbies online with true surfing, using kid-safe domains and considering Internet filters may be worthwhile but may also not be needed, depending on your child and the level of your involvement.

These kids can become intrigued by what they are not allowed to do.[2] Close supervision of what they are doing online is one safety net; the other is considering true filtering software as well as having frequent and honest discussions about the online world.

Nine to 12 Years: Training Wheels Optional

Meet the tweens! Ace gamers, independent, and likely your in-house tech support, these kids are sponges for technical accomplishments. Not only do they not take long to master new digital skills, devices, and software, they quickly find new ways to put them to use.

The issue, of course, is that tweens are not teens or adults. They are truly kids—big kids filled with ideas, curiosity, and a thirst for information about the world around them, but still kids. They want to be older than they are. They often look and act older than they are. And we sometimes forget they are not older because of how masterfully they can navigate the online world and digital off-line devices such as cell phones.

Supervision is still needed with the training wheels–optional kids, although a bit more at arm's length. This bunch responds well to being given rules to follow with clear consequences. If they know they are being monitored, often that is more powerful than any monitoring device we can install on our hard drives. Even more than monitoring, frank discussions about the online world and what you are worried about goes a long way with this age group. They are very rules-focused and eager to please the adults in their lives. Having clear expectations for use helps them understand the parameters but not in a vacuum. This group very much needs to understand why you have the views you have beyond "I say so" or "Because I'm the parent." This group tends to be all about fairness and equity and making sure rules are followed properly. To this end, if you have rules or know of rules that online sites have, it's important you follow them too, or you'll not only be going against how your kids are wired but how they expect you to behave. This will be covered more in Chapter 14.

With tweens, the online world becomes very intriguing. They yearn to be a part of it and become very interested in sites they may not be ready for, such as Facebook and MySpace. There are many other sites, though, for which they are ready (see Chapter 14). Helping them learn the rules of the cyber-road will help them not only online but off-line as well because social norms tend to be a challenge to them in general at this age.

Thirteen to 18 Years: Look, Mom, No Hands!

The much anticipated teen years have arrived, complete with newfound independence, rebellion and questioning of authority, and desire to be completely independent from the family once relied on for everything, including the ultimate litmus for right and wrong. Indeed, the teen years are when most of what we thought of our kids gets tossed out the window and we have to change and be much more flexible as well as realistic that prior expectations and assumptions may no longer hold true. Our kids as teens are not the same kids we once knew as tweens. This is just the natural evolution of becoming an adult. We all went through it, even if we want to block out those years!

The key to success in helping our kids negotiate the teen years is truly dependent on how we negotiated the prior years. Having discussions about Internet safety and the myriad issues of the online world for the first time in the teen years makes as much sense as waiting until the teen years to discuss caring for the body, puberty, or sexuality. It all is a process that has to build over time.

Teens are wired to overreact or not react at all. We did this to our parents and they will do this to us, especially when it comes to sorting out the details of their online lives. Freak out if you must on the inside or later on in private, but maintain the best poker face and cool and calm exterior despite what your teen tells you about his or her online life or what has been seen, heard, or read online. GetNetWise describes teens perfectly when it writes: "If your teen confides in you about something scary or inappropriate that he encountered online, your first response shouldn't be to take away his Internet privileges. Try to be supportive and work with your teen to help prevent this from happening in the future. And remember that your teen will soon be an adult and needs to know not just how to behave but how to exercise judgment, reaching her own conclusions on how to explore the Net and life in general in a safe and productive manner."[3]

With this age group, even Internet safety experts find things are not always the way they seem. Marian Merritt, Internet safety advocate for Symantec Corporation, found this out with her then 14-year-old daughter, Maddy: "We were one of the first beta testers for the new family safety service called [Norton Online Family]. When I first set it up on my teen daughter's laptop, I did so with her reluctant permission. We agreed that I would monitor what she did but not put the filters to block anything. And I didn't put the alerts on to send me notifications. I think both of us were worried that the new filters would be too restrictive or make a lot of mistakes and I didn't want a flood of messages about nothing.

"Soon after I set up the service, I logged into the account Web site to review her online activities and to make sure I could understand what I saw. My calm quickly turned to icy panic when I saw one item listed in red. It was a Web site my daughter had visited that broke our house rules. Even worse, it was a porn site.

"I was so reluctant to visit my daughter in her room to find out what was going on. So I took a careful note of what the activity report indicated had happened before she visited that porn site. That additional bit of information helped me realize that what I was seeing was the result of an unfortunate click on the wrong link, rather than evidence of a child with an interest in the wrong sort of online material.

"Once we did talk about what had happened, you can imagine how relieved she was to know that I understood how she'd mistakenly clicked the wrong link. She also wasn't sure about coming to me to talk about it, out of fear I wouldn't understand how she'd ended up on the site in the first place. I pointed out that we could adjust the settings in [Norton Online Family] so that even if she clicked on a link like that, instead of going through to the site, the service would block her. She was really happy and relieved to know we had that option and we agreed to adjust the settings to give her that further protection and confidence that she could use the Internet without running into trouble. And I was so grateful that we'd dealt with the situation without overreacting or being overly punitive for what was clearly an innocent mistake."

Talking with Marian about this episode reinforced some interesting points I was trying to research for this book.

1. It is very important to have the facts about what a child, particularly a teen, is doing online before confronting a child.
2. Filtering programs don't tell the entire story and you have to understand the information you are looking at to make sense of the time your child spends online.
3. Sometimes monitoring is better than filtering because it prompts conversation.
4. Teens often end up places online innocently but are fearful of letting us know out of shame, embarrassment, and concern over us overreacting or not believing their story.
5. Things are not always what they seem!

I'll get into filtering programs a bit more in Chapter 18, but this vignette is a good example of what many experts have shared about filtering programs in general—monitoring is better than filtering, and discussion always trumps both!

Resource

Internet by age and stage. Common Sense Media Web site. Available at: http://www.commonsense.com/internet-safety-tips/age-and-stage.php. Accessed March 4, 2010

References

1. Rideout VJ, Foehr UG, Roberts DF. *Generation M²: Media in the Lives of 8- to 18-Year-Olds.* Menlo Park, CA: Henry J. Kaiser Family Foundation; 2010. Available at: http://www.kff.org/entmedia/upload/8010.pdf. Accessed May 6, 2010
2. Getting started: ages and states of Internet use. Dell Web site. Available at: http://www.dell.com/content/topics/topic.aspx/global/learn/family_safety/started_ages?c=us&cs=19&l=en&s=dhs. Accessed March 4, 2010
3. Safety by age/maturity. GetNetWise Web site. Available at: http://kids.getnetwise.org/safetyguide/age. Accessed March 4, 2010

Chapter 11

Understanding Tweens and Teens

"They're gone!" my daughter, age 10, yelled a floor away.

"What's gone?" I yelped back from the kitchen.

"Most of my stuff on Webkinz!"

We logged on together and she was right—some of her valuable items were gone. We quickly changed her password and talked about being extra careful to not let friends trick her into giving it to them. But you know, we believed her that she hadn't given it out. Her behavior and emotions told us this was a clear situation of hacking. It was an upsetting lesson to learn so young, but we helped her understand she had taken all the necessary steps to protect her stuff and talked about good versus not-so-good passwords so that they would be harder for hackers and friends to guess.

Had we not been so involved with her online life, we wouldn't have even known what to search for or what Webkinz was, and it would not have been so easy to manage when the issue hit.

It's not enough to know the rules for online kids or age breakdowns when kids should go online. We have to know what drives our kids to be online and what drives them to do what they do in the first place! We do this so well when our kids are very small, as infants and toddlers. We almost second-guess their every move from when they are about to notice their hand for the first time, to when they will roll, to when they will take their first step or say "mama" or "dada."

Somewhere around kindergarten, though, we stop tracking quite as dogmatically. It's also around that time we relax as parents. Is it that our kids are just big and communicative enough that we don't need all that data? Are we just too busy? Or do we not know what data we should be looking for?

Part of the issue is that growth itself does slow and the developmental milestones become less dramatic and a bit more cerebral as kids enter the school years. Those early years are so hyperkinetic and dramatic, it's easy to get lulled into a sense that all is OK when the rapid-fire changes begin to ease and give way to a more manageable, albeit often intangible, pace of development.

Just as we start thinking of our kids as "big kids," so too does society at large. Even the language used to describe our kids changes quickly once they become tweens and teens, and it can quickly convince us our kids are ready for more than they developmentally can contend with.

One of the social trends is to push our kids into an adultlike world, then criticize them when they are not acting "mature." So let's not judge a tween by teen standards or teen by adult standards. This way it becomes easier to reset the clock to a more kid-friendly pace.

The Teen World Unraveled

In July 2009, when he was a 15-year-old intern with Morgan Stanley, Matthew Robson wrote about how teens use digital media.[1] Robson's report cracked adult assumptions and rocked the globe! He showed us that there's uniformity in industrial countries in how teens use digital media and that adult views of this generation are not always accurate.

Robson's report is one of the first to run through new and old media and give us a glimpse in how most teens are using the venues discussed. While based in the United Kingdom, his comments apply to the United States, and most of his comments are consistent with observations made by larger observational reports of teens by Pew, Kaiser, ComScore, Cox Communications, and Harris Interactive.

Here are Robson's conclusions.[1]

- **Radio:** Teens are not regular radio listeners. They prefer online music venues where they can pick their own music.
- **TV:** Teen TV watching is seasonal and dependent on TV series and sports season. Viewing often occurs in spurts depending on the show. The TiVo concept is also very popular.
- **Newspapers:** Teens don't have time for newspapers; they obtain their information online.
- **Gaming:** Wii is the most popular game console, followed by Xbox 360, then PS3. With the introduction of Wii, girls are now gaming as much as boys and at younger ages. PC gaming is not of interest to teens.

- **Internet:** Teens are all online at home and school. All teens are into social networking, with Facebook being the most popular. Teens are not into Twitter (see Chapter 15). All teens use the Internet for search, with Google the number 1 search engine. YouTube is popular for video viewing. Shopping is not prevalent because it requires a credit card.
- **Advertising:** Teens usually don't pay attention to banner ads and find them "annoying." They also ignore "outside" ads.
- **Music:** Music is very important to teens. They prefer to not pay for it and love to share it with friends. Illegal downloading is popular because iTunes is cost prohibitive for many teens.
- **Movies:** Teens love going to the movies because of "the experience." Robson notes this is more important than the film. The cost of going to the movies can keep older teens from seeing movies in the theatre, and pirated DVDs become more common.
- **Devices**
  - Ninety percent of teens have a cell phone.
  - Most popular cell phone features: calling and texting.
  - Teens normally don't upgrade phones too often due to cost.
  - Teens normally don't use Internet on their phones due to cost.
  - Most teens have a TV.
  - Most teens have computer access and those are PCs.
  - One-third of teens have game consoles, with 50% of those being Wii.
  - What they love: touch screens, phones that can hold music, devices that can connect to the Internet, big TVs.
  - What they hate: wires, black-and-white screens, big phones, phones with less than 10 hours of battery life.

Brain 101

When it comes to the online world, understanding brain development will help you appreciate why some of the popular social media sites have age guidelines and why, when parents look away from those guidelines, child health and safety advocates cringe. It's not that your child may not be safe; it's that we know what's just around the corner when your child becomes a teen.

What makes the teenage years so challenging to describe and even predict is that there is no one way to experience it and no exact age that starts the process for all teens. To make the situation even more complex, each teen's individual strengths and weaknesses, physical, emotional, and intellectual, drive the process in different and unique ways from other teens.

What we do know is that chronologically all kids become teens at 13 years of age and stay that way until 19 years of age. What we don't know is exactly what path each teen will take from 13 to 19. Each will have moments of amazing brilliance as well as incredible road bumps. Each teen will have moments where we, as parents, want to pull our hair out, and others where we are jumping for joy, completely amazed by our teen's maturity and reasoning. There will be times when our teen will be able to stand firm against the power of the peer, and others when our teen will crumble under the pressure.

Each and every one of these experiences is not only normal but expected, and we have to be realistic that our teen, regardless of how "good" she was or how "mature" he seemed as a tween, will be that way too.

Peers, hormones, neurobiological changes, and a growing sense of independence as the later teen years approach and preparation begins to leave home for college, a first job, or perhaps the armed services all create some very interesting and unpredictable moments. Some of these moments we can explain; others we'll have some trouble sorting out.

Reassuringly, though, this all boils down to some complex changes in teen brain development. While experts vary in the merit they place on the state of teen development research at the moment, what we do know is that teen brain development is complex and doesn't occur the same way in every teen due to how varied each teen's experiences are. We also know that they all end up doing fine if we support them as parents and a community!

Typical Tweens and Teens

If any parent of a teen tells you they have no issues with their teen, they're lying! Even "good" teens have difficult moments, and even the most "together" of parents of teens want to pull their hair out and send their teen to Siberia from time to time. That is honestly why most quotations about teens refer to them as an unpredictable bunch, with parents often dumbfounded and aging more in those 7 years than at any other time in their child's existence.

We're deluding ourselves if we think

A. We can raise our teens better than any other parent who has tried before us.
B. Our teens are going to be straight with us all the time.
C. Our teens are not going to do the dumb stuff we did as teens.

Teens are not this way by chance. They act as they do because of some specific changes in their brains.

Luckily for us, some very smart scientists and researchers have sorted this out. In doing so, it becomes easier to understand statements such as, "It's really not a good idea for an 11-year-old to be on Facebook, and a reason why 13 is set as the minimum, but older may be better."

The Tween Brain

On the Web site BrainConnection.com, Robert Sylwester, EdD, says brain development "encompasses two distinct 10-year periods—a childhood acceptance of dependence, and an adolescent reach for independence." He notes that childhood brain development occurs in two 10-year periods and that each "period begins slowly and awkwardly with a four-year initial activation of the brain systems that process the focus of that period, followed by a six-year developmental drive towards confident competence."[2]

The first 10-year period would include 4 preschool years and then kindergarten through fifth grade. The second 10 years would be the middle school years of sixth through eighth grades followed by the remainder of high school and early college.[2]

The part of the brain we are concerned with for tween and teen development is the actual cortex—the *cerebrum*. This is the meat of the brain we see in pictures. This part of the brain has 4 sections, with the most forward section called the *frontal lobe*. The areas on the side are called the *temporal lobes*. On the back, there are the *occipital lobes*. And the areas tucked between the front and back are the *parietal lobes*. They each have different functions.

- **Frontal:** reasoning and emotion, decision-making
- **Temporal:** our touch lobes
- **Occipital:** our vision lobes
- **Parietal:** our sensory and sound lobes

Sylwester notes that brains develop back to front during this 20-year phase. This is why in elementary school kids are so great with learning facts, while things like higher reasoning are not easy to master until high school and college. It's pure biology.

It's obviously complex, how our brain's different areas interact, but suffice it to say that there are limits to what a child can do at certain ages because of what's wired in and ready to go. It would be like asking a computer to do something it isn't programmed to do or doesn't have the memory for.

Comparing tween and teen brains, Sylwester describes them as follows: "An infant is a toddler, relative to walking—and a tween is a fumbler, relative to problem solving."[3] So, can a tween problem solve? Yes, but with lots of mistakes and starts and stops. We have to be realistic to the tasks we ask them to do and the expected outcome. For kids, the stakes are not very high when errors of judgment occur, but they become very high with teens and can lead to accidents, drug use, pregnancy, and issues with friends.

Many parents will say to me, "But he is so mature" at 11 years of age. This statement should help explain why that comment doesn't make sense: "(Tweens) are neither really smart children nor incompetent adolescents. They're just trying their best to enhance the maturation and integration of some very complex cognitive systems that can only mature through experience."[3]

The way their brains are wired, tweens can do some amazing things. But let's not for a moment think they are supremely mature or can begin to tackle much higher levels of reasoning. They just are not there yet and won't get there for about 8 more years, when their brains fully develop. Tweens are still concrete thinkers and their driving force, especially early in their tween-dom, is to please the grown-ups around them. For some precocious tweens the switch on teen-like independence gets turned on around age 12; it's later for others. That's the earliest teen independence emerges—precisely the time when we need to be careful about their online experiences.

The Teen Brain

Work in progress is the best description for any growing child, especially teenagers—and their brains! Teen brains are capable of amazing thought and creativity but are becoming rewired in a fast-paced and unique way that leaves them efficient one moment and clumsy the next.

New research using magnetic resonance imaging (MRI) technology is beginning to sort out the complex nature of the teen brain. It's becoming very clear that teenagers do not use the same areas of the adult, mature brain right away and are driven early in the teenage process by the centers in the brain responsible for gut reaction and impulse. This is important to understand because it helps us gain perspective about why our teens don't understand social consequences or emotional messages, yet they can be overachievers in school, sports, music, or any other event they set their mind to.

Jay Giedd, MD, notes on www.dana.org, "In many ways adolescence is the healthiest time of life. The immune system, resistance to cancer, tolerance for heat and cold and several other variables are at their peak."[4] At the same, time, Dr Giedd notes that mortality for teens has increased by 300% and in areas that are directly related to risk taking—driving resulting in accidents, weapon use resulting in homicide, and drug and alcohol use resulting in suicide. These are the number 1, 2, and 3 causes of death in this age group, according to the Centers for Disease Control and Prevention.

This isn't too surprising when you take a step back and consider what parts of the brain teens use for rational thought and decision-making compared with the fully mature brain of adults. Using MRI technology, researchers, including Dr Giedd, have been able to document that teens and adults use very different parts of the brain for similar activities, such as those involving reading of emotions, decision-making, and higher functioning.

As adults, we use our frontal lobe, the so-called CEO or executive center of our brains. Teens don't use that area of the brain for decision-making; they use a more primitive part of the brain called the *amygdala*. The amygdala is thought to be where our gut reactions originate. If this is where our teens' decision-making reactions are centered, it does help explain, to a degree, why they are so impulsive.

Gary Small, MD, who has studied the impact of technology on the brain and cowrote the book *iBrain,* agrees. Dr Small explained that the adolescent brain is still developing during the teenage years. Due to a process called pruning, 60% of the synaptic connections will be pruned away during these years. How our kids spend their time will likely affect this process, although, he explained, we don't yet fully understand how.

The prefrontal cortex is not fully developed in teens, so Dr Small feels that the major question we have to consider is what the effect of increased technology is on our teens' overall development, including social interactions and empathy. Dr Small wonders if the 40-year-old of tomorrow will be less empathetic than the 40-year-old of today because of this effect, and be less able to problem solve. He is seeing some of this play out now as he discusses the effect of technology on brains across the country. College professors have told Dr Small that students are less focused and are texting during class. "We jump from idea to idea like we jump from Web site to Web site," he explained in a phone interview. "We teach them ideas but it's hard to settle them down. As I was talking (in his lecture), they were texting."

Unplugging for Life

"Families are really struggling with this," noted Dr Small.

The good news is that the brain is incredibly resilient and further research will likely teach us much more about helping our teens and tweens negotiate the world with a prominent role of technology. "It takes us a while to give up what we want and technology is so alluring," he explained. "Change in behavior is a hard sell."

So not texting in class, going hands free, even unplugging once in a while will take time to relearn but are crucial for all of us, especially our growing kids.

Beyond allowing ourselves to be detached from technology, the other issue to consider is social. If we don't reclaim some unplugged time, how will our kids learn to communicate face-to-face? How will they learn to talk with each other and adults? How will they learn to settle their issues face-to-face and not with technology as an intermediary? (Dr Small's book has exercises as well as quizzes that help identify people at risk for social problems that are worth noting.)

Much ado about nothing? I don't think so. All the experts I spoke with had at least one experience with their own tween or teen that reminded them that their own kids are struggling with social skills, even with technology at play.

Rachel Dretzin, a producer for PBS Frontline, told me how her 11½-year-old son will answer the phone then hang up with a "Bye."

At 15, my daughter will sometimes answer the phone with "What?" Or if she calls, she will just dive into what's on her mind without saying "Hi" or "It's me."

The issue is reading faces and learning to express emotion. We can't let our kids off the hook with the difficult social and emotional tasks they will encounter growing up. Ask yourself this: are the future 40-somethings that Dr Small predicts the type of people you want to be parents to your future grandkids?

Technology may have an effect on our kids and their brains, but we can have a bigger effect if we pay more attention to the on and off switch!

Resources
- Interview: Deborah Yurgelun-Todd. Inside the Teenage Brain. PBS Frontline Web site. Available at: http://www.pbs.org/wgbh/pages/frontline/shows/teenbrain/interviews/todd.html. Accessed March 4, 2010
- Giedd JN. Structural magnetic resonance imaging of the adolescent brain. Ann N Y Acad Sci. 2004;1021:77–85. Available at: http://intramural.nimh.nih.gov/research/pubs/giedd05.pdf. Accessed March 4, 2010
- Spinks S. One reason teens respond differently to the world: immature brain circuitry. PBS Frontline Web site. Available at: http://www.pbs.org/wgbh/pages/frontline/shows/teenbrain/work/onereason.html. Accessed March 4, 2010

References

1. Robson M. How teenagers consume media: the report that shook the city. *The Guardian* UK Web site. Available at: http://www.guardian.co.uk/business/2009/jul/13/teenage-media-habits-morgan-stanley. Published July 13, 2009. Accessed March 4, 2010

2. Sylwester R. The tween brain: midway between infant dependency and adult autonomy: part 1. BrainConnection.com Web site. Available at: http://brainconnection.positscience.com/content/228_1. Published March 2006. Accessed March 4, 2010

3. Sylwester R. The tween brain: midway between infant dependency and adult autonomy: part 2. BrainConnection.com Web site. Available at: http://brainconnection.positscience.com/content/229_1. Published April 2006. Accessed March 4, 2010

4. Giedd JN. The teen brain: primed to learn, primed to take risks. The Dana Foundation Web site. Available at: http://www.dana.org/news/cerebrum/detail.aspx?id=19620. Published February 26, 2009. Accessed March 4, 2010

Part 2

The Teen/Tween-O-Sphere Uncensored

Section 2
Online Technologies

Chapter 12

The Internet and Web 2.0

W ould you go on a road trip without a map? Most of us do just that when we go online. Surfing the Web without a plan of attack is no different than attempting a road trip hoping to hit particular destinations but with no clue where they are or how to find them.

Our roads are, for the most part, labeled. We have a highway system we can understand, and planning a trip is as simple as taking out a map or plotting in our coordinates on MapQuest, Google Maps, Yahoo! Maps, or a handy GPS if we happen to have one. But if you didn't know where you were going, if you were trying to find something based on a notion of a vague place in a faraway land, you would have a heck of a time finding information.

The reason for this is simple—just like our highway and road system, the Internet has a definite organization complete with labels. Those labels include terms that may seem very technical and foreign, like Web 1.0, Web 2.0, user-generated information, social networking, texting, microblogging, blogging, bookmarking, RSS feeds, "share this," and "friend me." Way back when, terms like latitude, longitude, equator, poles, states, countries, mesas, rivers, volcanoes, and many other geographic terms sounded foreign too.

If we learn a bit more about the online world and how it's organized, we can help our kids make more of their time online, as well as help them stay a bit more safe.

What's in a Name?

Sorting out the name game online is half the battle to getting to where you want to be and mastering the venue. The 1.0 in Web 1.0 is a way of saying, "I was first." It refers to not only the original technology that was initially developed for the Internet, but the first Web sites that we all viewed when the World Wide Web came online and entered our homes as broadband started becoming more popular. Those initial Web sites were very simple, sparse, and text-oriented. They were meant to transmit information, not invite participation as our Web 2.0 sites do today. If you want to take a walk through the park of what some of the more popular sites like Google, Yahoo!, Twitter, and Facebook looked like when they launched, check out this link: www.telegraph.co.uk/technology/6125914/How-20-popular-websites-looked-when-they-launched.html.

Take Google, for example. In 1999, here's how it appeared.

No video. No links for personalization. No news. No images. Just search and white space. (Courtesy of Google.)

Web 2.0 sites, on the other hand, are made for sharing and personalizing. These are the sites we use today, including all the social networking sites we have online now—music, video, blogs, and pictures—as well as our current Web browsers that allow us to pull in RSS feeds for news, blogs, video, games, sports scores, movie times, and anything else that comes to mind. We can not only personalize our pages but share what we find with others via e-mail, posting to social networking sites, or saving to our social networking bookmark page. These are all basic properties of 2.0 sites.

Even the look of 1.0 and 2.0 sites is dramatically different. Web 1.0 sites tended to be professional but a bit stiff. Web 2.0 sites go for creativity. They are put online to draw people in. They are also easy to use, create, and maintain, which wasn't always the case with 1.0 sites—they often needed a designated Web team to help with development and maintenance. Web 1.0 sites also required some capitol to create. Web 2.0 sites can be created for free or very inexpensively, especially blogs and sites built on blog platforms. You can also think of Web 1.0 versus Web 2.0 like this.

Web 1.0	Web 2.0
Home pages	Blogs
Reading	Writing
Companies	Communities
HTML	XML (ie, a "feed")
Client server	Peer to peer
Lectures	Conversation
Advertising	Word of mouth
Wires	Can go wireless
Dial-up	Web via broadband
All about ownership	All about sharing

Courtesy of DarrenBarefoot.com; Courtesy of JoeDrumgoole.com

Web 2.0 lingo is now being applied to just about everything online, so that's really the only reason to understand what it means. Now when someone says, "This is a health 2.0," you'll understand right away that the person is talking about a health site with 2.0 features like blogs, social abilities, RSS feeds, and all sorts of sharing features. And it will likely look really cool and be easy to navigate.

The other reason you need to have some appreciation for the 2.0 world is that it is the world our kids and teens exist in all the time. Not only is this world made for them, but many of the most popular 2.0 applications have been invented by digital natives themselves! If our kids and teens are going to be this invested in this world, so too should we. Luckily, our digital natives leave a trail of high-tech bread crumbs so finding them online won't be that difficult. In fact, it's as easy as ordering from a menu at your local diner…except this one is high tech with a lot of bells and whistles.

Ordering From the 2.0 Menu: Where to Begin

If you are traveling down a highway, there are a few predictable stops you can expect to find—rest stops, exits to other destinations, restaurants, gas stations, scenic vista outlooks. Traveling around the Internet is really no different, except that our path will end up as clear as the keyword terms we put in the search bar. If we are clear with our terms, search results will get us fairly close to where we hope to be. If we're vague or haven't a clue what to put for a term, our end result will be equally hard to decipher and we may find ourselves on a wild goose chase through cyberspace, blindfolded.

Our off-line lives have addresses and names and so do online destinations. The online home of a site is called the URL and the name is just that—the site's name. Some sites will have a designated name, while others will have a common name that everyone shares and then divvies up with user names.

The difference between the two is like owning a home versus a condo. When you own a home you have a street address. When you own a condo you tend to have a subaddress for the property, something like Anywhere Village, Unit 747-9.

Online, self-standing sites will have specific URL addresses. For example, my Web site is www.pediatricsnow.com. Common sites that divvy up their space, such as social networking and social bookmarking sites, use user names. Those Web sites have addresses that look like www.nameofwebsite.com/username. For example, on Twitter you'd find me at http://twitter.com/drgwenn, and you can find my bookmarking links at http://delicious.com/drgwenn.

Knowing this helps you have an idea whether a site is common or free-standing. Common sites tend to be social networking sites, so understanding the lingo can be very useful!

But the online issue isn't just in understanding the lingo; it's in figuring out where to go and how to get there. This is where the rubber meets the road—if we don't do this right, we could end up on a slice of the Internet that is far from G rated and nothing we'd want our kids exposed to. This is one of the biggest reasons we need to be invested in understanding the online world.

Again, we have our off-line models to rely on. When you and your family decide to go to a movie or out to a restaurant for dinner, you consider a great deal of variables. For the movie, you'll consider the movie's rating and the age and temperament of your kids. You may consider a few reviews or opinions of people you know who have seen the film. You try to get a sense of whether the film is appropriate for your child. This isn't as easy as we'd like, but parents commonly give it a try before purchasing tickets. We go through similar reasoning for picking out a restaurant to dine at with our kids. Many are family friendly and offer something for everyone. Others are a bit more mature but do accommodate families with kids' menus.

And of course, there are the fanciest of restaurants that are priced in a very grown-up range with a comparable menu. Regardless of the type of restaurant you are at, you likely will notice very generational preferences for food choice and individual ones as well.

With its many Web sites, blogs, and social media sites, the Internet is no different than the myriad of restaurants we frequent. There's a huge variety of online destinations, each offering a different menu of options that will ultimately determine your online experience. Some destinations are for all ages, while others are clearly for particular ages and groups. Unlike menus in restaurants, however, it can be much more difficult online to discern which sites are always the best for kids, especially older tweens and teens who are able to handle more mature material and have better reading and computer skills.

There is a difference, however, between dining and traveling online that we can't ignore. When we go to a restaurant, it's easy to check it out beforehand to be sure it's appropriate for our kids. We don't often have that luxury with Web destinations. It's all too easy to end up somewhere unintended that is not age or developmentally appropriate for our kids. Even the most savvy of adult searchers can wind up on questionable sites, so you can imagine how challenging this is for kids.

With the help of groups that monitor how people use the Web, we can get a fairly good picture of our kids' online use and create a menu of sorts for their Internet travels. Each online child will have different portions and preferences for what they pick from that menu, but know it is the first step to helping our kids navigate the Web as they migrate through it.

One important issue to always remember—the more bells and whistles a site has, the more our kids are likely to want to explore it!

Chapter 13

Instant Communication Primer

Somewhere between the beginning of fourth grade and fifth grade, my oldest daughter and her friends replaced e-mail with instant messaging (IMing) in the blink of an eye. Not yet a cell phone owner, she and her friends had determined that e-mail was too slow and that IMing was much more convenient and fun. When the IM adventure first began, we were clear about the rules—we could check her IM log at any time; we would randomly check her IM list and if we found anyone on it we didn't know we'd shut it down; and it couldn't be used when she had homework to do.

Those rules worked well, and still do, even though IMing has expanded into the world of cell phone texting as the same kids became teens and entered their upper middle school and early high school years. What we didn't expect, however, was instant communication's amplifying effect on selective hearing.

When my oldest daughter was in fifth grade, just about a teen but not quite, I found I had to fight fire with fire to snap her out of her technologically induced haze. Once, she was IMing with her friends. I had called her multiple times to come downstairs for dinner, even once from her bedroom door, but to no avail. I found her at her computer with her fingers clicking away and her eyes glued on the screen. Every once in a while a faint "ping" would echo in the room as a response would come to her message. Before I exploded with frustration, a sudden aha occurred. I ran to my computer, hit the IM button, and typed, "Hello…cute girl on the computer, you are cordially invited to the kitchen for dinner." To her credit, she laughed and came downstairs with me. Three years later, she actually denies the incident!

It's no secret that we live in a very hurried society. Adults hurry as they move between work and home, their kids' various activities and home, or their home-based job commitments and home-based home commitments. Kids hurry as they move between school and their activities before finally arriving back home again. Our communications technologies have kept pace with our hurried lives, becoming faster and more portable as new iterations of technology emerge. We have no less than 5 ways to communicate with each other relatively quickly each and every day.

- E-mail
- Instant messaging and social networking site posting
- Texting
- Phone calls (landlines, cell lines, computer calls [video and microphone])
- Microblogging

Add to this list the more static forms of communication such as comments left on Web sites, blogs, and social networking sites, and this becomes one hefty list of communications tools, a veritable potpourri of ways to stay in touch—instantly.

Phones: Our Familiar Old Friend Paves the Way for Things to Come

Telephones are the technology we all intuitively know the best because we all grew up with them. Even our own parents had phones as kids, albeit in a different form and more generalized.

Our lives may be wireless today, but the philosophy phones represent dates back to a time in our history grounded by wires and a zeal for change and evolution that has managed to survive to this day. Many independent factors evolved to get us to where we are today, but the one that changed our lives the most occurred on March 10, 1876, when Alexander Graham Bell made the first audible telephone call to Thomas Watson. Bell's telephone was his attempt at improving communication from the telegraph and taking it to the next level by adding speech. Is that any different than more recent inventors and industry leaders taking the basic telephone and enhancing it by adding computer communications technology, or taking computer communications technology and applying it to the concept of telephone technology?

Our modern communication applications are part of our culture's long history of improving how we communicate. Technologies are much more advanced than Bell could even dream of, but the premise he used to create the telephone and the ideals he sought to achieve are the same.

Cell Phones: When in Doubt, Make It Smaller

One of the hallmarks of modern living is portability. Cell phones represent the finest in portability—smaller, sleeker, faster. No longer just a phone, today's cell phones are multimedia on the go.

In 1973, Motorola created the first handheld phone and made a wireless call based on handheld radio technology. Cell phones began to go public in 1977 with the testing of small groups. Within a decade, technologic changes allowed for standards to be created and a path to be paved that lead to where we are today, with cell phones in virtually every home.

Why History

Cell phones are now married to other technologies well-known to us, the computer and Internet. That's why it's important to understand these technologies and where we've been—so we can better know where we are going and keep an eye out for possible potholes. If you think back to history lessons of your youth, especially the industrial revolution, you'll recall that the best advances and progress in science and technology have as much to do with our thirst for information as they do with our desire to answer important questions or make our lives simpler. We don't always look before we leap. In fact, some of the best advances of our time have been by accident.

Mobile Phones and the Next Generation

My kids' school has a rule that cell phones cannot be used during the school day. I think this is a good rule. If something should occur with one of my children that necessitates a call home, I feel best if they go to a teacher or the school nurse during the school day. But I can't help but wonder what we've created in our kids by giving them cell phones and having them have such ready access to us during the day. Have we gone too far? Are there other issues that cell phones cause in the hands of teens? You bet! In fact, knowing how impulsive teens can be, perhaps they are not the group we should be entrusting with our latest and greatest technologies. Perhaps, if I may be so bold, we should limit them to just having the phone part of today's cell phones.

116

Chapter 13: Instant Communication Primer

The Teen Love Affair With the Phone

Since the phone has become a staple in family homes, teenagers every-where have been drawn to its power. When my parents were kids, there was typically only one phone per home. Part of the issue was the expense. Having more than one phone was often cost-prohibitive for the typical family. As teens, though, the only goal for my parents and their friends was their ability to connect. Despite the lack of privacy, they couldn't resist using the phone to talk in the same way with their friends that we did as teens and our kids do today—only they had to be a bit more careful because parents and siblings were most certainly in earshot. Nothing was sacred in a family home in the 1940s and 1950s!

Now our kids have cell phones that they use in their bedrooms instead of landlines. In fact, almost as soon as landline technology finally evolved to a point of true user ability by becoming wireless and affordable, cell phones have swooped in and taken over, with even more affordability, portability, and features.

Instant Communication: Pitfalls

Extreme Texting

I was stunned when I first heard the headline—one teen texted 14,000 times in one month. It sounded so surreal that for a moment I thought it was a teaser for an episode of *The Simpsons*.

Instant Messaging

Sometimes IM lingo can mean big trouble, the sort you don't want to think about your kids dabbling in. A while back, I noticed the ad on the next page on a few Web sites.

Clicking the add took me to Parents: The Anti-Drug (www.theantidrug.com), sponsored by the National Youth Anti-Drug Media Campaign, a group dedicated to helping parents help kids stay drug free.

If you look at your teens' IMs or text messages, they can be perplexing—part English, part foreign language, part alien. For help, check out the text lingo in Appendix A (a more complete list can be found on www.netlingo.com/acronyms.php). WiredSafety.org also has some useful translators so you can determine what your child's texts and IM conversations mean should you have the need to discern those.

It would be impossible to run down a complete list of text and IM-speak, but a few common examples include

- BFF = best friends forever
- BTW = by the way
- IMHO = in my humble opinion
- LOL = laugh out loud
- KFY = kiss for you
- ILY = I love you
- PAL = parents are listening
- POS = parent over shoulder
- WUF = where are you from?
- WYRN = what's your real name?

As you can see, there are a few common IM and text-isms that have become part of everyday language, such as BFF, IMHO, and BTW. This trend is likely to continue. (See Appendix A for a more thorough list.)

Kids sometimes use texting and IMing to flirt, and they also use it to talk about drug and alcohol use. You can find a complete list of codes kids use to talk about drugs at www.whitehousedrugpolicy.gov/streetterms. What

is alarming is how many different ways there are for our kids to use technology to hide that they are using or contemplating using drugs. We are truly our kids' best "antidrug" and can parent online in a few different ways.

1. Take the "How Tech Savvy Are You?" quiz (http://theantidrug.com/E-Monitoring/quiz. asp). If the quiz doesn't open your eyes, the answers sure will!
2. Talk to your kids each and every day about their lives. Kids with good relationships with their parents do better overall.
3. Keep your kids busy participating in activities they love to empower them to have solid self-esteem and stay busy and out of trouble.

Drug Policy Campaign public service announcement screen shot. (Source: Office of National Drug Control Policy media campaign ad. Available at: http://www. whitehousedrugpolicy.gov/mediacampaign/index.html.)

4. Be aware of what your teen is doing online and visit those sites yourself regularly. This isn't snooping; it is being involved. You can learn a great deal about your teen by reading what he or she writes on Facebook, a blog, or Web sites.

5. Talk with your teen about the importance of friending each other on sites that require this, such as Facebook. Most teens are OK with this; if yours is not, discuss why and see if you can arrive at a compromise.

What you may be noticing by now is that this advice is not unique to IMing; it's really a core set of digital family values we need to follow for all technologies.

Sexting: Texting With a Dangerous Twist

Teens and tweens love technology, and the temptation to push the envelope on the boundaries of those technologies is often too irresistible when they are caught in the heat of the moment. Teens and tweens can become completely swept away in what we would consider poor judgment in the blink of an eye, all under the umbrella of "this is so funny." But often what's being planned is not funny at all and can do some significant harm. That's the case with sexting, a trend in text messaging where teens send nude pictures of other teens via a text message from their cell phones.

Their young age blinds them to the repercussions of this impulsive act. They fail to recognize how humiliating the teen in the picture will feel being plastered on other people's phones. They fail to understand that this is a form of pornography and illegal. They fail to realize that this is a form of cyberbullying and harassment. In the click of a button, a cascade of lives are changed forever, with serious emotional and social harm to many.

Sexting seems to have come into our lives quite out of the blue. However, the dissemination of nude pictures or inappropriate content isn't new at all and has been occurring via e-mail and IM for a long while. It shouldn't surprise us that old practices end up on new technologies. That's the way things evolve for all forms of communication, good and bad.

Sexting is concerning not just because it's distasteful to think about but because it's incredibly common among teens. Recent data suggest that 1 in 5 teens have sent nude or seminude pictures of themselves or others to someone else. As if that statistic isn't enough to open our eyes to the significance of this issue, sexting is a crime in all 50 states, with the sender of the picture at risk for being charged as a sex offender. In the current legal system, many kids found with sexual images are charged with child pornography and labeled as sex offenders. Legal and health experts agree that this isn't the appropriate path to evaluate these situations with teens, but it is the current law and what we all have to abide by.

The issue at hand is that for teenagers this isn't about sex, sexuality, or sexual stimulation. Sexting becomes about power and embarrassment. The images themselves are just that—pictures. Charging teens who misused technology for their own personal gain as adults based on adult interpretation of possessing sexually charged material would only make sense if that is how teens themselves viewed the material. Because that's not the case, we need a better, more age- and developmentally appropriate punishment to fit this crime.

So until the laws change, we have to educate our kids as soon as they are old enough to have cell phones about the seriousness of sexting and what to do should an unwanted picture end up on their device. And we have to be more responsible about talking to kids about their sexuality so they can be safe and not have these images taken and disseminated in the first place.

We learned in 2009 of how deeply emotional this can become when Jesse Logan committed suicide after a picture she sent to her boyfriend was sexted to the school after they broke up. The off-line bullying and harassment she endured was too much for her.[1]

Because of the way the federal laws are written, many states are taking up the issue of sexting and trying to sort out a better way to handle it. A current list by state can be found at http://im.about.com/od/sexting/United_States_Sexting_Laws.htm. New laws with new definitions seems to be the best path.

The American Academy of Pediatrics offers tips to help you talk with your kids and teens about this new, uncharted territory (see Appendix F). Having the conversations as soon as your kids are old enough to have a cell phone coupled with healthy discussions of sex education is the best way to keep our kids safe.

We need to set good examples ourselves and not view images and Web sites that could be viewed as unsavory or illegal in any way. As our kids grow, we have to first teach them about their bodies, evolving sexual organ maturity, and evolving sexuality well before they learn to have full sexual relationships with anyone. We can often get in the way by superimposing our adult views on conversations we need to have with our younger kids and teens that really can be much more innocent and simple. At the same time, we have to realize that the teenage years are when our kids come alive as sexual beings. The more open we are to conversations, the easier it will be for them to turn to us when issues arise. This isn't easy stuff, but we can and often do make it worse by not allowing our teens to talk and process the chaotic changes they are experiencing. Add technology to the mix and it's no mystery that we're seeing some very serious consequences play out.

Real Kids, Real Stories

You only have to start talking with other parents or open your favorite news browser to see just how prevalent sexting has become. Debbie told me not long ago that her 15-year-old son's phone was stolen by another teen boy a few months ago. That teen boy went through her son's phone book and wrote down all the phone numbers of girls. Then he took a picture of his penis and sexted it to those girls from her son's phone. He then gave the phone back to her son bragging about what he had done.

Debbie's son was mortified and unusually quiet at home that night. Worried, she asked him what was up. He told her the story and she quickly went through his phone and called all the parents of the girls who were sent that x-rated picture to warn them and inform them of the story. Had she not done that, her son may have been accused of sexting at best and child pornography at worst.

Debbie feels this is a lesson to all parents to talk with their teens about the dangers that exist, like sexting. She credits being well tuned into her son and her son feeling comfortable enough to tell her the truth for averting a disaster.

Google your community and you'll find stories like this coast to coast.

Staying Safe With Cell Phones: No Wires Doesn't Mean No Control

With our kids using cell phones at record rates, safety issues have now gone where every tween and teen is venturing to go...and we have to somehow keep pace. Luckily, cell phone carriers are making that much easier for us with features you may not realize your cell phones services already have. It would take an entire book to review every cell phone carrier and every safety feature. In general, there is a range of safety features that are essentially filters. Some are free, while others cost a few extra dollars a month, but they all include a range of the following features:

- Filtering digital content
  - Web, movies, music
- Number blocking and allowing
- Time controls
  - Hours your child is allowed to use the phone
  - Total minutes your child is allowed to use the phone

Refer to Chapter 18 for more information about Internet safety on cell phones.

Most kids misinterpret parent controls, whether it be for cell phones or computers, as a sign of mistrust. For that reason, I strongly encourage all parents considering parent controls to use full disclosure and let their kids know they are going to be using parent controls and why.

If we ask our kids to follow rules, it's equally important that we follow rules in return. For this reason, signed cell phone agreements are incredibly valuable. One of the best around right now is from the Wireless Foundation, and it has a very interesting clause: "I will not take away my child's cell phone if my child comes to me about a problem concerning content or contact on a phone unless my child is in danger or has disregarded family rules. Instead, we will work together to try to solve the problem and to make sure my child makes good choices."[2]

The key is to gather information and reward our kids for turning to us. More times than not, there is a reasonable explanation for how content ended up on our kids' phones. Think about the courage and moral fiber it takes for children to come to parents when they know they've stumbled on challenging content. That's an act of responsibility, so we have to stay calm and get the facts and not just blindly react to the content.

References

1. Celizic M. Her teen committed suicide over 'sexting.' MSNBC Parenting and Family Online Web site. Available at: http://www.msnbc.msn.com/id/29546030. Published March 6, 2009. Accessed March 9, 2010
2. Contract for responsible cell phone use. The Wireless Foundation Web site. Available at: http://www.wirelessfoundation.org/WirelessOnlineSafety/ FamilyCellPhoneContract.pdf. Accessed March 9, 2010

Chapter 14

Social Networking 101

No doubt we live in a very connected time. At any given moment of a typical day, one of our family members is plugged into the digital world, communicating with people geographically far away. Some of these people are true friends off-line and well-known to each other; some others are simply known to each other by screen name or icon, with real names and real pictures almost becoming secondary. Adults tend to have some connection with the people they friend, although we all have a certain percentage of online friends we will never meet off-line. This is just the way the world of online friending goes and is the blessing and curse of social media of every kind. From the day they are born, our kids have come into this world with the digital age in full bloom. This is in stark contrast to the majority of parents, who grew up without much technology and had to learn to adapt and embrace the dawning of the digital age from its earliest seeds to its newest and sleekest technologies. Not having had to adapt to a new culture, our kids have found it very easy to just seamlessly live their lives socially online and off.

Today's kids and teens are referred to as *digital natives,* and their parents *digital immigrants,* to explain each generation's experience with technology. While not perfect, these labels explain each generation's comfort zone with using technology.

Being born into a media world is clearly different from being born into a world that later gives birth to media and then to "new" media. In the end, though, we all still have to learn to use these technologies in a healthy way, and as parents, we have to be able to guide our kids through the safety issues of the only world they know. This can be a huge challenge for us and our kids. We have to not only learn technologies and venues but figure out where our kids are hanging online. We also have to recognize that our kids may not be able to see the dangerous traps of these online places because they have grown up with them as part of the background noise of their childhoods. These are not new for them. These new social sites (at least new to us) are really different and more advanced flavors of what they've been exposed to since the moment they were born and were able to turn on their first computer toy!

If you look at those "first" computer toys, even those are social! Clearly Web 2.0 has taken hold in the toy marketplace as well as the computer marketplace. And with good reason—social media is where the true action of the Web is for kids and where the appeal is at all ages!

If you do a search for "computer" on your favorite online toy store, you may be surprised to discover that there are not only many products for kids aged birth to 2 years, but those products are all very social. They are true training grounds for a later real experience online.

You'll find "Baby's First Laptop" by Baby First Corporation, which comes with a boot-up sound, a crinkle mouse, and a touch pad that plays "Twinkle, Twinkle Little Star"—it really looks like a laptop. From there, you can advance to computerlike toys for older infants and toddlers with real buttons and a laptop feel that claim to teach kids all sorts of things. Some of these toys are character-themed. You'll also find early computer games and smiley faces at every turn to reinforce their interactive, social nature. These toys are intended to draw in the child so he or she wants to stay on the virtual online world the toy creates. Keep in mind, we're still talking about kids younger than 2 years! They can't even say "computer," let alone "Internet!"

Moving on to the 2- to 4-year-olds, the computerlike toys get more sophisticated but are still toys. There are more programs to choose from. There are more gaming systems all claiming a learning focus. And there is an introduction to the grown-up computer—the Fisher-Price "Easy Link Internet Launch Pad" uses characters to help kids find kid-safe Web sites. This type of technology is one type of tool parents can use to guide children at young ages to learn to use the Internet safely and smartly and will be discussed more in Chapter 18. You can often find other useful tools on your Internet browser and through your cable company called *parental controls;* "control," however, is a misnomer. It's really about helping our kids learn the rules of the Internet road and empowering them to be participants in that journey.

The Digital Age: No Longer Child's Play

Eventually, toys quickly become replaced by the real deal. The toys we've purchased for our kids and they have received as gifts become left in the corner of the room in a big old pile and as early as preschool, our kids start showing interest in our computer. However, for very young kids, a computer is really just one big flashing light—that's the attraction to them! That's the reason computers geared toward very young kids are often in the shape of animals!

What's amazing is how social all of these games are and how quickly our kids, regardless of our most disciplined attempts to shield them from the advertising and marketing effects of TV and toys, find popular Web sites such as Webkinz, Disney Club Penguin, and Shining Stars, to name a few. Like it or not, by the time our kids are in early elementary school, you'll be finding yourselves dealing with the slippery slope of what I've been calling the "junior social networking sites," or "social networking sites on training wheels," as some folks refer to them. While these sites may look innocent and youthful, don't kid yourselves; they are as interactive as the more mature social networking sites such as Facebook and MySpace but a bit more private and anonymous, which is very important for young Internet users. All these sites have a huge commercial element to which we do need to pay attention because they influence how our kids view themselves, food, purchases, and the world around them.

Social media use has become so important and commonplace in our global culture and society that it is now affecting education. Many schools already teach computer literacy at young ages, but some programs are now including actual social media lessons. The most dramatic to date is a proposal in March 2009 in England for elementary schoolchildren to study social media venues with less emphasis on traditional history, math, and geography. Authored by Sir Jim Rose, this proposed new curriculum seems more an exposé of today's modern life than just an overhaul of lesson plans. Along with the addition of social media, Sir Jim's proposal also contains lessons on healthy living and well-being including sexual education, drug and alcohol awareness, healthy eating, and sports that don't necessitate intense competition. In summary, Sir Jim's proposed curriculum seems to hit on the aspects of today's modern world that all children should be well-versed in starting at a young age, with computers and social media central to those lessons. Time will tell how successful these changes are in England, but it would behoove public school programs to take a step back and compare current lesson plans with our actual world. If social media and the health issues of today's world are missing, that could be a warning sign.[1]

You may be wondering what this has to do with social media and social networking. Everything! If we don't teach our kids the correct lessons and messages about being healthy and avoiding the more risky behaviors kids and teens are exposed to as they grow up, they will get their information from blogs, chats, instant messaging (IMing), Twitter, online communities, and social networking sites such as Facebook and MySpace. It behooves us as parents, health care providers, and educators to include the lessons our kids need to know when we have the opportunity to teach them, and to include in those lessons where and how to find information online (as you saw in Chapter 4). The topics surrounding social media range from the very technical to the esoteric. Inherent in all social media, though, is the social nature of the venue. That is the true allure for these sites for kids of all ages—and adults, if truth be told. What separates adults from kids, though, is life experience and an understanding of the greater social world. To help our kids and teens negotiate the world of social media, let's see that world from their eyes.

The Power of the Friend and the Allure of the Computer

Not having been born with a silver computer in our mouths, we had to learn the traditional way, with hard work. After enduring the endless frustration of typewriters and pen-and-paper drafting of essays and manuscripts, computers took some getting used to. I vividly remember my friends and I using them as glorified typewriters for a long while until programs, games, and the Internet became more accessible for the full power of the computer to be felt. True, not having to start a new page over at every mistake and battling with various forms of corrective tape was reason enough to jump for joy once we all figured out the word processing programs of our first home PCs. Back then, "tech" support was still live and often in person from friends and family.

In contrast, our kids have been born with digital media use in their souls. Using a computer has become as routine a childhood lesson as learning to crawl, run, and ride a bike. It isn't a question of "Will my child learn to use a computer?" but *"When* will my child learn to use a computer?"

Our children become so adept at using computers and the Internet at astoundingly young ages that it isn't at all unusual for them to know about a Web site or computer application well before we do. In fact, according to Pew Internet Life Project, kids are many times their parents' computer and Internet teachers! They are our home tech support.

Tech savvy they are; life savvy they are not. That is the black hole for kids and teens online, and we have to be ever vigilant to not mistake ability with understanding the finer points of social interaction. This is where kids at all ages need the most coaching and guiding and where we, as concerned adults, can make a huge difference in creating truly Web-savvy youth users. We talk with our kids about the ins and outs of crossing the street safely; outlets, the kitchen, and many other home safety areas; and general health and wellness issues about eating, fitness, and sexuality; we have to add Internet issues to the list.

As with all issues in childhood, one big discussion will fall on deaf ears. Our best path to success for Web issues, as with all important issues in our children's lives, is to have multiple discussions over time that start young and build as our children develop more sophistication themselves. Part and parcel to this issue is our ability to understand and use these technologies. For us to be truly "in the know," we have to not only know where our kids are occupying their time online but the ins and outs of those online spaces. We don't have to become experts, just savvy enough to have meaningful conversations and pick up a few warning signs should they arise.

We also have to realize that experience will play a huge role in our kids' abilities to negotiate these sites well. This is no different than learning to drive. Our kids may learn to be competent drivers on empty side streets initially, but negotiating traffic and highways takes more time and experience. For most areas of life, in fact, experience and patience are our best paths to maximizing fun and safety for a great experience!

Just as the sun rises and sets every day, you can be assured your kids will end up on a social networking site. As our kids get older, just using the computer and playing a few games won't be enough to satisfy their curiosity of what's on the other side of the Internet fence. Add to that curiosity the innate need to be ever connected with their friends and before you can blink, your kids will be on social media and using it. Typically this occurs without a big announcement or discussion or even great fanfare. It just pops up one day right before our eyes.

128

It starts differently for different kids. For some, the thirst to connect may occur from a seed planted from a game or an activity they've seen someone in their lives do online, such as a parent or an older sibling. They may have heard from a friend of a friend of a friend about "this place" online and before you can ask how the school day was, you see a blur darting to the computer muttering, "Just a sec, there's something I have to see." That's how kids think starting in the tween years and growing intensely into the teens years. It's all about the here and now and being where their friends are—now.

It's healthy and very normal for older elementary schoolkids and older to want to be connected with their peers in this way. In fact, that need to connect and be part of the pack was no different for us at the same ages. We used phones and passed notes in class as our "high-tech" ways to stay connected. That's all we had. Our kids use social media via computers and cell phones. That's what our kids have. And that's what we have to use to stay connected to our family, friends, and business associates too.

It's common to have a dawning moment when we realize our kids' boundaries have expanded well beyond the safe haven of our homes and communities. For me, it was the day I walked into my oldest daughter's room to see her video chatting with one friend, IMing another, shooting off an e-mail, and updating her Facebook page. She had been online and using social media for a couple years already, but it didn't hit me until that moment in time just how involved these technologies were in her day.

The problem with social media is in the name. While technologies may be social in that they all involve interaction, we are still talking about technologies that create relationships in cyberspace, not real space. We are still dealing with technologies that only tell part of a person's story, not the entire story. And we are still dealing with venues where social interactions are controlled, for the most part, and not organic, natural, spontaneous, and based on the interplay between people in real time and space. No matter how "real" some of these venues feel, something about the other person still gets lost in translation as it travels through cyberspace between keyboard clicks and fiber-optic cables.

We grew up using our phones to facilitate real-life encounters. For many kids, social media sometimes replace real-life encounters. Online conversations have their time and place but are truncated and often not grammatically correct. This doesn't always translate well to smooth and natural social interactions. There is no way a child can learn social cues and etiquette by being exclusively online. As parents and educators, we have to help kids not become so sucked into using social media that they fail to have real-world experiences. Social media should augment and enhance our lives, not replace them.

Some kids become absorbed with social media to the point of obsession. Internet and gaming addiction is a true disorder and I suspect we'll be seeing similar issues with social media before too long. The key is to watch for warning signs.

1. Does the use of social media cause your child to not enjoy the real world as much when off-line? That is, do you notice him more comfortable online than off?
2. Does the use of social media cause your child to skip real-world activities with family and friends?
3. Does the use of social media cause your child to have mood swings from posts made, posts not made, or friend counts?
4. Does the content of social media sites being explored contain risky behavior such as eating disorders, drug seeking, or alcohol abuse?
5. Does your child become upset if there isn't an Internet connection or you take away social media use for a while? Or does she become unusually upset if you disconnect the Internet?
6. Does your child become disrespectful or aggressive when you inquire about his online activities or ask to see his social networking profiles?

If any of these issues are occurring with your child, seek counseling from a licensed psychiatrist. If you are not sure how to locate one in your area, call your pediatrician for advice.

Before you do extensive online research on every site out there for your child's peer group, go on a hunting expedition and figure out what your kids are using. There are a few ways to approach this very important task.

1. Have a conversation with your family at dinner. Bringing up the topic of social media in a general way can be less intimidating to some kids than having a focused conversation that just involves you and your child. This strategy can be particularly useful if you have teens and older tweens. As a conversation starter you could say, "I read that a lot of kids in high school are using Facebook. Is that true? Are you on it?" You can change the age to match your child and "Facebook" to any venue you are hunting to confirm or deny.

2. Have a conversation with your child. Sometimes the best approach is the direct approach: "I know kids your age use social media. Show me what you and your friends use and what privacy settings you have set up. We want you to be involved with your friends but need to be comfortable with how you are using these technologies—some kids have gotten into a lot of trouble not understanding their proper uses." You can give examples of "Facebook firing" (kids have been fired from jobs for improper posting on Facebook walls); sexting; bullying by text, IM, or e-mail; and inappropriate images or video on social media sites.

3. Give your child a heads-up, then do a search of her computer, cell phone, and anything else that goes online: "In about an hour, I'm going to be checking your computer and cell phone logs. Feel free to join me if you'd like." You are paying the bills and own the technology. Your kids are still under age and learning the rules of the road. You don't need to apologize or rationalize parenting to your child. Spot-checking how they are spending their time online isn't snooping, it's keeping them safe. But I'd suggest you do it in the open and not behind their back. When you do hunt the hardware, areas to pay attention to are

    •   Web search and browsing histories.

    •   Text histories, sending and receiving. Pay particular attention to pictures and be sure they are not inappropriate. Images of a sexual nature by text are called *sexting*, which is covered in Chapter 13.

    •   Bookmarked social networking sites. Double-check the privacy settings yourself.

    •   Friend lists on social networking sites. What's the number? Does your child personally know everyone he's friended? Anyone on the list of concern to you? Are you listed among your child's friends? If not, you should be. One way to keep our kids safe is to be part of the conversation space they are on. Many families friend each other on Facebook; you are not asking your child to do something other parents haven't asked of their kids. This is a great way to build a community of trusted grown-ups to help with checks and balances.

    •   E-mail. We can easily forget "old-fashioned" e-mail with a clear trend toward social networking, but we do still use e-mail and so do our kids. Take a quick look to be sure there are no alarming e-mails saved in your child's inbox.

Social Networking: The New E-mail

In March 2009, Nielsen Online released a report, *Global Faces and Networked Places,* with some interesting yet unsurprising data—social networking sites are used much more than e-mail for our primary means of communication.[2] On the Nielsen Wire blog, the company wrote: "Two-thirds of the world's Internet population visit social networking or blogging sites, accounting for almost 10% of all Internet time."[3]

Other interesting points from the report include

- Social networking sites were visited once every 15 minutes online in 2008 and are now visited once every 11 minutes. In some areas like Brazil and the United Kingdom, they are visited much more frequently— every 4 and 6 minutes, respectively.
- Social networking sites and blogs are growing 3 times more than any other area on the Internet.
- Social networking sites are now multigenerational; 35- to 49-year-olds use Facebook to the same extent as 18- to 34-year-olds.
- Facebook use has increased 566% from December 2007 to December 2008 and replaced MySpace as the most popular social networking site.

Add to these data the fact that kids are using computers much more now than in the past. The March 2005 Kaiser Family Foundation report, *Generation M: Media in the Lives of 8–18 Year-Olds,* revealed a 44% increase in computer use from 1999 to 2004 (27 minutes per day in 1999 to 1 hour 2 minutes in 2004).[4] The January 2010 update of this report, Generation M^2, showed an increase in computer time by 27 more minutes a day.[5] In the original Generation M report, Kaiser revealed that our kids are spending 28% of their time each day using the computer. Not surprisingly, it confirms that most of the activities that kids do online beyond basic searches are social or involve communication—IMing, recreation, downloading music, or making a Web page. The big finding in Generation M^2 is how mobile our kids have become. M^2 revealed a dramatic increase in cell phone use, MP3 player use, and laptop use well beyond the other media venues discussed in the report.

What does this all mean? As Kaiser wrote in its original Generation M report: "Anything that takes up this much space in young people's lives deserves our full attention."

Since the first Generation M report came out, our kids are online even more, as Generation M^2 helps confirm, and are more on the go with their digital lives with cell phones and smartphone devices, including the iTouch. In 2009, kids and teens became even more digital, spending 63% more time online than when the original Kaiser Generation M report came out in 2005, according to Nielsen.[6] That May 2009 report gave us another staggering statistic—the growth of kids online outpaced the entire Internet population, with 18% growth for the 2- to 11-year-old sector compared with only 10% growth for the entire Internet population.

Viewed from this perspective, adults who are not online sorting out the social world of kids might as well let kids go out to recess without teacher chaperones!

To Friend or Not to Friend?

To friend or not to friend is the question of the moment when using a social media site. For adults, we try and gather a group of friends who will help us achieve our endgame for that site. If the goal is to reconnect with people or stay connected with friends and family, we tend to friend people we know or used to know but lost touch with for a myriad of life reasons. If the goal is business related, we will likely friend people who will help us advance our networking agenda. It isn't so much a numbers game for us but quality of contact.

For our kids, however, it's about quality, sort of, and numbers. If you look at a Facebook page of a typical middle or high schooler, you may be surprised just how may friends are listed—hundreds, if not more! Compare that most adults, with fewer than a couple hundred, and you can begin to see issues of discretion and screening start to play out.

I noticed a friend of my oldest daughter had more than 400 friends on his Facebook page and made a comment along the lines of, "Wow! That's a lot of people." My daughter, closing into 200 at this point, matter-of-factly explained, "Well, he's in high school and very popular. Of course he knows that many people." Who was I to argue, other than a mom who knew there was no way my daughter truly knew 200 kids well enough to call most of them friend or that her friend in high school really knew 400 people?

So what was happening? Simple. They were both being friended by people who knew someone they knew or by people they sort of knew but not well. That's enough in teen logic to friend someone on Facebook. As parents, our job is to be sure the people being friended are truly appropriate and that privacy settings are set so that only friends receive updates, not the entire Facebook world!

The other issue with friending is that it isn't always reciprocated. As adults, we don't get caught up in that too often. If I make a friend request of someone and they don't accept it, life goes on. We each have our own litmus and personal guidelines for how we want to use social networking. Kids and teens, however, can get emotionally crushed if someone they friended doesn't friend them back. They can take this very personally and feel rejected. Luckily, most teens happily reciprocate the friend gesture, so this sort of rejection doesn't happen often. But teens on the receiving end of not being friended, even if it only happens once in a blue moon, stings because their entire lives online and off are about friends. Teens and rejection don't mix well. As parents, be on the lookout for mood changes after your child has been on a social media site. A simple question such as, "What were you doing before you became so upset?" may give you the clue you need.

As the name implies, social networking sites are about interactions. If you think about how complicated off-line relationships can be, it's a curious phenomenon that we're signing on to this online craze and allowing our kids to participate as well. What we don't get in online friends is the depth and quality of off-line friends, but we still achieve social interaction and camaraderie, which many find very satisfying and fun.

Wikipedia defines social networking as a service that "focuses on building and reflecting of social networks or social relations among people, e.g., who share interests and/or activities. A social network service essentially consists of a representation of each user (often a profile), his/her social links, and a variety of additional services. Most social network services are web based and provide means for users to interact over the internet, such as e-mail and instant messaging."[7]

One of the most difficult parts of social networking for kids is the concept of friending. When my daughter started to become interested in Facebook around 13 or 14 years of age, we tried to explain to her that what makes social networking fun and interesting is the ability to stay in touch with people you know and get to know people you may not see as often. We suggested she not "friend the world," only people she really knows—people she actually hung out with at school or at her various school events. Within a short time on Facebook, we noticed her friend list was climbing to the

100+ range. Her explanation: "I know everyone on that list by name off-line!" She could not discern being in a class with someone and being a true friend—nor would we at 14 years of age.

Contrast that to my friend list and there is a big difference. At least on Facebook, my list is relatively small. I limit it to actual off-line friends and family and a few business associates I know well; I don't friend people I don't have some sort of real-world relationship with.

However, some of my other social networking sites are a bit different. The Twitter culture, for example, operates under the principle of "followers." That system is set up around Web acquaintances you likely don't know well, if at all. The key is to surround yourself with interesting contacts who you may only find via Twitter and related services.

We have to help our kids understand that each social networking site has different rules of the road with respect to building our own community. We also have to help them understand that there is no reason they have to feel pressure to friend anyone.

We have a great deal of control in what people see of our posts, and that is something we have to monitor not only on our kids' sites but our own.

Safety First

Teaching kids about online social safety is really no different than reinforcing off-line social issues. I'll talk more about this in Chapter 18, but it all boils down to being realistic with your kids about being honest with what they are doing online and off, and following the rules!

For every aspect of our kids' lives, we help them learn the rules of the road. We clear a path as they learn to roll and start crawling. We childproof everything in toddling range as our kids learn to walk. As they get older and more independent, we help them learn to look both ways when they cross the street, wear a helmet when riding a bike, and cook without burning the house down. The real challenges for our kids begin when they enter school and start having friends. Learning the social rules of friendships and schools is not always easy but is an essential element of life. Kids often become confused by boundaries and are quick to bond and part ways with other kids.

As parents, advising our kids about friendships and off-line activities is a major part of our day and helps our kids enormously in mastering the social tasks necessary in life. For them to be successful in the online social world, we have to have some familiarity with the online social world our kids travel through and advise our kids in that world like we do off-line.

Privacy in Social Settings

Given their popularity and the social trends in use, it's important we all have a sense of what these sites are about, including the privacy policies and safety controls you can build in at home. As you'll see, some of these sites sound scarier than they are, and most have more control than you realize. In the end, there are 2 big dangers to kids with these sites—your child's young age and inability to understand proper and improper posting, and parents not understanding age issues related to these sites and allowing kids to participate younger than they should.

For each social media site, know where the privacy settings are and what it means to enable or disable them. For groups like Facebook or MySpace, the issue of even having your child join becomes the first privacy question to answer. Keep in mind that nothing is truly private on cyberspace, so before you allow your child to sign on to any site, know what the site is and isn't about. For younger kids, sites that allow anonymity and parental consent provide better peace of mind and security than simply joining Facebook or MySpace and hoping for the best. For teens, it's important that they learn to understand how anything written anywhere online and the appearance they give online represent who they are, not just today but perhaps in the future. This holds true for video and picture posts as well. The concept of *permanence* of online material is not easy for kids to grasp but crucial for them to begin to learn. Their online person is their calling card or online fingerprint. One way to explain online behavior to kids is to remind them not to say online what they would not say off-line to anyone. I've seen e-mails and texts in which people call others names. We need to help our kids understand that if name-calling isn't OK off-line, don't do it online. If insulting someone off-line isn't acceptable, it's not acceptable online either. We have to help them learn to have polite conversations online, even if they disagree with the person they are communicating with, just as they do in the off-line world.

All sites have carefully worded privacy statements and most require parent permission for kids younger than 13 years to participate. I've actually been impressed by what I've seen on some of my kids' sites in terms of patrolling and enforcing of rules and regulations.

At the same time, privacy rules only go so far. What really keeps kids safe is ensuring that you and your kids have a well-understood plan of use for any social networking site.

1. **User names and passwords:** Make sure your kids never use their real names for user names and have passwords that are not easy to track, such as birthdays, towns, or names of streets. For added safety, make sure you know your child's user name and password for all sites so you can go on once in a while and make sure everything is as safe as you are told it should be. For teens, as added protection, I suggest you have them friend you on sites such as Facebook and consider not allowing them to go on sites on which you do not have a profile. They will be much safer if you are on the same social site as they are.

2. **Friends:** On sites that allow you to friend others, you need to have a frank discussion with your kids. True friends are people you know in off-line life. Just seeing a name on someone else's profile is not enough to warrant a friending.

3. **Profiles:** On sites that have complex networks, such as Facebook, set up preferences so only your friends can see what you post. You don't want your child's words, pictures, or information going to the entire site.

4. **Personal information:** Never post personal information such as e-mails, home address, or phone numbers on social networking sites. For teens using Facebook, you can negotiate with them what they will be putting on their profile and help them limit to a reasonable amount of information without offering too much.

5. **Stranger safety:** This doesn't happen as often as you think, especially if you have the privacy settings set up appropriately. The safest rule to follow is this—if you do not know the person off-line, do not friend the person online! However, if a stranger does try and contact your child, simply have your child inform you so you can look into the situation. If the situation warrants, contact the site. All sites have a way of reporting suspicious activity. Predators do exist on these sites and we have to be sure our kids are safe.

Social Networking Site Roll

The honest truth is that keeping up with the list of social networking sites for our kids, tweens, and teens is about as worthwhile a task as trying to memorize all the clouds in the sky today and hoping to see the same configuration tomorrow. Your children are cyber-bees pollinating whatever cyber-sites are attractive at that moment; today's sites will differ from tomorrow's.

There is a good chance your child is interested in whatever site is popular today, so those should be the ones you worry about. And it is possible that the sites that are popular by the time you read this chapter are not the ones I mention; that's the nature of the social networking landscape.

Instead of trying to tackle every site out there, there's a lot we can learn from the tried-and-true sites today that will help us when a new one enters the landscape. These sites differ in appearance and bells and whistles but are the same in what they offer for user-generated content and the ability to control a person's privacy and online safety. Those are the features that trump all others.

Kids

Kids love character-oriented sites and sites with games and activities. They seek out ways to interact with other online characters and don't care so much about the ability to connect with real friends. Social networking sites for this age group tend to be parent-protected in that a parent must agree to allow the child to participate. Most are moderated by adults to keep the site clean and bully free. User-generated content is very much controlled and limited by the site to only a few choices, such as decorating a banner or certificate. Webkinz and Club Penguin are two of the best sites for the young elementary school-aged group, but there are many others online.

Many of these sites are highly commercial, though, and you have to buy a doll to gain access to the site or buy a subscription to join. If a site allows a free trial, do that so you can check the site out with your child. One of the best ways to screen a site is to figure out what is popular with your child's friends. Because these sites are social, your child will likely want to be part of whatever site his friends are using, but resist the temptation to join them all. That is not only site overload for a small child but will get expensive, online and off.

Tweens

During the tween years, sites become more sophisticated, but they are still very character-related. Examples for this age group include Barbie, LEGO, Webkinz, Shining Stars, and Club Penguin. For this age group, the options become a bit more socially sophisticated, while there is still that layer of anonymity.

Teens: The Facebook and MySpace Generation

The teen years are the years we begin to see MySpace and Facebook. This is for 2 good reasons. First, the minimum age for these sites is 13 years. Second, the teen years are really the youngest that kids can understand enough about social behavior to dip a toe into the online social world. Let's start with the most popular teen site that many adults are currently using to understand the ins and outs.

Facebook

One of the most popular social networking sites online today, Facebook actually began as a Harvard University project by founder and computer science major Mark Zuckerberg to help college students stay in touch in a more high-tech way than printed college yearbooks. While founded in 2004, the company we are familiar with in name and scope, allowing anyone 13 years or older with a valid e-mail address to join, was launched in 2006.[8]

Because of the need for a valid e-mail, by the time your child is 13, you should have a well-defined way of handling how your child gives out her e-mail address. Facebook is a great first trial for being able to responsibly sign up for a third-party site and choose a password. Facebook doesn't allow dual profiles for the same e-mail, so your child can only use your e-mail if you have multiple e-mail accounts. Otherwise, you won't be able to sign up for Facebook and friend your child, which I highly recommend!

There are a lot of features on Facebook and many unlock or are optional. For Facebook, as well as any new social networking site, get to know the basics and try a few fun and games now and again just for giggles! If nothing else, these sites can provide wonderful distraction and are a great way to toss some cheer and appreciation to the true friends on your list. For example, you can send a virtual cupcake or a bouquet of flowers. You can personalize a button, called a "flair," and shoot it to folks on your list that may get some meaning from your message.

Facebook's hallmark used to be a simple statement at the top which gave your name followed by is…. So for me, my Facebook prompt would have read, "Gwenn Schurgin O'Keeffe is…" and I'd add a comment from there. It was a fantastic prompt and a great conversation starter. I could write anything from "…writing," to "…enjoying time with my family," to "…annoyed it's still snowing in Massachusetts!" People could then comment on your prompts if they'd like and mini-conversations would ensue.

In early 2009, Facebook tossed out a few site and appearance tweaks. Not all were well-received and after a vote of the Facebook community, many of the "old" features returned. However, our familiar prompt of "is" was replaced with "What's on your mind?" or "Write something," depending on whether you are on your home page, wall, or profile page. This has taken some getting used to! Being stuck in my ways, I still think in terms of the old Facebook "is" prompt, but others have emerged from their shells with full-blown sentences exploring what's on their mind in the full sense of the phrase.

In terms of communication, you have a few options. There's the comment section of a friend's wall; this is a great way to toss back an idea or a quip, but it is public, so other people your friend has friended will be able to read this. For a more private communication, you can send a message similar to an e-mail via your inbox or do a true chat if you notice your friend is on-line. Facebook has prompts alerting you to friends online and who commented last so you can keep track of who has commented on your posts and quickly comment back, if you wish.

Your profile is where you tell your Facebook world all about yourself and you decide 100% the level of detail you want to share. I've seen some people tell their entire life story and others tell just the highlights and give people a snapshot.

Other cool features include

1. **Blog RSS feed:** I can pull in my daily blog post automatically via this feed. Kids don't use these too often but they are helpful in following multiple sites at one time. As our kids get older, they will learn about RSS feeds. What will help them make good decisions is gaining an understanding about good sites versus bad sites.
2. **Video uploading:** This is one of the most popular venues for tweens and teens. Video watching and creation is absurdly popular. Beyond the entertainment value, videos allow for message transmission, which is important for this age group.

3. **Photo uploading:** Another important technology for today's digital youth; one of the ways today's kids express themselves is via pictures, and sharing them online is easy, quick, and fun. Moreover, it can be done by e-mail, Twitter, Facebook, blogs, or just about any other Web 2.0 venue you can think of.
4. **Sharing of links:** Teens and tweens search for information a bit differently than we do as adults, but they do love sharing e-mails and links of stories and ideas when they find them.
5. **Music:** Downloading and sharing music is a hallmark of today's society but especially today's youngest generation.

Pitfalls and Health Risks

Kids tend to try some sites like clothes and leave a great many of them behind. What's important is to not become too hung up in becoming an expert on any one site, but learning to stay on top of what sites your kids want to explore and to have a plan in place for monitoring those sites. While your kids may buck this at times, especially as teens, we have to be involved to catch health issues should they arise.

While health issues using social networking are rare and tend to include addiction, we have to remember that tweens and teens are obsessive by nature. Before we worry about addiction we have to look at the big picture of a child's life. Is the child happy? Is she participating in other activities? Are her grades acceptable?

The other issue to remember with teens is that it is normal for them to be withdrawn from adults and moody at times. When gauging whether this is within the range of normal, ask how your child is doing in other settings. As long as your child comes out of her shell appropriately with friends, in school, with activities, and with family, you have little to worry about. However, if the withdrawn behavior is interfering with other domains of life, such as home, school, or friends, call your pediatrician for advice and check your child's computer and cell phone to see what your child has been up to online.

Stranger danger is real and is always something to be mindful of online. Today's digital youth have been raised learning these issues so it's less frequent than headlines may make you think, but there is a subset of vulnerable kids who are very impressionable and needy. These kids are using the Internet to seek out friends and crave attention. These are the types of kid who tend to get into trouble with people they don't know well. These kids may be loners in the real world or have trouble making friends. If your child falls into this category and is spending a great deal of time online, you'll want to monitor what he is doing carefully.

The other group of kids to worry about is those getting into trouble off-line who are seeking similar trouble online. Kids battling major issues in school, with academics, drugs, alcohol, or eating disorders, sometimes use the Internet to feed their habits.

Final Take on Social Media

Social media is about connections and conversation, and it's clearly here to stay. While some of the names and faces of online venues have changed here and there, a clear core group has emerged that is becoming very popular with our kids. If we start with that core group of sites and understand how to use them and how our kids are using them, we'll be a step ahead in the growing social media slice of cyberspace.

References

1. Cohen T. Exit Winston Churchill, enter Twitter…yes, it's the new primary school curriculum. Mail Online Web site. Available at: http://www.dailymail.co.uk/news/article-1164682/Exit-Winston-Churchill-enter-Twitter---Yes-new-primary-school-curriculum.html. Published March 25, 2009. Accessed March 9, 2010
2. Global faces and networked places. Nielsen Wire Web site. Available at: http://blog.nielsen.com/nielsenwire/wp-content/uploads/2009/03/nielsen_globalfaces_mar09.pdf. Published March 2009. Accessed March 9, 2010
3. Social networking's new global footprint. Nielsen Wire Web site. Available at: http://blog.nielsen.com/nielsenwire/nielsen-news/social-networking-new-global-footprint. Published March 9, 2009. Accessed March 9, 2010
4. Roberts DF, Foehr UG, Rideout V. *Generation M: Media in the Lives of 8–18 Year-Olds.* Menlo Park, CA: Henry J. Kaiser Family Foundation; 2005. Available at: http://www.kff.org/entmedia/upload/Generation-M-Media-in-the-Lives-of-8-18-Year-olds-Report.pdf. Accessed May 7, 2010
5. Rideout VJ, Foehr UG, Roberts DF. *Generation M²: Media in the Lives of 8- to 18-Year-Olds.* Menlo Park, CA: Henry J. Kaiser Family Foundation; 2010. Available at: http://www.kff.org/entmedia/upload/8010.pdf. Accessed May 6, 2010
6. Growing up, and growing fast: kids 2-11 spending more time online. Nielsen Wire Web site. Available at: http://blog.nielsen.com/nielsenwire/online_mobile/growing-up-and-growing-fast-kids-2-11-spending-more-time-online. Published July 6, 2009. Accessed March 9, 2010

7. Social network service. Wikipedia: The Free Encyclopedia Web site. Available at: http://en.wikipedia.org/wiki/Social_network_service. Modified March 8, 2010. Accessed March 9, 2010

8. Facebook. Wikipedia: The Free Encyclopedia Web site. Available at: http://en.wikipedia.org/wiki/Facebook. Modified March 9, 2010. Accessed March 9, 2010

Chapter 15

Twitter 101

Courtesy of Twitter

I first heard about Twitter during a conference of medical communicators in 2008. At that point, Twitter was only 2 years old and just starting to take hold online and within the medical community.

What was evident from that early Twitter discussion was the ability to connect with many people. What wasn't yet evident was just how to connect and whether it would truly catch on.

Conceptualized in 2006 and built in only 2 weeks, Twitter took off in popularity in just about as much time. And it is one of the most interesting, addicting, and often perplexing social media applications to enter the scene lately. According to Twitter.com, "Twitter is a service for friends, family, and coworkers to communicate and stay connected through the exchange of quick, frequent messages."

According to Pew Internet and American Life Project, 11% of adults are currently using Twitter, with the breakdown slanting toward younger generations. Of all Twitter users, 19% are 18 to 24 years old, 20% are 25 to 35 years old, and 10% are 35 to 44 years old. However, according to Pew, Twitter users are not as young as other social media venues—the average age falls around 31, compared with 26 for Facebook and 27 for MySpace.

The typical Twitter user is very mobile and has a thirst for information. According to Pew, 75% of Twitter users use the Internet wirelessly and

82% of Twitter users use their cell phones to go online and use applications to tweet and text. And the more other social media venues someone uses, like blogging, the more likely a person is to use Twitter.[1]

Twitter embodies the very essence of how we use technology today. Centered around the question, "What are you doing?" Twitter marries our need for instant communication and connectedness with succinctness. Basic tweets are really just glorified instant messages (IMs) limited to 140 characters and able to reach many people at once or a designated group of people, depending on how we build our list of followers and refer to our followers in our tweets.

Twitter explains how people use the prompt, "What are you doing?" like this: "The answers to this question are for the most part rhetorical. In other words, users do not expect a response when they send a message to Twitter. On the receiving end, Twitter is ambient—updates from your friends and relatives float to your phone, IM, or Web site and you are only expected to pay as much or as little attention to them as you see fit."

Twitter flows in real time, so unlike e-mail, IMs, or texts, you only see the tweets that you catch when you log on. Twitter built this by design. The point is to be able to tune in and out without feeling the pressure to respond.

I've heard people complain that they worry that they will "miss a tweet" or "miss something important," but Twitter was never intended for this purpose. It was designed to be a place were people could put out their musings in real time and people could respond to those musings, or not. According to the Twitter team, "Just remember, how you use Twitter is completely up to you. Follow hundreds of people. Follow a dozen. Post every hour. Post never. Search for your favorite topics and create lists. Or not. You are in control on Twitter."

The actual Twitter Web site is very simple, but there are Twitter Web applications that do allow you to sort your Twitter followers into sub-groups so you can track conversations and people of interest more easily. Still, keeping up with all conversations does become a challenge if you have a lot of followers and are following a lot of people.

Everyone uses Twitter differently and there is no one right way to use this tool. It has great use in getting out information about what you are doing, connecting with people in your industry groups in business, and keeping in touch with friends. There are ways to connect with people privately, which is very similar to one-on-one texting or IMing, called a direct message or DM.

I joined Twitter late in the game compared with some of my social media and blogger friends. Since joining in early 2009, life as I know it in online communication has changed dramatically. I receive far fewer e-mails and far more tweets and am connected to a wider array and greater variety of people in my industry groups than I ever thought possible in a short amount of time. There is a clear and powerful entropy to this tool that quickly lures you in and doesn't let go.

Compared with other social media sites I've been involved with (and I've been involved with many), Twitter trumps them all, hands down.

When you look at a Twitter page, you'll notice a thread of comments made by the Twitter author, as you see in my Twitter page screen shot on page 143. To see the Tweets of other people, you have to be a registered user of Twitter and start following other users. To tweet, you have to be logged on to your own user page. The top will appear like this (courtesy of Twitter).

Type your tweet, limited to 140 characters, including letters and spaces, in the "What are you doing?" box.

Twitter has been called *microblogging*. Unlike true blogs, however, it allows for social interaction and real-time responses. By use of the @ sign, you can direct a tweet to a specific follower and have a conversation with a follower in response to another tweet. If you see the phrase RT, that indicates re-tweet and is a way to tip your hat to a tweeter who posted something that you want to rebroadcast because of the importance of its message to you. It allows for a message to be passed down the tweet chain without retyping all of it yourself, while giving credit to the original poster.

Twitter does allow for personalization, as you can see from my Twitter page. You can add logos, change colors, and include your Web site in your small biographic corner.

What's important to remember about tweets is that unless you make your profile private, everything you post is public and can be viewed from your user page. If you make your profile private, only people to whom you grant permission can view your tweets.

If you had to compare Twitter to the many technologies already in existence, it's a cross between blogging, chat, text, and IMing. While called microblogging, it has definite features of instant communications that you find in chat rooms, IMing, and texting. Unlike traditional blogging where the goal is to post daily or a few times a week, people will tweet many times a day.

Twitter Uses for Health and News

You can think about Twitter in a number of ways. One author on About.com wrote that it is a "quick journal of what she is doing day to day." Some use it to network with others in their field to form a bigger network. Many journalists are on Twitter now and use it to find experts, story leads, and guests for segments. Other people are on it because they are interested in the world at large and want to network globally. It does seem to be a powerful tool for disseminating information quickly to a large amount of people.

Some of the unique uses so far include

- **Political:** Twitter was instrumental during President Obama's campaign.
- **Science:** In May 2009 astronaut Michael Massimino sent the first tweets from space to update the status of the Hubble Space Telescope repair.
- **News:** Many news and media venues are on Twitter to update stories, ask for input, and try to find guests.
- **Headlines:** Twitter has broken headlines. Swine flu stories broke on Twitter. In January 2009, a passenger on United 1549 had a Twitpic taken before the main media had official pictures.
- **Conferences:** Many people are using Twitter to "live tweet" events.
- **Public relations:** Users in many industries use Twitter to publicize events, goods, and services.
- **Connect:** Twitter is used daily to inform people of "tweet-ups" (meetings between Twitter users) and about goings-on in towns and cities globally.

- **Health:** Doctors on Twitter update their blogs, posts, and podcast. Health groups tweet their new information and campaigns. Hospitals have used Twitter to live tweet surgeries. Twitter was instrumental in disseminating information quickly during the H1N1 outbreak.

During TV shows, the presidential inauguration, news conferences, and even award shows and conferences, people have started to live tweet events, bringing real-time coverage and commentary to events that formerly only produced static response after the fact or the following day.

Twitter fills people's thirst for information and need to know all at once. But unlike other social networking sites, there is one population who hasn't yet jumped onto the Twitter bandwagon—teens and kids younger than 18.

Teens and kids love instant and quick, so in many ways Twitter would be the perfect application for them. But if you compare Twitter with other social media sites teens are on such as Facebook and MySpace, some noticeable differences emerge that give us important clues as to why teens and kids are not gravitating to Twitter in the same way they are flocking to the others. Teens and older kids like a boundary between their life and their parents and other grown-ups. On Facebook and MySpace, for example, you can set your settings to allow only your friends to see your page; the general public will be locked out. On Twitter, your tweets become public unless your privacy setting is on, and the vast majority of people never engage that feature.

Tweens and teens love to personalize and add applications. Twitter is very basic in that regard. In my own Twitter experience, the only teens I've seen on Twitter have been there for business reasons—true young entrepreneurs or journalists. I have yet to find a teen on Twitter for the sake of the venue itself.

One caveat to keep in mind is that Twitter has a minimum age of 13, so allowing a child to be on Twitter before 13 is a violation of Twitter's terms of service. This is not an insignificant issue and one I'll discuss more fully in Chapter 21.

To get a deeper sense of the generation gap in Twitter usage, I turned to Google.

Web Images Videos Maps News Shopping Gmail more ▼   Web History | Se

Google why kids don't use Twitter   Search Advanced Search

Web ⊕Show options...   Results 1 - 10 of about 91,400,000 for why kids don't use Twitter.

Why the kids don't use Twitter (and other insights on online ...
Mar 11, 2009 ... In case you don't know of danah boyd - the online communities academic
who recently joined Microsoft - you should.
onlinejournalismblog.com/.../why-the-kids-dont-use-twitter-and-other- insights-on-online-
community/ - Cached - Similar

Why Don't Teens Tweet? We Asked Over 10000 of Them.
Aug 30, 2009 ... Most teens don't use Twitter because it doesn't enable them to do ..... not
some life changing event, anyone with kids will tell you, ...
techcrunch.com/.../why-dont-teens-tweet-we-asked-over-10000-of-them/ - Cached - Similar

Teens Don't Tweet; Twitter's Growth Not Fueled By Youth | Nielsen Wire
Does it matter that the kids don't use Twitter? | iMod said: [...] reported, " Twitter's footprint
has expanded impressively in the first half of 2009, ...
blog.nielsen.com › Home › Nielsen News - Cached - Similar

5 Reasons Why Many Kids Don't Use Twitter | TechXav
I think the single biggest reason why kids don't use Twitter is the reverse network effect –
they've got their circle of RL friends, which is the same as ...
www.techxav.com/2009/.../5-reasons-why-many-kids-dont-use-twitter/ - Cached

Social media experts seem to agree with my rudimentary observations of why teens and older kids are not on Twitter. (Copyright Google.)

According to Microsoft researcher danah boyd: "While it's possible to make Twitter 'private,' the culture of Twitter is all about participation in a large public square. From the digerati seeking widespread attention to the politically minded hoping to appear on CNN, many are leveraging Twitter to be part of a broad dialogue. Teens are much more motivated to talk only with their friends and they learned a harsh lesson with social network sites. Even if they are just trying to talk to their friends, those who hold power over them are going to access everything they wrote if it's in public. While the ethos among teens is 'public by default, private when necessary,' many are learning that it's just not worth it to have a worrying mother obsess over every mood you seek to convey. This dynamic showcases how social factors are key to the adoption of new forms of social media."[2]

Teens who have commented about how teens use digital media have confirmed this view. According to Daniel Brusilovsky, a 16-year-old teen who writes online for TechCrunch, Twitter is just "too open": "...Twitter is a different type of social network than Facebook. Facebook is about connecting people, and sharing information with each other. The way my friends and I see it, Facebook is a closed network. It's a network of people and friends that you trust to be connected to, and to share information like your e-mail address, AIM screen name, and phone number. You know who's getting your status messages, because you either approved or added each person to your network.

"With Twitter, it's the exact opposite. Anyone can follow your status updates. It's a completely open network that makes teenagers feel 'unsafe' about posting their content there, because who knows who will read it. Sure, you get e-mails notifying you when you have new followers, but that doesn't compare to the level of detail you get when someone on Facebook adds you, and you get their information."[3]

Fifteen-year-old Morgan Stanley intern Matthew Robson noted a similar sentiment about Twitter: "Most have signed up to the service but then just leave it as they realize that they are not going to update it (mostly because texting twitter uses up credit, and they would rather text friends with that credit). In addition, they realize that no one is viewing their profile, so their 'tweets' are pointless."[4]

While huge numbers of teens are not on Twitter for these reasons, some are starting to become intrigued enough to follow their favorite celebrities and rock stars. Celebrities and bands are using Twitter for giveaways and promotions, which is attractive to this age group and may begin to lure more teens to Twitter. We'll have to stay tuned and see what happens!

As parents, should we ignore this venue because our kids and teens are not spending a considerable amount of time on it at the moment? In my opinion, no. Our teens and kids have not found a big use for Twitter today, but we don't know what tomorrow will bring. Following our "never say never" philosophy of online use adoption, teens may well find a use for Twitter or a use may be found for them in the educational arena. It behooves us to understand Twitter so we have a sense of what it's about.

Furthermore, Twitter can help us out enormously as parents in our hunt for reliable information on health trends and current topics in parenting and the well-being of our kids. Using Twitter, we can find resources in our communities, experts to help our kids, experts to help ourselves, and information to help us stay up-to-date. It's a powerful venue that way. Twitter can also help us connect with other people who have shared experiences with us in whatever area we seek communal support.

Of course, like with any social media tool, do your homework and check your followers carefully. There is a great deal of spam on Twitter and not all experts are what they seem. Take the time to link through and check the parent site listed on a potential follower's profile. And don't feel the need to follow someone because they follow you. Only follow people who help build your network toward your goal, whatever that may be.

With other social networking tools, we typically start discussing potential health risks or consequences at this point in our tour of the tool, but there really isn't anything yet to worry about with Twitter. It is very transparent with a group focus that keeps the site very clean and up front. You may not find every post to be up your alley, but you are also not going to find as much in the way of real health risks from the posts either.

For your college students on Twitter, the biggest risk is in stranger danger and in helping your older teen/young adult sort out the qualities of a follower that makes that follower's posts seem reasonable to read and consider.

Twitter is most certainly a venue to play with and consider using. Although our kids and teens are not using it, some families have dabbled in it for family connections via the private tweet channel. This seems to work best when there are older teens and college students at home.

To Tweet or Not to Tweet?

Does this mean you should be part of Twitter? Maybe. It has many uses for following and finding information, and for that reason alone it may be beneficial for your own personal use. For our kids and teens, though, it is still a venue whose story has yet to be written. It may just be one of the few high-tech venues us digital immigrants gain more experience with before the digital natives; wouldn't that be a twist to the pattern we've seen so far?

References

1. Lenhart A, Fox S. Twitter and status updating. Pew Internet and American Life Project Web site. Available at: http://www.pewinternet.org/Reports/2009/Twitter-and-status-updating.aspx. Published February 12, 2009. Accessed March 9, 2010

2. Boyd D. Social media is here to stay...now what? Microsoft Research Tech Fest, Redmond, Washington. February 26, 2009. Available at: http://www.danah.org/papers/talks/MSRTechFest2009.html. Accessed March 9, 2010

3. Brusilovsky D. Why teens aren't using Twitter: it doesn't feel safe. Available at: http://www.washingtonpost.com/wp-dyn/content/article/2009/07/13/AR2009071302437.html. Published July 13, 2009. Accessed April 1, 2010

4. Robson M. How teenagers consume media: the report that shook the city. *The Guardian UK* Web site. Available at: http://www.guardian.co.uk/business/2009/jul/13/teenage-media-habits-morgan-stanley. Published July 13, 2009. Accessed March 9, 2010

Chapter 16

How Digital Kids Share, Think, and Organize

W acky Packages. Those were the rage when I was growing up, at least for the girls. For the boys, they spent hours collecting, sorting, and trading baseball cards.

Wacky Packages became so popular that for many years, they actually outsold baseball cards. What made them a blast was the social element. Anyone who collected became part of our network. We'd chat about these by phone and around the school lunch table, pass notes in school in the hallway walking to our next class.

There were even sightings out of state and in other countries to extend the circle a bit more. That was always exciting—when someone would come back from family travels with stories of Wacky Package collecting far away.

This was sort of the grandmother (or father!) of social networking, pre-digital. We didn't rely on technology but each other. We didn't have Facebook, blogs, or Twitter but phones hooked to walls and face-to-face connections. We used to swap in person. Today's kids swap things online and virtually. But it's all the same—social networking and connection.

What made this so exciting for us was the ability to be together, to *engage* with one another and be *creative*. This kept us *entertained* for hours on end and *communicating* with one another about all sorts of things. Today's digital natives—kids, tweens, and teens—are no different. They gravitate to the same activities, summarized by the mnemonic I call the 2 Cs and the 2 Es: create, communicate, engage, entertain.

Create

Digital natives are not just able creators; they are extraordinaire! This skill is applied in their non-digital lives as well; watch the care with which kids today put together a school project. It's not just about the end result, such as a race car in tech ed or face mask in art, but that extra touch that makes it their own.

In the online world, creativity is the name of the game. When my oldest digital native was only in fifth grade, she didn't just manipulate her own music online; she created it. We found a music composition program that musicians and students use, and within hours she had mastered it. Once in middle school, now a tween, she had the opportunity to take part in a state competition with other young composers. The most striking feature of the final performance, beyond the sheer talent of these kids, was the amount of digital technology kids used as they got older. It's like a switch was tossed around age 11 or 12 years. For some young composers, the creative process was digital. For others, the recording of the final product contained the digital elements. In the end, though, almost all entries contained something digital that lead to the final product in a substantial way beyond just being a recording device.

Communicate

Have you ever been near a middle or high school around dismissal time? It truly is a site to behold. Regardless of age and grade, these digital natives will barely have a toe outside the building of the school before they have cell phones in hand and fingers tapping. A few may actually be listening to their phones because their parents still use the voice message feature. And a good amount of others have earbuds in place as they plug in to tunes for the long ride or walk home. In many instances, this is taking place while chatting with friends.

When my teen and tween arrive in the car, it usually takes less than 5 seconds for one of their cell phones to make the familiar "veep" sound of a text coming through. I'm always amazed that something that wasn't just chatted about could need to be texted. I'm told that "stuff" comes up that can't wait until the next day. That "stuff" can amount to dozens of texts in a short amount of time on average!

We joke in our home that our cell phones don't ring, they "veep," since it's rare for our kids to get phone calls or voice messages.

Engage

Tweens and teens are happiest when they travel in a pack. This engagement is important developmentally and a huge aspect of their lives online and off. Most of what drives them is the power of the peer and the need to be social. This power can be so great it can make smart kids do things they otherwise wouldn't. So teens' and tweens' social lives should be a parent's concern, online and off.

Entertain

In addition to the social aspect of their lives, digital natives thrive on fun. This is the age of gaming and video downloads, of putting everything to music and sharing the latest and greatest MP3 singles. Digital natives find themselves on iTunes immediately after *American Idol,* downloading their favorite contestants' latest MP3 singles.

Everything digital natives do is driven by one of the 2 Cs and 2 Es. Many times these areas happen at the same time or overlap, but one of these areas is always being expressed when our kids are spending time in the digital world.

You only have to watch a tween or teen for a short while to figure out that a digital life includes

- Videos
- Music
- Instant messaging and texting
- Cell phone use—calling, texting, sometimes surfing the 'net, gaming
- E-mail
- TV watching
- Computer use—surfing, searching, blogging
- Gaming
- Social networking sites—MySpace, Facebook

Kids use these differently and put themselves at risk in ways you may not have thought of.

- Videos and gaming
  - Use: creativity, engagement with others, entertainment
  - Risk: exposure to material inappropriate for age about sex, sexuality, violence, body image; games that mimic real-life activities have the added risk of overuse injuries.
- Music
  - Use: creativity, engagement with others, entertainment
  - Risk: lyrics not appropriate for age (many times, kids don't even know the lyrics or why they are inappropriate); hearing issues from not listening at safe decibel levels or with proper earbuds or earphones
- Instant messaging and texting
  - Use: creativity, communication, engagement with others, entertainment
  - Risk: extreme texting; distraction from schoolwork, other activities, and friends; sexting; cyberbullying; communicating with peers about dangerous and destructive behaviors such as promiscuity, eating disorders, or drug use
- Cell phone use—calling, texting, sometimes surfing the 'net, gaming
  - Use: creativity, communication, engagement with others, entertainment
  - Risk: extreme texting; distraction from schoolwork, other activities, and friends; sexting; cyberbullying; communicating with peers about dangerous and destructive behaviors such as promiscuity, eating disorders, or drug use; accidents if using while driving or biking
- E-mail
  - Use: communication, engagement with others
  - Risk: cyberbullying, obtaining incorrect information from other people about issues, not understanding issues of anonymity and boundaries with replies
- TV watching
  - Use: engagement with others in room, entertainment
  - Risk: too much TV linked to obesity, violence, unhealthy habits, inattention, early smoking and drinking, early sexual experiences
- Computer use—surfing, searching, blogging
  - Use: creativity, entertainment
  - Risk: not understanding how to search and finding faulty information

- Social networking sites—MySpace, Facebook
  - Use: creativity, communication, engagement with others, entertainment
  - Risk: not understanding friending; Facebook depression; stranger danger; sexting; inappropriate posts leading to bullying or issues with others, even years away (eg, during interviews)

Sharing in the Digital World

This is a sharing generation. Kids love to share the goings-on of their days; that's why we see them texting and chatting so much about small details that we, as their parents, don't find that important. They also love to share the stuff in their lives they find interesting, like links, music, and videos. Music and links deserve some special attention because they are staples for our digital natives. Music drives all digital kids in one way or another and they all have something on their MP3 they love to not just tune in but share with others. And links are the backbone of the Internet and play an interesting social role that even the youngest digital natives have begun to latch onto.

Links and URLs

Not too long ago, I asked my 14-year-old how she and her friend share Web site URLs and videos. She looked at me and initially said, "We just do." This generation shares seamlessly and mindlessly. It is hardwired into their beings and they don't have a conscious idea of the process initially.

They also don't keep records of sites they find that are cool the way we do. In the adult culture of online work, we love to bookmark. Some of us do so on our computer Web browsers, organizing our finds in folders, while others use social bookmarking sites such as http://delicious.com or http://digg.com, both of which organize by keyword, just like you are searching.

While young and middle teens may not yet know about bookmarking, they will need to soon enough. It is a good idea to have a sense of what this is all about so you can help your child organize the online world a bit. Kids may have some of the nuts and bolts sorted out before us, but we know how to take notes and organize; there is a lot they can learn from us about how to streamline and make sense of their digital lives. This isn't just academic— with kids being so busy so young, helping them organize their digital lives will make them more efficient off-line. And off-line time is where our refueling occurs. So anything we can do to minimize digital time and get our kids some off-line time, we should do!

File Sharing 2.0: Bookmarking Goes Social

Our need to organize extends to our online lives. Whether it is our cell phone contacts or favorite Web sites, our need to de-clutter is hardwired into us.

Online file systems are more cumbersome to keep tabs of than off-line systems. Invisible to the eye, we can pile endless reams of data in these systems without blinking an eye and not even know if we are anywhere near capacity. At least our off-line systems have a few telltale signs we need to sort and toss—drawers that won't close, files that explode!

If you've ever attempted to organize a bookmark on your computer's Web browser, you'll know that it is simple to do, but it's a bear to locate that bookmark quickly later on. Unless we are efficient with the bookmarks we keep on our computer Web browser, the list of URLs to sites can quickly pile up.

Why the leap to social bookmarking? What advantage does it have over our computer?

One obvious advantage is not having it saved on our computer. We can organize this virtual pile of our preselected Web sites and references from any computer or digital device that has Internet access, 24/7, anywhere in the world.

The second advantage is that bookmarks are not organized by big, bulky files but by keywords and tags, the labels we used to identify the Web site or URL as if we needed to find it again doing a Google search.

Third is the ability to share bookmarks with others and to see what other people have found in similar categories or tags that interest us. This comes in really handy with research!

Finally, the Web is now set up for these services and actually encourages us to use them over our built-in computer systems. Those are still viable options but less robust and more difficult to organize. Most Web 2.0 sites now have a list of the popular social bookmarking and networking sites and allow you to bookmark those Web pages easily. The most popular program for this is called AddThis (www.addthis.com).

Courtesy of AddThis.com, www.addthis.com/web-button-select

Clicking one of these icons on any Web page opens up a larger box with links to all the popular social media and sharing sites. You can post to all of your social media accounts, print, e-mail, and save to your computer from this one location. It's truly one-click posting!

Let me use my Web site as an example so you can see how this works. If I want to share my new column with my Twitter feed or Facebook, I would go to my column page and hit the "add this" or "share" button at the top of the page, whichever is present.

www.pediatricsnow.com

Now, a larger box appears that looks like this.

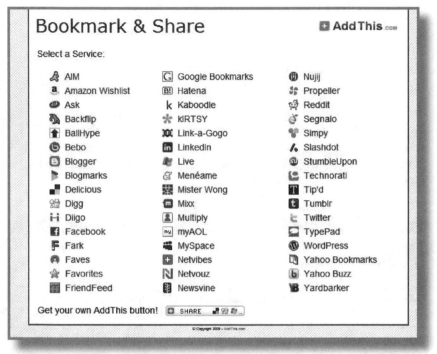

Courtesy of AddThis.com

From this one screen, I can add my new column to my blog on Blogger, my Twitter feed, Facebook, Google Bookmarks, Delicious, Favorites, FriendFeed, and LinkedIn, where I have active feeds. From the original "add this" button, I can also print, which is handy at times. It really is that simple!

Social media venues all have different purposes, which is why I have a few active feeds, but most people just manage one feed and call it a day! For bookmarking, all the sites are similar. I happen to find that Delicious meets my needs; you may find another site suits you better. You may have to play around with the sites a bit and see what works for you. It truly does boil down to personal preference with bookmarking.

Some families are finding bookmarking on computers useful as a road map so younger family members know where to go online safely. Using a special toolbar or folder for each child is a great way to organize a few sites for children who are able to read so they can be a bit more independent on the computer.

Why Be Social With Links?

By making your bookmarks social, you allow yourself to create an online community of resources. Say you find 5 amazing sites on the H1N1 virus, but a few of your friends locate a few more you hadn't stumbled on. Being part of a social bookmarking site allows you to all enjoy the benefits of all of these resources. This creates an amazing online collaboration and a pooling of ideas and perspectives. Since we all search the Web a bit uniquely, we are likely to find a group of sites for any given topic that others haven't discovered.

Overlapping areas are what create the social networking part of any social bookmarking site. There will be times I'll stumble on your sites or our colleagues' sites, but other times we'll all meet in the middle and share. That middle zone is like a full online library of Web sites and information.

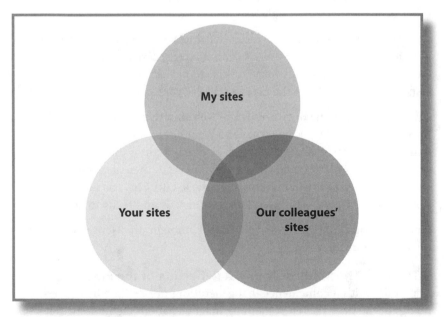

Venn diagram of social bookmarking site

But how do we find the sites we are looking for? That is where labeling comes in. When you put a site onto one of the bookmarking sites, you are asked to tag it. That's the same thing as a keyword for a blog post or Web site article. Our tags are really our folders for the sites we find and bookmark. So the only catch with finding each other's sites is figuring out the tags. The more common and simple, the better!

Keeping Kids Safe With Bookmark and Share

Bookmarking per se isn't dangerous or unhealthy. In its simplest online form, it's no different than placing a traditional bookmark or placeholder in a book. Any risk comes into play on the social end. Because tweens and teens can share links, a Web site or link someone else suggests may not be appropriate in one way or another.

For kids who want to venture into cyberspace, a frank conversation about the online dangers of social networking is needed because that's what this is. They have to be aware that sharing information in cyberspace isn't as simple as it seems. They have to be respectful of the content they share with friends and be careful of the content they accept and look at from other people, especially people they don't know.

One great online tool is the privacy setting. You can make an entire account private so outside friends cannot have access to it without an invitation. That is the best way for your kids to protect their information and to not have anyone from the great world of cyberspace trolling their links.

There is also the issue of viruses from Web sites they don't know well. It's important to help kids know what and what not to bookmark. Sites they may use all the time are reasonable to bookmark. Sites that are needed for research for a project are fantastic to bookmark. Other sites may be cool and fun, but the utility in bookmarking those URLs isn't as useful and not be something we want to encourage our kids and teens to do.

Once your kids go to a true social network, though, that sense of security tosses right out the window.

MTV to Go! The Music of Today: A Reflection of the Past

I don't think it's a coincidence that generations are defined by the technology of the day. There's something magnetic about technology that pulls people together, binds families, and encourages teens to express themselves.

When my grandparents were first arriving in the United States from Russia, radio was the mainstay media venue of the day. One of my favorite Normal Rockwell paintings shows a family gathered around an old radio; it reminds me of stories I remember hearing when I was a child from my grandparents and parents about what it was like to huddle around that type of radio and listen to the news and various shows.

In my childhood, music primarily revolved around records. We were in heaven when home recording became available so we could recreate our lists and play them back endlessly!

For our kids, swapping music is as daily a ritual as brushing teeth and as natural as saying "Hi" to each other. They don't have the technologic issues we had. MP3 players themselves can be a bit pricey, but the music is often as free as a click on your keyboard.

The agelessness of listening to and sharing music shouldn't blind us to the fact that music does have some properties to pay attention to.

1. Appropriateness for age and development
2. Legality of sharing
3. Volume
4. Effect on kids' behavior

Appropriateness for Age and Development
When was the last time you actually listened to the same music as your tweens and teens? Do you know the names of the groups? Have you really heard the lyrics?

We had an experience awhile back that was eye-opening. Our 14-year-old had downloaded the lyrics of a song that she loved the beat to. In reviewing the lyrics, I noticed some images that were very dark and degrading toward women. There were other images that were just downright violent and a few times guns and other weapons were mentioned. We asked her why she hadn't picked up on the lyrics and her response was, "I just liked the song. I wasn't really focused on the lyrics."

Research has confirmed that kids and teens really do pay more attention to music than lyrics and that it's the tune that attracts them to a particular song. Most times when kids sing a song, they don't really focus on the lyrics, even if we are stunned by what they are singing.

Studies are clear, however, that listening to lyrics with degrading tone or that are sexually explicit can cause harm. Those are the lyrics we have to be careful of.[1-4]

To help our kids tune in to the right attributes of a song, help them understand these issues.

Legality of Sharing

Where some kids and teens can get into trouble isn't so much in illegally sharing music or downloading it from illegal sites but in using music for purposes they are not supposed to, like using copyrighted music for a podcast.

Volume

Simply put, the longer our kids listen to blasting music, the more at risk they are for hearing issues. Volume also makes our kids unaware of their surroundings, placing them at risk for harm from all sorts of intentional and unintentional accidents.[5,6]

Effect on Kids' Behavior

Music doesn't make our kids misbehave. Rather, the intensity of the music experience can be hypnotic; coupled with the impressionable nature of teens, this becomes a combustible combination.

Listen Up!

So how do we help our kids have good and appropriate listening habits? First, we have to be good role models. Be sure to listen to music in a way that is safe. If you're wearing earbuds, keep the volume low so you can hear others talking or oncoming traffic.

Use music as a conversation tool. MP3 players, cell phones, and computers are a guide to kids' listening patterns and taste. If we hear something inappropriate, it will be tempting to freak out and flip out. That will backfire, that much I can promise you. A more sound approach is to try and point out why lyrics are inappropriate, perhaps citing current events. Most kids will arrive at their own reasonable conclusion when you point out the actual meaning.

Finally, pick your battles. My brother went through a phase in high school and college in which the music he listened to sounded like mooing cows. We dubbed that his "cow phase." He had very eclectic taste in music and since it was otherwise clean, my parents found a way to tolerate it.

With our kids' musical lives being so portable and mobile, laying down firm dictates honestly won't work. We don't have to like what our kids listen to—just tolerate most of it and put your foot down when it truly becomes dangerous, destructive, derogatory, or damaging.

References

1. Martino SC, Collins RL, Elliott MN, Strachman A, Kanouse DE, Berry SH. Exposure to degrading versus nondegrading music lyrics and sexual behavior among youth. *Pediatrics.* 2006;118:e430–e441
2. American Academy of Pediatrics Council on Communications and Media. Impact of music, music lyrics, and music videos on children and youth. *Pediatrics.* 2009;124:1488–1494
3. Brown JD, L'Engle KL, Pardun CJ, Guo G, Kenneavy K, Jackson C. Sexy media matter: exposure to sexual content in music, movies, television, and magazines predicts black and white adolescents' sexual behavior. *Pediatrics.* 2006;117:1018–1027
4. McIlhaney JS Jr. Problems and solutions associated with media consumption: the role of the practitioner. *Pediatrics.* 2005;116:327–328
5. Vogel I, Verschuure H, van der Ploeg CP, Brug J, Raat H. Adolescents and MP3 players: too many risks, too few precautions. *Pediatrics.* 2009;123:e953–e958
6. Vogel I, Brug J, van der Ploeg CP, Raat H. Strategies for the prevention of MP3-induced hearing loss among adolescents: expert opinions from a Delphi study. *Pediatrics.* 2009;123:1257–1262

Part 3

Safety Is a State of Mind

Chapter 17

The Digital Footprint

When I was growing up in the pre-digital days, capturing memories involved taking pictures, keeping journals or diaries, and creating picture albums or scrapbooks of our special moments. We did these activities for our daily lives and school.

Time capsules have been in existence a very long time and people still use them today. They are a fun way to try and capture a moment and hope it will represent to the future what life was like for us the day we closed the capsule door. Unlike the time capsule I was part of in 1975, today's time capsules often involve very high-tech stuff—movies, digital snapshots, pieces of technology. We've gone so far as to put some time capsules into space for our very distant relatives to open, and others have been launched deeper into space by NASA as calling cards to other worlds that life does exist on Earth.[1,2]

Leaving a footprint of our existence has always been important to us. With the evolution of the digital age, we certainly have easier ways to accomplish that.

One of the best snapshots of our life is actually our online history. With so much of our collective lives online, we can learn a great deal about our priorities and values by the types of Web sites we visit.

Alexa tracks these sorts of data and actually does so by country. What's as interesting as seeing the Web site trends in your own country is comparing those trends with other countries. The digital world has connected our global community in ways we could never have thought possible, other than in sci-fi movies. It's truly intriguing to see not only the list but learn how we are similar and different around the globe.

As we explore the Internet, then, we have to be aware that we are not just connected with the people we know but people all over the globe—because they are using the same technologies. This becomes very important for our kids to be aware of as they learn to explore the world. Everything they do online creates a digital footprint that will etch their presence in cyberspace and be hard to erase.

Time capsules often don't accomplish the goal they seek. More often than not, the capsule succumbs to the elements long before it is unearthed and its contents revealed. A digital footprint doesn't have this issue as dramatically. Even deleting material doesn't provide 100% assurance that material will be eliminated—it may have been backed up somewhere, a copy of which people were unaware. The rule of thumb is that nothing really goes away on cyberspace—it can always return to haunt you.

When our kids go online, we have a vague awareness that they could potentially connect with someone far from our home. The protective nature of parenting makes it difficult for us to imagine the feasibility of this occurring. We naively surmise that at worst, they'll connect with another teen in town or another state.

But we can no longer ignore the fact that we are a global community and that families in other countries are using the exact same Web programs and technologies we are. It's not a question of whether our kids will connect with someone in another country while spending time in the digital world, but when.

If we look at the US top 20 sites from the eyes of tweens and teens, those that are important to focus on include

- Google
- Yahoo!
- Facebook
- MySpace
- YouTube
- Wikipedia
- Blogger
- Amazon.com
- WordPress.com

If we add music to this list, these sites represent how our young generation spends its time online. If we spend some of our time learning a bit about these venues and the categories they represent, we'll be better prepared to help the younger generation negotiate the digital world and stay safe within it.

What Happens Online, Stays Online

We all know the importance of backing up our material and have felt the pang of loss when our computer freezes just before our last save of a big project. Today's computer programs all come with handy "autosave" features so these stressful moments are becoming a thing of the past.

Large Web sites back up their databases too, as well as any material that any of us may have added to the Web world. Whether a commercial Web site, blog, or social media site such as Facebook, MySpace, or Twitter, all sites should have a comprehensive backup system in place.

Therein lies the paradox of the digital footprint (or imprint, as some folks call it). What we put on cyberspace never truly goes away. We have to consider it permanent because there is likely a copy somewhere; to think otherwise is foolish.

Digitial Footprint Defined

Wikipedia defines digital footprint as "the data trace or trail left by someone's activity in a digital environment."[3] It turns out that digital footprints can be made actively or passively. We make active digital footprints by creating profiles, posting on blogs, leaving comments, and setting up accounts. Passive digital footprints are created when our information is copied by other Web sites and stored.

The concept isn't just one of being "findable," according to Pew Internet, but also being "knowable." What's interesting is that adults are aware they have a digital footprint, but few care about it. In fact, according to Pew Internet, "Fully 60% of internet users say they are not worried about how much information is available about them online. Similarly, the majority of online adults (61%) do not feel compelled to limit the amount of information that can be found about them online." So it's no wonder that parents haven't been dogmatic about stressing the importance of monitoring the digital footprint with their kids.

An interesting twist in these findings is that teens are more private with their online profiles than adults. Pew noted that 40% of teens have their social media profiles viewable by anyone, compared with 60% of adults. Fifty-nine percent of teens have their profiles set to friends only, compared with 38% of adults.[4]

Creating a Positive Path

When we teach our kids to negotiate the off-line world, we teach them about ways to create a good impression. We help them understand manners, body language, etiquette, and social rules. We help them learn to negotiate tricky social situations as they get older and start to explore the world on their own. They sometimes shine and sometimes stumble, but we help them stand back up and get on the right path.

Learning to negotiate the online world is similar; by helping our kids learn the rules of the online road their digital footprint trail will head in a positive direction. To manage their digital life and footprint, kids need to know the following before posting anything online:

1. Stop to think before you hit send.
2. Don't write online what you wouldn't say off-line.
3. If you saw your online friend off-line, would you be embarrassed by what you wrote, sent, or said?
4. If something isn't funny off-line, it isn't funny online.
5. Comments that have a dangerous or destructive meaning toward another are never OK—they are always harmful and could get you into a lot of trouble.
6. Bullies are bullies, even online.
7. Follow posted rules.
8. Follow age restrictions.
9. Ask yourself if what you post is something OK for parents to see.
10. If you were a future employer, what impression would you have of your digital footprint?
11. What you post can be altered by others—pictures, videos, comments, and text.

How can you help your kids understand the importance of the digital footprint? First, take it seriously yourself. Monitor your posts and be a bit more concerned about the material you are posting and who is reading it. Second, find headlines about other teens gone astray with things like "Facebook firings." These are very real and do occur. Venting online happens and we all have done it, but discretion is key.

Finding Your Footprint

The phrase *digital footprint* may sound intimidating, but finding our online footprints is easy. You've actually hunted for your digital footprint before and found it but never really thought of it in this way. Every time we go online to Google ourselves and find something we have done somewhere on cyberspace, we are tracking down a piece of our own digital footprint. Every time we Google a person we know, in or out of our family, we are stepping on the trail of that person's digital footprint.

Locating one's digital footsteps is easy. What's more important, though, is understanding what the footsteps mean and whether you should worry. This is more important if you are trying to hunt down your child's digital footprint or if you find a surprise.

Googling my kids, I discovered they were not anywhere they shouldn't be or that we didn't already know about. What would I have done had I found a surprise in the digital footprint? For example, what if I had found my name or one of my kids' names on a site I wasn't aware of? Here's a way to evaluate the digital footprint.

1. **Don't panic!** Things are not always as they seem. You need to take a deep breath and evaluate the situation a bit more.
2. **Name check:** Many people today share the same name. Go to the link and see if the name you see in the search result is actually you, your child, or the person you were searching for. More times than not you'll discover it is all one big case of mistaken identity. If not, go to step 3.
3. **Site check:** What type of site is it? Perhaps it's a social media site and your child signed up without knowing. Perhaps it's a site that pulls information from other sites without the originator of the information's knowledge or permission. Perhaps a third party supplied the information.

There is usually a good and credible explanation. For adults, many times other sites do pull in information from sites to which you have already granted permission. This is typical for blogs, for example. So I'm not surprised if I see a blog post I've written or an article I've given to another site show up somewhere else. Sometimes I track it down for removal; other times I don't. It depends on the nature of the site and the circumstances under which it was posted.

If I discovered one of my kids' names and learned that they had signed up for a site that I was not aware of, like Facebook, MySpace, or a free gaming site, I would find a calm time to ask them about it. The goal here is to not prejudge. I've learned that kids have a way of asking us indirectly if it's OK to do things online, or they will assume that if their friends are on a site, they can be on the same site. Worst case, they assumed they would not be caught. If we freak out as parents, if we become too authoritative, they will shut us out so firmly that we lose credibility in their eyes. The key is to learn what they were thinking, find a solution, and set clear expectations for the future.

For example, if the site is OK for your children's age, perhaps their unauthorized use caused no harm, but you need a better plan for learning what your kids are up to online. If, however, you discover they are on a site they should not be on, talk to them about why the violation of the family rule occurred. Was it an accident? That sometimes happens. It can be easy to end up on a site accidentally from a trail of searching. If a true violation of house rules did occur, most experts advise taking away TV time or increasing off-line chores as opposed to shutting down the digital world. The idea is to reinforce values, not cause a power struggle over technology.

We Are Their First Footprint Manager

Kevin, dad of digital tween Cam from Chapter 8, is in the parenting trenches like all of us, trying to balance the gift of freedom to his digital native child while waiting in the wings to help out when needed. Kevin feels that it's a parent's job to be the mediator of the digital footprint: "We have to manage the digital imprint as parents until he is ready to take it over. The goal is to find the middle of [the] road before he does and test it out like driving."

Kevin mentioned, "Many parents abdicate responsibility to kids and don't want to know." I'd have to agree. Many parents don't try to drive the online world or speak the online language, and this is when issues occur and our kids' digital footprints veer off course and get covered in mud. We toss over control of the technology and the all-important digital footprint to someone else.

Our kids are too young initially to process future implications of things like silly posts or pictures. They need us to help guide them to appropriate behavior. They need us to help them understand that we live in a day and age in which it isn't uncommon for college admissions officers and future employers to hunt for "digital dirt" before making an important decision about college admission or job offers. What about privacy controls on things like Facebook? Even if our kids have their accounts locked down, their friends may not. Glimpses of images in which they have been tagged may end up online. References to them may pop up on other people's walls, Web sites, and blogs. Our kids won't know these are not such great practices unless we help them see the future trail to which these digital footprints will someday lead.

Believe it or not, I was able to find a reference to Googling someone's history for potential employment dating back to 2006 on CollegeGrad.com![5] The article points out that job seekers need to be mindful of their social media posts and that employers are looking!

A 2007 commentary noted that this practice is legal and information found online by an employer can actually be used for employee termination.[6] Googling isn't just a matter of interest; it's now considered a tried-and-true, and legal, background check!

As BusinessWeek noted in "You Are What You Post," "Schools are warning parents about Google's danger to the MySpace generation, for whom the Internet functions as a virtual diary-meets-barstool confessional. Adolescents try on identities and new behaviors like sweaters….The teenagers on the 'companies and co-workers' section of MySpace who are talking smack about employers…are clearly unaware of the implications."[7]

A study done by the University of Massachusetts Dartmouth Center for Marketing Research center confirms that college admissions officers are watching. In fact, 23% are checking out prospective students via traditional searching, while 17% are hunting into social media. Google and Yahoo! were the search engines most commonly used, and Facebook and MySpace are the social media sites most commonly looked over.[8]

What's interesting about these data is that they show that admissions officers are nosy but that social media hunts are not the primary source for college admissions acceptance information. This is reassuring, given the many factors important for college acceptance.

That said, the digital footprint is clearly of interest to people and something being explored as a decision tool. And it's not just being used for that. With online dating becoming popular, digging up digital dirt is part of the pre-date ritual, certainly in college and beyond.

It's up to us to help our teens understand what this all means—how to use social media venues and manage their online presence responsibly, in a way that creates a lifelong asset and not a closeted skeleton that will resurface unexpectedly from time to time.

The Temperature of the Headlines

Have you noticed that whenever you're worried about one of your kids being sick, regardless of age, you put your hand to his forehead and check for a temperature? It's almost an automatic parenting reflex. Whether there are overt or implied signs of sickness, we hunt for that all-important fever because that is a true telltale sign of serious illness and helps us gauge how concerned we should be and our course of action.

It turns out we can take the temperature of headlines and issues too, thanks to something called Google Alerts. You can set these up to track any keyword, phrase, or name imaginable as well as the frequency you'd like the alerts (daily, weekly, monthly). Google will track these topics for you and shoot an update to your inbox with the headlines for those keywords.

If you follow your Google Alerts for a long enough period, you start to sense whether the issue you are following is really hot, a flash in the pan, or old news that someone is trying to reinvent. These give voice to an issue and recognize it is real, and not just a worry we may have.

Tracking some important new media concepts with Google Alerts such as sexting, social media and teens, and cell phones and kids has allowed me to take the temperature of the new media landscape while doing research for this book. It's clear by the amount of headlines on all of these topics that these are no fly-by-night issues; these are real. And some issues like sexting are so hot that the temperature is actually rising, with the amount of head-lines increasing and expanding around the entire globe.

For example, during one month in spring 2009, there were more than 50 sexting headlines for news stories, representing every geographic region in the United States. Based on these headlines, the American Academy of

Pediatrics created "Talking to Kids and Teens About Social Media and Sexting" (see Appendix F.) What can we do to help turn the situation around?

Make our own headlines!

We have to be willing to change the headline landscape for the better by learning from the experiences of others. Past headlines are lessons for what we should and shouldn't be doing. If we pay attention, we can glean some pearls of wisdom that should spare our teens the embarrassment and pain others had to endure.

1. Put a face to it.
2. Name it.

As we've seen, many online issues with teens and tweens occur because of the power of anonymity. If they are reminded that there is a real person behind the computer, that often changes their behavior and outlook considerably. In addition to talking with kids about their digital footprints, I use the mnemonic RITE to make kids pause and think about what they are posting online.

Is the Digital Message RITE?

Reread your message to be sure it sounds OK.

Imagine if you were receiving the message—would you be upset or hurt?

Think about whether it needs to be sent now or can wait a bit.

Enter button time.

Remember, what happens in cyberspace, stays on cyberspace and can be seen by anyone, any time. Cyberspace never closes. The onus is on us to make sure the current and future digital footprints of our digital natives always show a proud path.

References

1. Time capsule. Wikipedia: The Free Encyclopedia Web site. Available at: http://en.wikipedia.org/wiki/Time_capsule. Modified March 7, 2010. Accessed March 10, 2010
2. Capsule history. *American Heritage* Web site. Available at: http://www.americanheritage.com/articles/magazine/ah/1999/7/1999_7_88.shtml. Accessed March 10, 2010
3. Digital footprint. Wikipedia: The Free Encyclopedia Web site. Available at: http://en.wikipedia.org/wiki/Digital_footprint. Modified March 1, 2010. Accessed March 10, 2010
4. Madden M, Fox S, Smith A, Vitak J. Digital footprints. Pew Internet and American Life Project Web site. Available at: http://www.pewinternet.org/Reports/2007/Digital-Footprints.aspx. Published December 16, 2007. Accessed March 10, 2010
5. Entry level job seeker, Google thyself! CollegeGrad.com Web site. Available at: http://www.collegegrad.com/press/google-thyself.shtml. Published June 13, 2006. Accessed March 10, 2010
6. Longino C. Judges say Google background checks are okay. Techdirt Web site. Available at: http://www.techdirt.com/articles/20070509/103950.shtml. Published May 9, 2007. Accessed March 10, 2010
7. You are what you post. BusinessWeek Web site. Available at: http://www.businessweek.com/magazine/content/06_13/b3977071.htm. Published March 27, 2006. Accessed March 10, 2010
8. Barnes NG, Mattson E. Social media and college admissions: the first longitudinal study. University of Massachusetts Dartmouth Center for Marketing Research Web site. Available at: http://www.umassd.edu/cmr/studiesresearch/mediaandadmissions.pdf. Published 2008. Accessed March 10, 2010

Internet Safety Tools

For most things in life, we make sure our kids have experience before we unleash them on the world. We are with them holding their fingers before they let go and take steps on their own. We teach them to look both ways before crossing the street and then cross with them for a good long while until they are old enough to understand, remember it, and follow it. Once they are in school, they start to learn about more worldly safety issues such as fires and when to call for help from a grown-up, or being in a dangerous or destructive situation. Dangerous and destructive are often referred to as the 2 Ds, but in reality there are 4—dangerous, destructive, derogatory, and damaging comments, behaviors, or actions.

Whether online or off, when one of the 4 D situations occurs, our kids need to know to inform a parent or a trusted grown-up such as a teacher. Despite how much rope we give them, the 4 Ds are where we should draw the line.

Another Mnemonic Device: TECH Is the Word

I was driving home one evening around dusk. While waiting at an intersection for a red light to turn green so I could make a right-hand turn, I noticed a teen on his bike on the other side of the road. He missed the walk signal and was watching the lights expectantly. No sooner did the light turn green for me to turn than he darted across the street heading toward me on his bike. He was wearing a very dark sweatshirt and dusk was quickly becoming early evening. He barely missed my car's back end as I completed my turn. He looked unfazed and was not wearing a helmet. I got the sense his decision to dart across the street was a last-minute impulse.

That's the teen way! They tend to act without thinking about repercussions. This is true online and off. In fact, online kids tend to be more risky—the anonymity gives them a badge of courage! So how do we keep kids safe online when they feel even more invincible? It isn't easy given the teen persona, but it's not impossible. Think TECH.

T: Talk to your child about what he is doing online and ask him specifically about online safety issues.

E: Educate yourself on online safety issues, programs you need to know, and tools you can use

C: Check your child's computer and be willing to follow through on consequences.

H: Have a family use plan *(house rules)* so everyone understands what is and isn't allowed for computer and Internet use.

TECH is a great starting point, but be prepared for curveballs thanks to the power of the peer. I found this out myself when my youngest was in sixth grade, 11 years old going on 12. We learned a few interesting things that year. Some kids in her grade were on Facebook, despite a minimum age of 13 to join, and some were on sites that had a minimum age of 14 to join.

How do we feel about families allowing their preteens to fudge the rules to use these sites? Is it wise or is there a reason that these ages are picked in the first place?

If we give our kids permission to fudge their age on the Internet, the implicit message is that those age limits are up for interpretation. How can we, then, help them understand age minimums for getting a driver's license, drinking, or becoming a legal adult?

Whether online or off, age limits are created for a good reason—to keep our kids safe. Those are the ages studies and experts have determined that kids have to be at a minimum to participate in that activity safely.

As we saw with everything from social networking to bookmarking, there is a steep learning curve in how kids view and use each venue as well as their understanding of what's appropriate to post. It's our job as parents to realize that even good kids are limited by their ages. It's straightforward biology—they can't be older than they are, and we have to realize that.

If they are online before they are ready and before the recommended ages of these sites, they are hanging with much older kids and, potentially, adults. If teens have trouble figuring out boundaries, who to friend, and how to post appropriately, we can't expect a preteen or someone younger to do so.

Eventually our kids will have a digital footprint that will grow and march in all sorts of directions. It can be difficult to control the path of that footprint, so it's best to hold off until our kids are on sure footing online and understand the important issues about posting.

Keep in mind that social media sites do not ask for proof of age or police the medium to be sure everyone is the age they state. It would be a daunting, if not impossible, task to verify every user's age to be sure they are who they say they are. This is a problem in the adult population too. We really have no way of knowing if people are who they say they are at any age. (See Chapter 21.)

Internet and Social Media House Rules 101

In TECH, the H is to have house Internet rules that everyone agrees to follow, including adults! Even though ages of kids and specific activities will vary within a family, the actual rules are likely going to be very similar because healthy digital and online venue use within every family will be the same.

One of the first issues to consider is your own Internet habits, especially those that relate to safety. Do you know the proper uses for Web sites, blogs, and social networking sites such as Twitter and Facebook? What are your use habits? Do you text while you drive? Do you use your cell phone or laptop in the car? Do you use earbuds with your MP3 player in the car or while walking or running? Do you know what cyberbullying and sexting are? Do you know proper online posting etiquette?

At the beginning and end of the day, the best way to keep our kids safe online is to parent them. Kids learn best with small lessons over time as opposed to one big lecture or sit-down talk. Looking for teachable moments when your kids are using the computer will have much more staying power than talking about the issue out of the blue. Similarly, bringing up a headline from the news about a child in the same peer bracket can pack a powerful teaching punch.

Possible sets of house rules or family media use pledges that you can use for your family are included in the appendixes—mine is in Appendix G; a couple leading Internet safety groups agreed to have theirs reprinted for this book (appendixes H and I). Look at these as starting points and modify as needed for your family's needs. The goal is to incorporate technology into our lives in a meaningful way that allows us to have a healthy balance of online and off-line time. At the heart, all Internet safety pledges have the same fundamentals. Find one that works for your family and stick with it.

Freedom in the Digital World

As they get older, tweens and teens want to maximize time with their friends and minimize time with their family. This is a natural process that occurs at different speeds and starts at slightly different times for all kids. But it is one of the fundamental tasks of the later teenage years. From wanting a cell phone to walking independently to school, walking to the nearby pizza shop to going to the mall or a movie with friends without a parent in sight or even present, our kids will start to push the envelope on independence and push us out of our comfort zones into uncharted waters before we're ready.

Parents handle this emerging independence differently. Some parents create more rules; others, less. Some parents try to resist the trends they see in their kids' peer groups; others feel more comfortable going with the flow and allowing their kids more freedom to experience the greater digital world with some controls in place. In an ideal world, we'll all find a way to accomplish the latter.

As our kids enter the later middle school and high school years, we have to become very aware of our own fears and insecurities and try and separate those out from what is best for our kids. We have to recognize that it's OK to feel a bit antsy about giving our kids more freedom. We are setting ourselves up for teenage rebellion if we try to hold our teens down too much and be too overprotective. At the same time, our teens have to recognize that this is a two-way street and there will be consequences for violations of agreed-on freedoms.

Well before they are teens, how can we help them stay safe and understand the rules of the road? With conversation and technology, it's not as difficult as you might think. In fact, the two actually go hand in hand. Let's take a tour of various products in the Internet safety industry and see how easy the features are to use and fit into your family life.

Filters, Tools, and Online Safety Systems

Active parenting, following TECH, and being sure your kids understand the 4 Ds are the best way to ensure your kids' safety online. But extra layers of protection can come in handy when we are dealing with kids who are still sorting out how to live in a world that keeps getting bigger thanks to the World Wide Web and digital technology. That's just what filters, tools, and parenting "control" software are designed to do.

I put control in quotes because the goal isn't to control your kids' experiences; it's to empower them to make good decisions while putting in reasonable safeguards. This is no different than starting your kids off in the shallow end of the swimming pool before allowing them to swim in the deep end or dive off the board. Sometimes a graduated entry into a situation is the best way to gain the experience needed to participate safely and have the most fun!

There are many tools available to you, and most of them are free. While these tools do work admirably, it's important that you know the pros and cons of the tool you are considering as well as the price, if you opt for a commercial product. So before you spend a dime, do your homework and be sure that tool offers you something the free tools do not.

You also have to be realistic about the fact that none of these tools is 100% foolproof. There are going to be lapses in what filters can block and limitations in what you can control. And you have to consider the ingenuity of kids who are old enough to know that parental controls are in effect. A smart, determined, computer-savvy digital native will eventually find an end run around even the most sophisticated of filtering systems.

For a thorough and comprehensive review of current parental control systems on the market, I suggest checking out *PCMag Digital Network,* http://go.pcmag.com/parentalcontrol.

PCMag Digital Network's Neil Rubenking, author of the parenting control reviews and a computer expert, explained to me that effective parent control systems have the following features:

1. **Time control:** This allows you to control how much time your child is on the computer or playing a game, but it has to be independent of the clock on your computer to work correctly.
2. **Remote access:** This feature allows you to view and configure parental control settings on the children's computer from any other Internet-equipped computer.
3. **Extent of control:** This includes gaming, the Internet, search filters, and the ability to block specific sites and games.
4. **Parental interaction:** Your operating system itself, Mac or Windows XP/Vista/7, likely has parental control that you can enable to see if it fits your needs.

5. **Parental notification of events:** This is a helpful feature; you will be alerted when violations occur. This will allow you to assess if the filters are working for your child. For example, perhaps your child's homework involves extensive Internet searches but the program won't allow it—that would be a real issue for your child that can be avoided by altering the settings to allow for more robust searches.
6. **Instant message (IM) filtering/monitoring:** Evidently, these filters are easy for kids to do an end run around.
7. **Web site blocking:** Rubenking emphasized that this feature has to be "browser independent" or it won't be able to block Web sites.

So which parental control tool should you choose? In many areas of life, we tend to think of free as second best, but this is not the case with Internet safety programs. When free is a service provided by the largest and most respected Internet safety groups, I highly recommend you start with those programs first. They may fit your needs and if they do, you have saved yourself a few bucks! There are many fantastic free tools available today. Let me highlight a couple that stand out for accomplishing their goals and being very user friendly.

Free Internet Parent Control Filtering and Monitoring Programs

Norton Online Family
Norton Online Family is Symantec's free family Internet safety product. You can learn about it and download it at https://onlinefamily.norton.com/familysafety/loginStart.fs.

PCMag Digital Network's Neil Rubenking speaks very highly of this tool because "[it] has a good concept—make this a collaboration. Tell the kids the rules, let them know you will know if rules are broken, work with them."

Norton Online Family is a monitoring program that allows you to get a snapshot of where your kids have traveled online. In addition, it allows you to set up age-appropriate limits for your kids and helps facilitate healthy digital conversations to empower your kids to be better digital citizens.

With Norton Online Family, you choose the settings that best fit your child's age and the types of sites she typically visits—Web sites, chat rooms, social networking sites, or video sites, to name a few. You can further establish filters if needed or if your child is very young. You can set time limits and e-mail alerts so you are notified when something is detected. More information can be found at http://onlinefamilyinfo. norton.com/features.php.

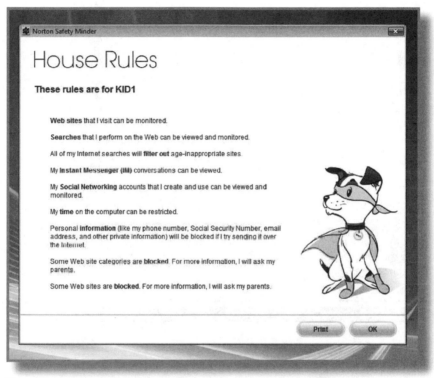

House Rules is configurable for each child. It's written to encourage discussion with your kids. (Courtesy of Norton Online Family.)

Activity Summary is what you see when you log into your account. Note the summary of the child's searchers and log-ins. (Courtesy of Norton Online Family.)

With Notification Settings, you can customize when and how you'll be notified of various activities the programs detects your child doing. (Courtesy of Norton Online Family.)

K9 Web Protection

K9 Web Protection, by Blue Coat Systems, is a free Internet filter worth considering. You can learn more about it and download the latest version at www1.k9webprotection.com. This product is simply a filter and the key is to remember is that it's only one tool that should complement conversations at home. So even if we filter, we have to help our kids understand the bigger Internet picture.

From the start-up page, you can choose to see what your child is up to under "View Internet Activity," or "Setup," where you can tailor what the program filters. (Courtesy of Blue Coat Systems.)

Chapter 18: Internet Safety Tools

On the Web Categories to Block page, you pick what you don't want your kids to have access to. The categories are in phrases and terms you use all the time. (Courtesy of Blue Coat Systems.)

Custom Select your own set of categories to block.

Place a check next to the categories you wish to block. (Click category name for description.)

Commonly Blocked Categories   Unblock All   Block All

☑ Abortion	☑ Illegal Drugs	☑ Pornography
☑ Adult / Mature Content	☑ Intimate Apparel / Swimsuit	☑ Proxy Avoidance
☑ Alternative Sexuality / Lifestyles	☑ LGBT	☑ Sex Education
☑ Alternative Spirituality / Occult	☑ Nudity	☑ Social Networking
☑ Extreme	☑ Open Image / Media Search	☑ Spyware / Malware Sources
☑ Gambling	☑ Peer-to-Peer (P2P)	☑ Spyware Effects
☑ Hacking	☑ Personals / Dating	☑ Suspicious
☑ Illegal / Questionable	☑ Phishing	☑ Violence / Hate / Racism

Other Categories   Unblock All   Block All

☑ Alcohol	☐ Health	☐ Remote Access Tools
☐ Arts / Entertainment	☐ Humor / Jokes	☐ Restaurants / Dining / Food
☐ Auctions	☐ Job Search / Careers	☐ Search Engines / Portals
☐ Brokerage / Trading	☐ Military	☐ Shopping
☐ Business / Economy	☐ News / Media	☐ Society / Daily Living
☐ Chat / Instant Messaging	☐ Newsgroups / Forums	☐ Software Downloads
☐ Computers / Internet	☐ Non-viewable	☐ Sports / Recreation
☐ Content Servers	☐ Online Storage	☐ Streaming Media / MP3
☐ Cultural / Charitable Organizations	☑ Pay to Surf	☑ Tobacco
☐ Education	☐ Personal Pages / Blogs	☐ Travel
☐ Email	☐ Placeholders	☐ Vehicles
☐ Financial Services	☐ Political / Activist Groups	☐ Weapons
☐ For Kids	☐ Real Estate	☐ Web Applications

The Custom category page allows even more fine-tuning of the categories, which may nor may not be needed depending on what your kids are into online. (Courtesy of Blue Coat Systems.)

K9 can also block things like MP3 files; if you were able to scroll a bit you'd see it can block spyware and sites that try to obtain sensitive information like user names, passwords, and credit cards. (Posing as a credible site to get your sensitive information is known as *phishing.*)

If you do enable K9, be sure to tell your kids.

McGruff SafeGuard

McGruff SafeGuard is a free Internet monitoring system from the National Crime Prevention Council. It can be found at www.gomcgruff.com.

Similar to the other free programs, its emphasis is on empowering conversation between parents and kids, not spying or locking down the Internet or going behind kids' and teens' backs. The goal is to help control the access kids have to the World Wide Web until they are able to manage their online time independently. At the same time, it fosters media literacy skills for parents by providing explanations for common phrases kids use.

The McGruff SafeGuard Parent Dashboard presents a snapshot of the entire monitoring system as well as tips about online lingo and statistics. So this becomes an educational place for parents as well as a place to check into what your kids have been up to. (Courtesy of McGruff SafeGuard.)

The McGruff SafeGuard download operates in the background of your computer. It monitors Web sites, social networking sites including Facebook and MySpace, chats, e-mails, and search engines, and tallies time spent online.

Via daily e-mails, the program alerts you to issues such as predators, drug use, crime, credit card spending, and illegal sexual activity. If the issue is a serious threat, such as a predator, it alerts the proper law enforcement agency. In addition, you can create custom alerts based on your family's needs.

The premium version of McGruff SafeGuard allows you to grab passwords, get alerts via cell phone, e-mail and print activity, schedule preset times for kids to use the computer, and block Web sites. Pricing is based on the number of computers being monitored and duration of monitoring time (ie, 3 months, 6 months, lifetime). More information can be found at www.gomcgruff.com/m/upgrade.asp.

You tell McGruff Safeguard what to monitor for and what online behaviors to be on the lookout for. (Courtesy of McGruff SafeGuard.)

| Conversation: | Friday, April 02, 2010 9:00:00 AM |
| Between | Christine90009 & Ingrid9 |

Sender	Message
Christine90009: 9:00:00 AM	hows it going?
Ingrid9: 9:01:00 AM	not bad – parents left on vacation
Christine90009: 9:02:00 AM	who watching u {You}
Ingrid9: 9:03:00 AM	grandparents
Christine90009: 9:04:00 AM	and they have nfc
Ingrid9: 9:05:00 AM	what u {You} mean?
Christine90009: 9:06:00 AM	skipping school tomorrow – off to city w/ {With} brad
Ingrid9: 9:07:00 AM	lol {Laughing out loud} what u {You} tell them?
Christine90009: 9:08:00 AM	field trip to museum. bus may be late getting back
Ingrid9: 9:09:00 AM	rofl {Rolling on floor laughing} {roll on the floor laughing}

If you click the Chat button on the McGruff SafeGuard dashboard, you can see snapshots of chat conversations your kids have had, if any. This can alert you to any issues you need to discuss with your kids. In this example, a child is talking about going to a party and buying drugs. (Courtesy of McGruff SafeGuard.)

Fee-Based Filtering and Monitoring Internet Safety Programs

There are a number of fee-based options on the market. The major question to ask yourself as you evaluate programs is whether they offer more than free programs. That is a personal decision you will have to make.

If a company offers a free trial, that is a great way to try one of these programs risk-free. Otherwise, make sure there is a money-back guarantee so you can obtain a refund if you are not satisfied.

There are many well-respected fee-based Internet safety programs on the market, but 2 stand out for features, price point, and receiving awards: Spector Pro and Safe Eyes.

Spector Pro

Spector Pro by SpectorSoft has every filtering and monitoring feature you can think of, but it is a tad pricey compared with other programs on the market. It comes as a CD-ROM in Windows and Mac OS formats. You can purchase it from the company for immediate download or on CD at www.spectorsoft.com/products/SpectorPro_Windows/index.asp.

Spector Pro allows you to look at what your child is doing online; it will also look for and find true trouble such as hackers and cyberbullies. Beyond tracking, this program grabs the information needed by law enforcement should a substantial issue develop. It can be set up to e-mail parents with alerts as to what kids are doing and lock out areas of concern.

Here's a look under the hood (all screen shots courtesy of SpectorSoft Corporation).

Spector Pro can be set to monitor your child's online use for keywords and alert you if found.

Clicking MySpace Chat/IM will show you the latest conversations your child has had.

You can see the top Web sites your child visits via the Web Sites Visited tab.

Clicking View Details in Web Sites Where the Most Time Was Spent gives you a report with this type of information.

Spector Pro allows filtering of content as well as time controls. Its downsides are cost and the fact that it only controls one computer.

Safe Eyes

Safe Eyes, from InternetSafety.com, provides parental controls, monitoring, and blocking for up to 3 computers in your home for an annual fee. A similar product is offered for iPhones. You can find more about both products at www.internetsafety.com/index.php.

The goal of Safe Eyes is to be intuitive enough that people can use it without a manual. Similar to Norton Online Family and K9, this product is about empowering families to come together to discuss the safety plan and work on it as a group. InternetSafety.com calls its Internet safety plan Gameplan; it's a great concept for approaching the online world. You can download Gameplan at www.internetsafety.com/internet-monitoring-game-plan.php; it is also included here as Appendix I.

Safe Eyes allows you to control any area of the online experience, including games, e-mail, and music. The following screen shots illustrate family summary, activity reports, and how to set time limits. You can also control news sites and other places your child visits as well as YouTube videos. (All screen shots courtesy of InternetSafety.com, Inc.)

Settings For: CSDemo

Activity Reports

Email Summary Report

Send Email Reports: Daily   Last Report Sent: Never

Send Reports To: [   ]   Add Email Address

Remove Selected Addresses

Report Storage and Access

Storage Location: My Computer

Keep Reports for: 30 days.   Save Days

Advanced Settings
You are protected until: 02-09-2013

Family Summary	CSDemo	csdemo4	csdemo2	csdemo3
Web Sites	Custom	Custom	Custom	Custom
Videos	Custom	Custom	Custom	Custom
Music	Off	Off	Off	Off
Instant Messaging	Medium	Medium	Medium	Medium
Games	Off	Off	Off	Off
Social Networking	Monitored	Off	Off	Monitored
Email	Allowed	Allowed	Allowed	Allowed
Time Limits	On	Off	On	Off
Activity Reports	On	On	On	On
Instant Alerts	On	On	Off	On

Higher settings provide stronger protection.

Add a New User   Get Uninstall Code

Advanced Settings
You are protected until: 02-09-2013

CyberSafe: Protecting and Empowering Kids in the Digital World
of Texting, Gaming, and Social Media

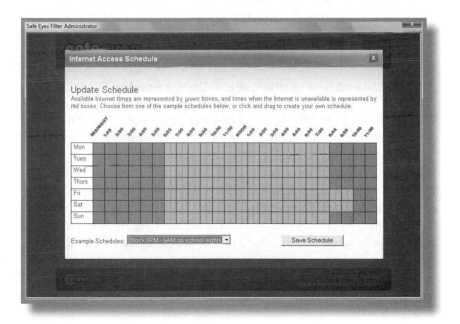

As you can see by the menu on the far left column, virtually every online area can be controlled and monitored if needed or desired. In addition, InternetSafety.com offers a program (for a fee) for the iPhone and iTouch so you can add parental controls to these devices. This will prevent access to the Web and downloads of music and other content. It can be accessed from the iTunes store.

Cables and TVs and Search Engines...Oh My!

Robust tools are one strategy, but there are others tools you can use that you actually already have on your cell phones, Web browsers, and TV. Knowing how to enable them and what they can and cannot do are the final parts of our tour of tools.

There is remarkable consistency in what the major groups, including AT&T, Sprint, Verizon, Google, and Optenet, provide as features, so I'm going to focus on those. Knowing what they are doing will give you a solid understanding of the entire cable and wireless safety landscape. In addition, there are some interesting safety developments on the horizon that are worth knowing.

When Old and New Media Collide: Do We Need to Filter TV?

When you were kids, did you have cable TV? Likely not. Most of us grew up in the pre-cable days and remember all too well adjusting the antenna to get good reception. Cable has been around since 1948 and some homes did have access to it. The evolution of coaxial and fiber-optic cables during the 1990s allowed more homes to have cable TV. But the broadband explosion at the turn of the new millennium (1999–2000) revolutionized the cable industry. This is also when we saw a marriage of cable TV and Internet; we had both media offered by the same companies through the same cables. Before long, TV was offered on our computers and the Internet on our TVs. And that's just where many of us find ourselves today with the Internet in our living rooms, on our computers, and on our TV sets!

When I sit down to watch a TV show, I just want to watch the show. Having access to the Internet from my TV doesn't add any value to my viewing experience. For kids and teens, however, those features are very cool! So we need to know they exist and the ways we can control them to ensure they are safe and appropriate.

Beyond just computer access, though, there are other parental controls that cable companies offer with our TV subscriptions—ratings of shows, gaming access and ratings, and adult content controls. This is important because our kids not only have access to all these features on our TV sets, but they can often access TV features on our computers via our cable subscriptions. Indeed, the world of TV and cable are now one!

Here's a quick rundown of what safety features big cable providers offer, as well as wireless safety features offered if they are full digital providers.

Verizon
Verizon FiOS offers parental controls from your TV for adult content, games, ratings, downloads, and Internet access to things like Facebook and Twitter. The following screen shots illustrate these features. If you have a different cable provider, find the parental controls to see the exact features your company provides. (All screen shots courtesy of of Verizon Communications, Inc.)

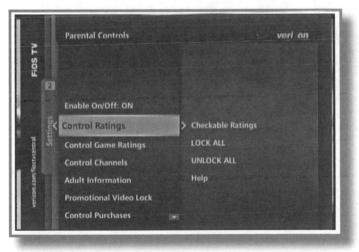

From the main parental control page, you can choose which feature you want to enable. Here the Control Ratings feature is picked to control the global ratings a child can access for all TV shows. (The TV rating selections include descriptions to help you pick by age and content.)

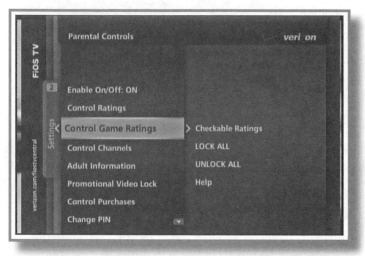

Game ratings are important; you control the types of games your kids can play.

Adult content controls allow you to block your child from finding and seeing any show with content inappropriate for their age.

The Control Purchases feature allows you to block the ability to block the ability to
purchase games or movies with fees.

For cell phones, Verizon offers free filters that allow you to block out content by rating; usage control features to block numbers and control time can be added to subscriptions for a small fee. More information can be found at https://wbillpay.verizonwireless.com/vzw/nos/uc/uc_overview.jsp.

AT&T

AT&T offers safety features for TV, wireless devices, home phones, and high-speed Internet. Its safety program, Smart Limits (www.att.com/gen/landing-pages?pid=6456), includes parental controls and information guides so you can learn more about topics relevant for each technology (eg, texting for cell phones, identity issues and viruses for the Internet).

Smart Limits is free for Internet and TV programming; wireless protection is a monthly fee. For AT&T wireless customers who use MEdia Net for Internet access on their wireless devices, there are free parental controls (www.wireless.att.com/learn/messaging-internet/media-entertainment/faq.jsp#controls). MEdia Net allows you to restrict access to mature content that is not appropriate for children and restrict purchase of downloads such as games, ring tones, and graphics.

Smart Limits looks like this. (Courtesy of AT&T.)

Clicking on each tab gives you reference information and links to the parent control pages.

From this page, you can learn the parental control features for each technology.

For the Internet, you can set up a profile for each child, useful if you have kids of different ages with different viewing, content, and developmental needs. In addition to standard Internet control features, there is one called "permission slips" that allows kids to request access. This feature recognizes that filters and blocks are not foolproof and ratings are not 100% accurate or always reliable, keeping doors of communication open.

TV controls are dependent on what service you have. If you have DIRECTV you can block shows and set up viewing times. AT&T U-verse provides some Internet-sourced content. The parental controls allow you to manage who in your family watches what content. You can hide shows from the guide, lock channels, and set up a PIN for on-demand videos.

AT&T supports groups that specialize in online education and works with law enforcement to keep the digital space safer, especially when incidents arise.

Optenet

AT&T and Verizon develop tools that integrate into their existing systems. Other companies are developing technologies that cable companies can integrate seamlessly with their systems and monitor in the background. Optenet is one such group. In this model, the cable or Internet service provider (ISP) contracts Optenet to provide monitoring and security products, and subscribers decide whether to opt in or out. Subscribers do not need to download any additional products or pay a fee because the Optenet system is part of their existing cable service. For most cable providers, subscribers would enable Optenet services with just one click in the cable provider services page.

Key features of the Optenet system can be seen in the following screen shot (courtesy of Optenet):

Optenet Solution for Telcos includes an all-in-one service that allows ISPs to offer parental control and full security to their subscribers, along with the ability to deliver security policies that are enforced for all their subscribers. The company offers a parental control service for residential customers, plus a security suite that prevents emerging Web 2.0 security threats. Optenet works with each country to tailor its program to its language and laws. It also integrates with direct contacts to law enforcement so if an online incident needs to be reported, it can be seamlessly and with the right information passed on digitally. This has worked successfully in Europe for a number of cyber-issues, including cyberbullying.

Sprint

As with all the major cell phone carriers, Sprint offers a number of parental controls for your child's cell phone usage. Areas you can control include Web access, purchase ability, camera access, texting, and calling. Some of these features are plan-specific so it's important to check with your plan as well as your phone's manual so you know how to enable what you have. More information can be found at www.nextel.com/en/services/safety_security/parental_control.shtml.

In addition to phone-specific features and subscriber benefits, Sprint has partnered with the National Center for Missing & Exploited Children and the National Education Association Health Information Network to produce an online public awareness campaign about Internet and cell phone safety called 4NetSafety (www.sprint.com/4netsafety). The program has a unique funding source—old cell phones from any carrier. People are asked to send old phones, and they are recycled or refurbished. The money generated from anything sent to this program goes directly back into 4NetSafety to develop its online safety programs, NSTeens (www.nsteens. org), a site for tweens and teens to learn to stay safe online via cartoons and peer-created videos, and bNetS@vvy (http://bnetsavvy.org/wp), a site with tools for adults to help kids learn to be safe online. Envelopes for donating cell phones, batteries, or accessories can be picked up at any Sprint store.

In fact, accessing the Web is just a cell phone away. And even if we don't enable Web access for our kids' phones, they likely have a friend who does have Web access from a phone. We have to be realistic that living in a community, it isn't just about the choices we make for our children but the choices other people make for their children. Sprint developed an awareness program for that and partnered with groups to not only create content to educate parents and kids but do so in ways each group thinks and talks. The target audience of NSTeens is actually tweens and young teens, the group emerging in the digital world and still learning how to use it properly. It is driven by peer-to-peer communication via cartoons or by real kids. Through games, videos, and comics, the site covers important issues of the online world—privacy, social networking sites, off-line consequences of online actions, sharing, gaming, and issues of peer-to-peer harm such as cyberbullying. Complementary teaching materials provided by NSTeens partner NetSmarts (www.netsmartz.org/education) breaks down the materials by age from young childhood through the teen years.

NSTeens and bNetS@vvy will help you close the digital divide in some really fun and creative ways.

Google
Google has conglomerated almost all of the most frequented online experiences into one place. It may have begun as a search engine, but Google also powers many of the user-generated technologies online today, namely Blogger and YouTube. So it's no surprise that Google is also pushing the envelope in ways we can control our experiences in those areas and keep kids of all ages safe when they venture into these digital arenas.

Google tries to provide enough information and tools so that people can protect themselves online but if needed, the company has a team that can be contacted to report a situation and intervene if necessary.

From YouTube, it's easy to find the Safety Center—there is a clear link at the bottom of each page. From www.google.com, however, safety information is a little more challenging to find. Here are links to it.

- Search history and settings: Search preferences: www.google.com/support/websearch/bin/answer.py?hl=en&answer=35892
- YouTube Safety Center: www.google.com/support/youtube/bin/request.py?contact_type=abuse
- YouTube Help and Safety Tool: www.youtube.com/safety_help

Google has an Internet filter. As you can see in the following screen shot (copyright Google), there are 3 settings: moderate, strict, and no filter. You can access this filter from the upper right-hand corner of www.google.com under Search settings. The filter is very straightforward; the moderate setting applies to pictures but not search, while strict applies to pictures and search. If you need any monitoring or the ability to tailor the filter in more detail, you'll need to add an additional product, such as those discussed earlier in the chapter.

Given how popular YouTube is among kids of all ages, its content controls are a great way to teach safety concepts, control content, and report abuses should they occur. The Safety Center landing page gives you educational information as well as the latest educational video up-front. The video in the following screen shot, "Playing and Staying Safe Online" (copyright YouTube, LLC), is one of a new series targeted for teens that is simple and a good launching point for discussion. Coupled with other informational videos, it can help your emerging digital natives get a good handle on some complex topics in a familiar form. And by previewing the videos ahead of time, you'll be prepared for questions, should they arise.

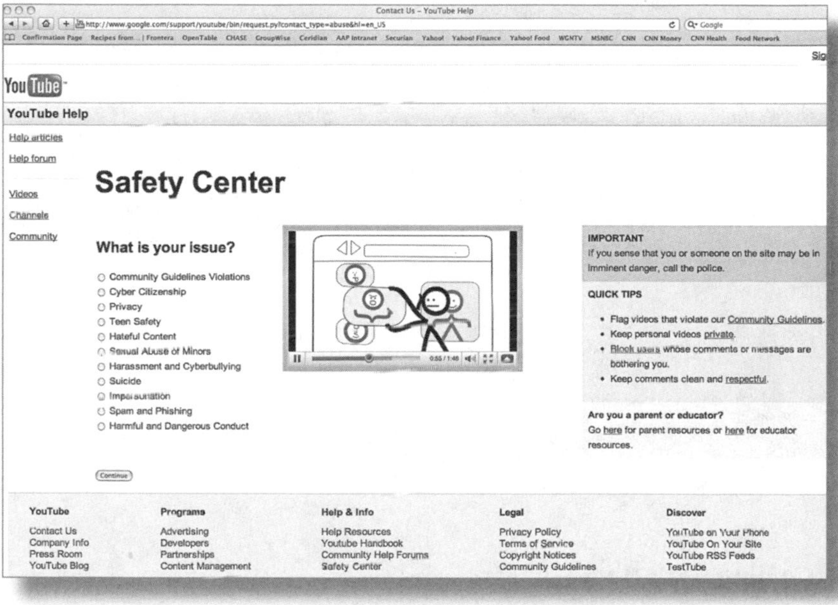

One issue to keep in mind is that according to YouTube's terms of service, 13 years is the minimum age for having an account. Use your discretion and consider screening any content before you allow younger children to view videos.

Given the user-generated content on YouTube and the fact that it is a community as well as a video viewing site, it's important to have a way to report issues such as harassment or hate speech. This applies to the content of the videos as well as comments that may be left on video pages. Following is the YouTube Help and Safety Tool, which allows any user to easily report an issue directly to Google (copyright YouTube, LLC). This tool is important because it puts control in the user's hand. So if you or one of your kids feels you've been victimized somewhere on YouTube, use this tool. As with all sites today, Google takes these issues very seriously. It's important for our kids to understand that even big companies such as Google have zero tolerance for dangerous and destructive online activity and want to help us stay safe.

Coming Back Home

In Steven Spielberg's film, *E.T.: The Extra-Terrestrial*, all E.T. wanted was to "phone home." In the end, that's what we want our kids to be able to do with whatever tools they are using today and tomorrow. We want them to be able to feel comfortable enough to communicate with us if a problem arises, regardless of the issue, using whatever technology is at their fingertips. We'll only be successful if we make ourselves available in an empowering and nurturing way.

That's one of the reasons it is so important for us to learn to discuss Internet safety the *right* way with our kids. This is much more than just safety—it's about communication and empowering all of us to make good and sound digital decisions. These tools are designed to give your kids training wheels as they get more life experience and learn to manage the world around them with and without technology. It's important, though, that the tools aren't viewed as a punishment or to set random limitations. There should be sound rationale behind why we want to use these tools based on our child's needs as well as our concerns. And those concerns should have facts to support them, not be driven by fear.

This is most definitely not a situation in which one tool will work for every family or the same tool will work for every member of every family. You may find you don't need a tool right now. What's important is that you're aware of what's available.

At the end of the analysis, the best Internet safety tool is you and your ability to use this information as a launching pad for family discussion. Even if you just start there, your family will be more 'net savvy and 'net smart than when you began!

Chapter 19

Online Gaming and Virtual Worlds

W hy should we pay attention to video and computer games? Because they're some of the handfuls of activities that just about all kids do!

Eighty-six percent of tweens and teens had video games on their holiday lists for the 2009 holiday season, according to a survey of more than 1,000 kids by Weekly Reader Research.[1]

Online games are just as popular. eMarketer reported that 8 million kids (aged 3–11 years) were visiting online virtual worlds in 2008 and 10 million in 2009, with projections of 15 million by 2013. By percentages, 28% of kids were visiting online worlds in 2008, and 17% of teens enjoyed the same activity; in 2009, those numbers grew to 37% of kids and 18% of teens. Projections have these percentages at 54% of kids and 25% of teens by 2013.[2] These numbers are not surprising when you consider that the vast majority of virtual worlds are targeted to the tween and slightly younger age group, and this is the age when children find these worlds the most fun and worthwhile.

Preteen time is all about fun and connection, so gaming becomes important. While for teens we pay attention to the social networking sites such as Facebook and MySpace, for our tweens and younger kids it's all about online games and virtual worlds—especially virtual worlds.

The popularity of these sites can be seen by the amount of development occurring in the industry; more than 200 sites are online and available for our kids to participate in, with more being developed daily. To give you a sense of the growth, Virtual Worlds News reported 150 new sites for kids as of August 2008, and 200 new sites launched in January 2009.[3]

If we dissect the 200 virtual online words online as of January 2009, just over half were developed for the kid bracket (under-7 age group), with the tween group (8–12 years) close behind. There is a bit of a blurring between these 2 groups in use—they may be 1 group in the end, which would mean a huge majority of these sites are for the under 12 age group compared with teens. A full list of virtual worlds can be found at www. engagedigitalmedia.com/research/2009/youth-01-26-2009.html

What we have to keep in mind is that the draw to these games at all ages is the social contact. Most kids go on these games with their friends. I've seen that play out with my kids. They would essentially arrange online playdates at predetermined times and meeting spots within the virtual world. I've seen these virtual worlds host wonderful virtual playdates in situations in which people have moved and the virtual world is the only environment where the children can visit with each other, and I have heard other parents report the same.

These games do come with a price, though. Most have fees, and many of those fees are billed monthly, so that's a consideration. And there's the price of something not going well if a social interaction goes south. However, given the way these virtual worlds are structured for our younger kids, I'd argue that it's OK to let them have those experiences before we given them the go-ahead to explore the broader social Web 2.0 world because many of these sites have wonderful safety features that allow our kids to step into a few online potholes and learn some valuable lessons.

It's not possible to talk about all virtual worlds, but I do want to mention one with features you can try to find on other sites as you do your homework—Club Penguin (www.clubpenguin.com).

Club Penguin: Early Lessons in Citizenship, Online and Off

It's hard to not know about Club Penguin these days. Most kids starting around the age of 8 find the site completely mesmerizing because it has all the aspects of gaming for this age—strategy, fun, cute critters, rewards for following the rules, and a safe environment.

Behind the cute facade, though, it is a complex virtual world that also has elements of communication, making it a social networking-like site with the brakes applied. Indeed, it allows peer-to-peer play and communication, but all the communication is controlled and the site is monitored for penguins pushing the brink on poor netiquette.

The site's safety features are worth noting because they are one of the things that make Club Penguin a good first experience with online social sites. One of the best features from my perspective is that the virtual world the kids are exposed to is 100% advertising free. That is unique in today's

All Club Penguin images used with permission, © Disney Enterprises, Inc.

online world. So kids spending time on Club Penguin won't have the added side effects of marketing, which are usually more negative than positive.

Another feature is that kids can't link off the virtual world of Club Penguin to other places on the Internet once they are in the virtual world. This prevents unwanted exposure to content inappropriate for their ages. The only area in the Club Penguin Web site that allows link-offs is from the www. clubpenguin.com gateway site; it includes links to shopping ("Toys") and Internet safety sites in the parent section.

The sign-up process actively involves parents, which is not always true with virtual worlds. To sign up, the only information asked is the penguin name, password, and a parent's e-mail address. No personally identifying information about the child is collected at all, at any time. Reassuring.

The site is moderated 7 days a week by adults who have had criminal background checks and work onsite in 5 locations around the world. An on-screen M tells players that moderators are on duty.

© Disney Enterprises, Inc.

Another unique feature of Club Penguin is the ability for parents to be involved in monitoring their kids' experience. Parents can set up an account and have access to controls to determine chat features and time limits, as well as changing their child's password if they feel that necessary. The timer allows parents to set the amount of time and time of day, which can be useful for kids who are old enough to be home alone. Parents can also see if their kids have been banned and why.

Timer	We know you want to balance your child's time. This feature lets you: • set the hours your child can play on Club Penguin • decide the daily total of time your child can spend
Enable Timer?	○ Yes ● No
Current Time:	3:52 pm
Set Play Hours:	From: 9:00 AM ⊕ To: 7:00 PM ⊕
Daily Total:	Hours: 02 ⊕ Minutes: 00 ⊕
	SUBMIT

© Disney Enterprises, Inc.

© Disney Enterprises, Inc.

To acknowledge that we live in a global community, the site is available in English, French, Spanish, and Portuguese and played in 190 countries.

The entire Club Penguin world is built around the concept that if you give, you will get back in wonderful ways. There is a great deal of role-playing and penguins even have virtual jobs to do. The concept is to reinforce the value of contributing to your community, as well as having fun!

In 2007, Club Penguin went a step beyond the typical virtual world play parameters and launched Coins for Change, an online giving campaign that now occurs each December.

At that time, more than 2.5 million players participated by donating 2 billion virtual coins. The following year more than 2.5 million players participated with more than 3 billion coins donated.

Teens are naturally drawn to games that have a civic goal at the core. This is important because it helps us understand that teens who play video games with a civic element are more likely to vote, be charitable, and be more civic minded. It stands to reason that the same lessons can be judiciously reinforced at slightly younger ages when kids are engaged in virtual worlds.[4,5]

Other Virtual Worlds

There are many other fantastic virtual worlds. You can extrapolate from the features I highlighted about Club Penguin to check on the following:

1. Is there a commercial component to the site? Look for ads or banners that market to kids or requirements to sign up for extra features.
2. What are the social features of the site and the controls for the features?
   - Does the site have a chat feature, and if so, is real or filtered language used?
   - Does the site have a forum, and if so, is it moderated? For young children and tweens, moderated site are safer and provide an extra layer of protection.
   - Does the site have a general moderator watching for overall good gaming behavior?
3. Does the site encourage good citizenship? What is the motto of the site and its overall theme? A site that focuses on good citizenship will tend to embrace themes of giving, responsibility, and good behavior.
4. How does the site punish irresponsible or bad behavior?
   - Are there clear rules that need to be followed and a way to report broken rules and abuse?
   - Is there a way to contact moderators for help if they are present?
   - Is there a clear statement of repercussions for broken rules?
5. Is there a parent channel? If so, what controls are present?
   - Gaming sites for children and tweens should allow you to control time, chat, and which areas of the site your child can access.
   - Know where parent controls are and discuss with your kids which ones you are going to use. It's the judicious use of these tools with conversation that keep our kids safe with all games.
6. What is the site's rating?
   - For games, check out the site's Entertainment Software Rating Board (ESRB) rating and description at www.esrb.org before allowing your child to play the game. (ESRB is the self-regulatory body that assigns computer and video game ratings that are recognized as the industry standards.) For additional information, you should also visit Common Sense Media's site at www.commonsensemedia.org. (This is a national organization of parents and individuals with child advocacy, public policy, education, and media entertainment experience.)
     - For Club Penguin, the ESRB rating is E for everyone with the content descriptor, Comic Mischief. This indicates that the game

is appropriate for ages 6 and up. In the rating summary, "players can dress up their own penguin, explore a snow-covered island, and interact with friends in this game set on a snow-covered virtual island. Players can also engage in a variety of mini-games including puzzles, mazes and card games. In one scene, a penguin becomes charred and its beak gets spun around when a boombox explodes." The description makes note that in one game a penguin gets charred during an explosion, which would be upsetting to a younger child.[6] Common Sense Media goes a step further, recommending the site for ages 8 and up, which makes more sense given the nature of the game and the fact that things explode! There is also an element of earning money, which is a difficult concept for younger children.[7] Combined, the sites give a very realistic snapshot of Club Penguin, which I found accurate with my kids' experiences and the information provided to me by Club Penguin.

7. What are some other considerations?

- Make sure your gaming system is in a public area of the house so you can monitor which games your child is playing and when.
- Talk to your kids and be sure there are clearly established rules of use around the games. Later in this chapter I'll discuss a fantastic tool called the PACT that can help facilitate conversation and hold everyone in the family accountable for following the rules!

Before You Hit Play, Do Your Homework

For any virtual world in which you consider allowing your kids to take part, it can be daunting to figure out where to begin. You will want to determine appropriateness and sort out how to encourage your kids to join you in your quest to play and have fun within certain boundaries.

You are not alone. Other parents and experts like me share your concern, as does the entire gaming and Internet industry. To that end, a number of key industry leaders have stepped forward to provide some of the best online tools and rating systems for gaming systems and online virtual worlds.

As mentioned, the ESRB assigns the well-known ratings to computer and video games. These ratings can be found on the front of the box and the content descriptors can be found on the back. Additionally, the rating summaries provide a brief, descriptive explanation of the content in the game and can be found on the ESRB Web site, on its mobile site at m.esrb. org, or through a free iPhone application. In addition, this group oversees the industry to be sure advertising guidelines and privacy practices the industry agreed to follow are actually followed. While voluntary, the vast majority of games sold in the United States and Canada have been rated by the ESRB, and the majority of major retailers, online and off, will not stock games unless they are rated by the ESRB.

The goal of the ESRB is to provide parents enough information to make an informed decision about a game for their child in their family. Around since 1994, the ESRB ratings have become trusted by parents, as indicated by the fact that 87% are aware of the ratings and 76% check them before making a game purchase.[8]

To find out if a game has been rated, go to www.esrb.org and search for the game. If it has been rated, you'll find the rating and content description to guide you to inappropriate content, which is important.

Insert game publisher or game title here.

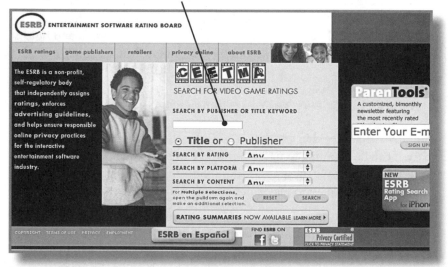

Courtesy of ESRB

Rating Category Content Descriptors

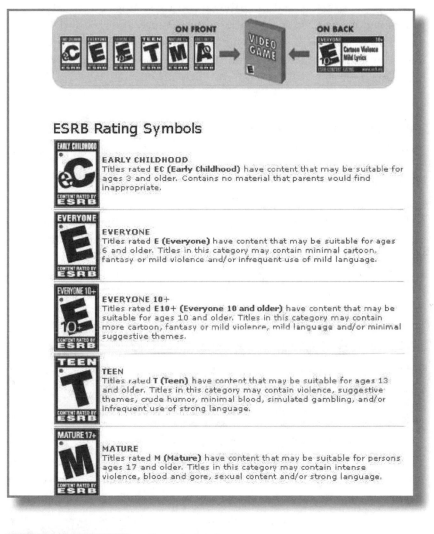

Content descriptors found on the back of the box.

Courtesy of ESRB

In addition to providing ratings, the ESRB provides step-by-step instructions on how to set up and use parental control settings on the latest generation of game consoles to ensure a fun, secure, and appropriate video game experience. I've listed links for the common gaming systems such as Sony PlayStation 2 and 3, Nintendo Wii and DSi, and Xbox in the resource list in Appendix J.

Beyond the Ratings: Empowering Parents and Kids to Play Smart

So you have the parental controls in place. Now what?

Microsoft and Xbox 360 pulled together a fantastic resource called GetGameSmart.com (www.getgamesmart.com) in partnership with other industry leaders including the ESRB, National Center for Missing & Exploited Children, NetSmartz Workshop, and GetNetWise, to name a few, to help families with the "now what."

Courtesy of Microsoft Corporation

According to the GetGameSmart.com team, the goal of the site is to help families establish healthy habits when it comes to playing video games, watching TV, and browsing the Web. One of the first initiatives was to create a challenge to help families commit to actions that help them become smarter about the gaming world. As you can see on the home page screen shot, it's still a prominent feature of the site because of its effectiveness for the 8,000 families who took part in the trial in early 2009. The complete list of challenges is at www.getgamesmart.com/challenge/list/. Once you are done with the challenges, check out the PACT at www.getgamesmart.com/tools/pact/start/.

Courtesy of Microsoft Corporation

The PACT is a tool that will help you and your kids empower each other to be more responsible gamers and play by the same rules. The PACT spells out that everyone will make sound choices and the parameters from ratings to time limits. The best way to use the tool is not to sit down and have a preexisting plan in mind for your kids but to ask them what they feel is reasonable. Do this after you've all completed the other challenges, and your kids will understand concepts such as ratings, time limits, and parental controls, and the spirit of the PACT.

If the PACT is broken, discuss and write down the consequences ahead of time. Hold yourself to the same rules! Parents play computer and video games too; our family should have acceptable expectations for our online use. Discussing the PACT is a fantastic way to identify hot-button online gaming issues.

Family Game Night 2.0

Family game night used to be weekly puzzles and board games; it was a wonderful way to bond and spend time with the kids. I can't emphasize enough how important those unplugged times can be. Even with fancy online gaming systems, don't toss out the board games just yet! There is still a role for off-line games and I'd encourage you to find a time at least once a month for gaming 1.0 play.

What's cool, though, is that some of our favorite board games are available for our favorite gaming systems—Operation, Connect Four, Battleship, Bop It, Yahtzee, Boggle, Monopoly. In this digital age, we may have to fight fire with fire and meet our kids online with some of our favorite games from time to time. If the end result is family bonding, why not? Make a bargain with your kids—one week you'll play an online game, and the following week you'll all play together off line. After all, if you are going to meet them in "their world" to play games, it's only fair they come to "ours" once in a while. Within a few minutes, they'll remember that our old-fashioned games are still in their world, relax, and even have fun!

References

1. Game Crazy reveals which video games top kids' wish lists this holiday season. PR Newswire Web site. Available at: http://www.prnewswire.com/news-releases/game-crazy-reveals-which-video-games-top-kids-wish-lists-this-holiday-season-66372162.html. Published October 27, 2009. Accessed March 12, 2010
2. Real kids in virtual worlds. eMarketer Web site. Available at: http://www.emarketer.com/Article.aspx?R=1007095. Published May 21, 2009. Accessed March 12, 2010
3. Virutal World Management report: 200+ youth-oriented worlds live or developing. Virtual Worlds News Web site. Available at: http://www.virtualworldsnews.com/2009/01/virtual-worlds-management-today-released-its-updated-youth-worlds-analysis-based-on-comprehensive-research-available-through.html. Published January 26, 2009. Accessed March 12, 2010
4. Lenhart A, Kahne J, Middaugh E, Macgill A, Evans C, Vitak J. Teens, video games and civics. Pew Internet and American Life Project Web site. Available at: http://www.pewinternet.org/Reports/2008/Teens-Video-Games-and-Civics.aspx. Published September 16, 2008. Accessed March 12, 2010

5. Kahne J, Middaugh E, Evans C. The civic potential of video games. Civic Engagement Research Group at Mills College Web site. Available at: http://www.civicsurvey.org/White_paper_link_text.pdf. Published September 7, 2008. Accessed March 12, 2010

6. ESRB Club Penguin game ratings. Entertainment Software Rating Board Web site. Available at: http://www.esrb.org/ratings/search.jsp?titleOrPublisher=club+penguin&rating=&ratingsCriteria=&platforms=&platformsCriteria=&searchVersion=compact&content=&searchType=title&contentCriteria=&newSearch.x=0&newSearch.y=0#. Accessed March 12, 2010

7. Club Penguin. Common Sense Media Web site. Available at: http://www.commonsensemedia.org/website-reviews/club-penguin. Accessed March 12, 2010

8. ESRB-related research. Entertainment Software Rating Board Web site. Available at: http://www.esrb.org/about/awareness.jsp. Accessed March 12, 2010

Chapter 20

The Risks of New Media Culture

Toward the end of 2009, I noticed that some car ads took a clever twist and focused on the life moments that a particular car facilitated, as well as the high-tech extras provided, from GPSs to MP3s. We saw families exploring nature, going to youth sporting events and other after-school activities, couples having dates, and parents teaching teens to drive. It was a great depiction of technology in our lives. The mottos of those ad campaigns spoke more to living a good life than buying a car.

If I were creating an ad to depict how to manage the inclusion of digital technology, I might pick a motto such as "Stop and smell the roses!" and show people with various digital gizmos in use as they went about all the parts of their day. As adults, we learn how to create some balance and avoid the thorns. Not our kids; not knowing what life was like unplugged, they can't recognize the thorns in their digital lives.

Another equally important issue is helping our kids understand that we live in one world and common sense and basic rules of safety apply in any space we visit, digital or not.

Finally, we are our worst enemies in that we see thorns where there aren't any. Think of it like this—we teach our kids that "knives are dangerous," but that's not 100% true. Sharp knives are extremely dangerous; butter knives, not so much; plastic knives, not at all. So we have to be careful how we frame online dangers and their relative risk. If we communicate effectively, we will have peace of mind and our kids will be safer than they are today

Our Unplugged Lives: Just as Thorn-Filled as Our Online Lives

Regardless of our digital background as parents, the concerns for our children's safety in the online world are remarkably similar to those in the real world. Talking with parents over the years, I've come to see a striking similarity in shared concerns among parents, independent of socioeconomic status and educational level. All parents worry about the physical well-being of their kids, especially when they are young. Falls, kitchen safety, water safety, crossing the street, bike safety, car safety, walking to school for the first time, and going to the mall alone for the first time are all examples of the type of concerns all parents express. This is by no means an exhaustive list, but it represents a sampling of the issues we think about in the off-line world.

Despite our group acknowledgment of these issues, parents have different styles and some worry more than others. I've noticed a few parenting types.

There's the parent who sees thorns everywhere. Over the past few years, this type of parent has been most commonly referred to as the "helicopter parent" but is sometimes simply referred to as overprotective. There is no question that these parents love their children, but they do so almost desperately that they can't imagine anything happening to them or their children learning to become independent without their help. In the off-line world, these parents are hypervigilant with grades and have been reported to do their college-aged child's laundry. In the digital world, these parents may pull the plug and say "No" altogether or hover so much that their kids find ways to do end runs around the myriad rules.

On the other end of the spectrum are the parents who can't see the thorns at all. These parents are perhaps the most worrisome because they can't see any danger when it does exist and often write the danger off as hype even in the face of data. These parents can sometimes leave you scratching your head because they will let younger kids do things at earlier ages than seems appropriate, such as babysitting younger siblings or other children. Online, this group will put 10- or 11-year-olds on Facebook and think it's perfectly OK. While other parents do this too, these are the parents 100% convinced of the "rightness" of what they are doing.

In between these extremes fall the majority of parents who see most thorns and do the best they can but struggle sometimes. These parents want to do the right thing and recognize some issues but readily admit they don't have all the answers. When it comes to our current tweens and teens, this is the group whose parents are currently tossing up their hands in frustration, knowing they should be doing more but not sure exactly what they should be doing. They may be following the pack and allowing their 12-year-old onto Facebook, but they know it may not be the best decision. These parents are willing to learn from their mistakes and ask for help.

What type of parent are you? Most of us flow between these groups but tend to have a dominate type. If you can identify where you fit, it can help you be a more effective parent. I guarantee your kids know your style—and they learn to work it. So be a step ahead of them and look in the mirror. It's not a criticism to be truthful to who you are. I believe we are relatively hardwired this way; it's our temperament. We can all learn to modify our behaviors, but first we have to be true to who we are.

Kids Will Be Kids

One of the most difficult moments for any parent is the realization that our child is not only not perfect but will defy our wishes at some point. Let's consider Facebook. The stated minimum age for use is 13 years, but we know that many younger kids are on. For example, "!zzy - Anilover" on Yahoo! Answers writes: "oh, come ON! im 11 and i hav a facebook!!!! i have like 30 friends on facebook (my age.) its not that hard to change your birth year from 1997 to maybe 1990. like anyone will ever know."[1]

"Like anyone will ever know." Therein lies the problem. If parents are not involved with what their kids are doing online, and the security on the site isn't foolproof and the age can easily be fudged, and parent involvement isn't outwardly needed, who really will know? Are our kids and teens playing out a modern-day Little Red Riding Hood, with media—especially new media—playing the part of the Big Bad Wolf? That's what studies seem to imply.

The Roses

So are there perks for all this online stuff? Or are these pitfalls just too great to risk the chance that something "bad" will happen to our kids?

There's no doubt that there is some real risk with digital use, and there's also no doubt that there are people online who will take advantage of our kids if they get the chance. But our kids' online lives did not just start today. We didn't just wake up and recognize there are issues that need to be addressed. Online issues are well-identified with everyone from law enforcement to the social networking sites themselves on board. In fact, the Internet Safety Technical Task Force, hosted by the Berkman Center, was charged with looking at this issue and sorting out just where we are today and where we need to go tomorrow.[2]

While no clear-cut solutions were found that fit every site's need, there was a general consensus that each and every site involved in the task force would address its unique issues and work diligently to keep underage kids safe while participating on their venues. This includes keeping kids off who don't meet minimum age requirements. The days of cheating their systems are hopefully coming to an end.

For our kids, the benefit of these sites is clear—socialization. If used properly, these sites can have a positive effect on our kids' self-esteem and overall development. These sites are designed to meet the needs of our developing digital generation and to foster the 2 Cs and 2 Es (see Appendix A).

Risks Don't Hide

There are no official rules for parenting or raising kids, but there are a few golden rules of sorts that are remarkably reliable.

1. Never say never.
2. A busy teen (tween) is a happy teen (tween), and one out of trouble!
3. At-risk kids are at risk regardless of whether the activity involves some form of media.

I've talked about rule number 1 in earlier chapters. The minute you hear yourself say, "Never will I let my child do…" you have just doomed yourself to eat your words! I cannot tell you how many times I have heard friends, relatives, and acquaintances say those words when raising their kids in reference to all sorts of issues, from child care, to cell phones, to driving, only to have to explain their 180-degree turn later. Why? Because nothing any of us are doing with our own children is new. And we won't do it better or different than any other parent we know!

The second rule is the core to surviving parenting our children through middle childhood and teen life. Kids gravitate toward "busy" as soon as the hormone years begin, which can be as young as 8! As soon as our kids become tweens, they yearn for busy, for those extracurricular activities that create our maddening after-school lives. Even kids who don't have those lives want them. And the ones who are at home are busy online creating, texting, or Facebooking. The tween years start the busy and the teen years help fine-tune our children's interests. One of the major reasons variety is so important developmentally is that it helps our kids develop interests and skills that will be important later in life.

Busy is also how kids stay out of trouble and what keeps kids who would otherwise get into trouble, out of trouble! This is a fact, proven time and again. Starting in the tween years, kids who are busy and involved are much less likely to delve into substance abuse or early sexual activity, or develop eating disorders or emotional issues.

One interesting concept to wonder about is the connection between un-plugged time and these issues. Is there one? There actually is. All of these areas are where our kids are at risk with too much media. When they are busy and not involved with too much media, these risks are much lower.

In our minds, though, we don't typically think of issues like obesity or sub-stance abuse as media issues. When we think of the online world, we worry about things like stranger contact or predators. It turns out that we twist in our mind what the risks are to our kids, underplaying the true risks and exaggerating those our kids are actually not at risk for unless they have other at-risk issues.

Kids and teens who are going to get into trouble involving underage sex and drugs are going to do that whether they are involved online or not. These kids usually have off-line issues that can be negatively encouraged in the online word. So let's not think for a second that the online world turns a child evil or makes the core rotten, so to speak; the core had issues to begin with.

Similarly, we have to remember that media exposure isn't without risk and as parents, we have to monitor the amount and type of that exposure. The right exposure in the right dose can be very helpful to our kids' self-esteem, learning, and overall sense of understanding of how the general world works.

So yes, there are issues online and we do need to pay attention to them, but we also need to keep them in perspective, stay involved with our kids, and pay attention to what they are doing online just as we do off.

When figuring out risk, we also have to remember that a great deal of its potential has to do with our kids. Truly vulnerable kids will be at the most risk for any issues, but all kids entering the digital world are at risk. All too often we forget that because we become a bit blinded by their online prowess.

True Internet safety has a number of factors.

1. **Technologic factors:** From the online program you are using to the settings you enable for privacy, there are a host of technologic factors that can assist us in protecting ourselves and our kids online.
2. **Parent factors:** Do we understand the online world? Do we know how to help our kids understand the online world? What we don't know puts our kids at risk and leads to us not truly understanding the real risks.
3. **Child factors:** Similar to parent factors, our kids have different levels of media literacy, and while they can use technology and learn it very well, they don't always understand the effect of privacy and safety issues even in the teen years.

At the core of all these factors is the question on everyone's mind—what are the true risks to us online? As it turns out, our perception doesn't match reality, and once you get acclimated to the reality, you'll have such a major light bulb moment, you're sure to never look at the Internet the same way again!

Blinded by Fear: Perception Versus Reality With Common Online Risk

Do you have a *cyber-fear*—a concern about what could happen to your kids when they go online? I asked our families from Chapter 8 about their online fears.

When I initially talked with Kevin, I was struck by his confidence in Cam's abilities. Kevin truly had no concerns about Cam and felt he had a good handle on the online world and was very digitally literate. Kevin was so confident in Cam's abilities that he allowed him to go onto Facebook and Twitter at age 12, a year younger than truly allowed, through Kevin's account and e-mail.

When I touched base with Kevin 4 months later, this is what he reported: "I recently went to an 'Internet Crimes Against Children' seminar conducted by local authorities and Cam's school. It has really rocked our view on things. My wife and I are very concerned about the potential for predators and we need to formulate a plan."

For Dylan's mom Krithi, the fears were slightly different: "What concerns me most is the potential for exposure to sexually explicit, violent, and racially biased content."

Dylan's fears are similar to his mom's but in a slightly different way. Krithi related to me in an e-mail: "I just spoke to Dylan and he said he understands netiquette, and follows online safety, privacy, and security rules, [so] he is not as much worried. But if he has to pick one, he says the thought that worries him most is the potential for someone (a predator) disguised as someone else to engage in chats. This, he says, is somewhat of a concern for him because he works with people around the globe (for his nonprofit and school) and he is working with them purely online and cannot relate a user ID to a face.

"So far, he has had no negative experiences because the e-mails and other communications are filtered to ensure the contact is reasonably authentic and that they are who they portray themselves to be. Other concerns seem to have died down completely as a result of the filtering and security software installed on his computers."

Mike expressed concerns that were very different and showed an awareness of the digital footprint: "I worry mainly about what future employers will find, and also what other people can find about me on the Internet. Some things I said when I was younger can still be found, and they are rather embarrassing. I also worry about getting viruses from untrustworthy (porn) sites. Also, I will forward this e-mail to my parents to get their opinion on the subject."

Unlike the parents of the younger kids, Mike's mother Barbara expressed a very different set of concerns: "I worry that it is too time consuming. Some days we don't talk because he is on the computer so much. I am worried that sometimes instead of facing life and socializing that he is more comfortable on the computer. I worry that because of the computer he is not advancing socially. I feel the computer is a good thing, and you can learn a tremendous amount on the computer, but time on it needs to be limited."

Marian Merritt, Norton's Internet safety advocate, asked her family, "What worries you online?" and shared with me the following responses: "My husband and I mostly worry about the kids posting things that might embarrass them (photos or comments). Occasionally we've asked them to take Facebook comments or status messages down because they gave the wrong impression. [M]y kids had very different attitudes about online safety:

- 15-year-old daughter worries about people seeing her private information (this is likely because I'm always telling her that in Facebook, the application developers get her profile information).
- 13-year-old son (a gamer) isn't really worried about anything online since he's only talking and socializing online with people he knows in the real world.
- 8-year-old daughter worries about people she doesn't know asking to be friends on Webkinz and Pixie Hollow."

I wasn't surprised that the majority of parents of younger digital natives that I spoke with had predators in the back of their minds with online danger, and that the parent of the emerging young adult had more global and social issues in mind. Nor was I surprised that Marian didn't; as an informed Internet educator she understands the data and is working in the field along with people like me to help other parents put risks into a more healthy mindset.

I was pleasantly surprised by the responses of the teens. They get it! Now it's time we all catch up and the best way to start is with a fresh look at the online landscape and where the risks to our kids truly are.

News headlines and shows such as NBC's *To Catch a Predator* can easily give the impression that strangers are lurking at every corner and poised to do harm to our kids in a multitude of ways. While we don't want to minimize this issue, we need to understand the true risk of this situation occurring to our kids if we are to make sound decisions about the online world.

When you cut the issue down to its most basic elements, it's about relative risks. We know that walking alone at night in the park is more dangerous than walking with friends during the day in the same park. The park isn't the problem; it's the time of day the walk is taken. The same is true with the online world. It's not that social networking sites or cell phone communication tools are "bad" or "dangerous," but communicating with them in certain ways, such as talking with strangers and not having privacy settings adjusted correctly, ups the risk.

In addition, our fear of stranger abductions is out of proportion with how often they actually occur. It is one of the more rare online incidents that can occur to any child.

Risks Defined

Online risks to our kids fall into a few broad groups—personal harm, social issues, commerce issues, and direct and secondary risks from media exposure

If we were to rank these risks in terms of actual threat to our kids, from most to least likely to occur, they would be ordered as follows:

1. **Direct risks:** Media violence; exposure to inappropriate content (eg, text, music, videos); dangerous and destructive behaviors (eg, cyberbullying, sexting)
2. **Secondary risks:** Sexual precocity, drug abuse, eating disorders, body image issues
3. **Commerce issues:** Marketing to kids, effect of ads on growth and development
4. **Social issues:** Communication, isolation, privacy, depression, digital footprint
5. **Personal harm:** Predator risks

It's not just that the direct risks to our kids are more common than predator risks; we have to understand that the relative risk of the events at the bottom of the list occurring is far less than the events at the top of the list. This list is presented visually in Appendix E.

Online predators may be foremost on our minds as parents, but the reality is that only 1 in 7 kids are solicited by online predators. If you look closely at the 2005 study from the University of New Hampshire that produced these results, you'll discover that most kids were not contacted by predators at all. According to the study's authors, approximately half of the encounters were from other youth and not intended to lure at all, but were simply lewd comments that were not at all at the level of intensity we think of for solicitation. The example the authors give, "What's your bra size?" shows the discrepancy in how adults and kids view lewd. More importantly, the youth contacted were aptly able to handle the solicitation and did not report being fearful, indicating that education and awareness messages have been successful.[3] In contrast, cyberbullying has been reported by 40% of kids and is a growing problem, with short- and long-term issues in the daily lives of kids.

We don't make our kids fearful of water because of the risk of drowning; we learn the risks and teach them to swim. It's time we apply the same

sound mentality to the dangers of the online world. We have to have
a realistic handle on what the dangers are if we are to ward off risks
thoughtfully.

A Tour of Risks

When tough decisions have to be made, we can just lay down the law, or
we can talk with our kids and enlist their help in their own safety. Sometimes we have to put our foot down and just ensure that our kids are safe;
truly dangerous and destructive or 911 moments fall into this category. In
most other situations we have the luxury of time to talk with our kids and
empower them to be part of the conversation, which is how they will learn
to be part of their own solution for safety.

Think about it in terms of what you did long ago when preparing your
child to cross the street alone for the first time. That moment didn't occur
out of the blue. Early in life, you would talk to your child about the road,
cars, lights, signs, and pedestrians. As you crossed the street holding your
child's hand you would find yourself saying, "Remember to look both
ways before crossing the street."

With the Internet and digital world, we have to take the same approach—
teach our kids about the rules and what they need to know to stay safe.
Part of this is a discussion of risks. Just as you once discussed wanting to
avoid being hit by a car, you need to discuss avoiding online problems
such as cyberbullying, predators, and everything in between. We have
to provide full disclosure if our kids are to be informed.

We talk about most risks with our kids as we teach them about the world
in general, but there are 3 unique to the digital world that bear mentioning
and some special discussion—cyberbullying, sexting, and media violence.

Cyberbullying

Experiencing bullying is challenging and upsetting. It's one of those
situations that leaves a permanent mark on a person's inner fabric and
can forever alter the path a person takes, depending on how the situation
is handled.

It's no surprise that as more of life has become digital and online, bullies
have gone there too. The problem with online bullies is that they are

faceless and often harder to identify and stop than bullies in the off-line realm. The effect, though, is no less significant, especially on children. In fact, online bullying—*cyberbullying*—is the most common negative situation that can happen in the online space to any of our kids.

What makes cyberbullying so challenging is that kids don't report it to adults and don't want to rat out their friends. To add insult to injury, schools uniformly don't have great strategies for handling it.

The Cyberbullying Research Center released a study in 2009, *Bullying Beyond the Schoolyard: Preventing and Responding to Cyberbullying,* for which 2,000 middle school students (grades 6–9) were surveyed from a large US school district. One-third of students admitted to posting something that was defined as bullying behavior toward another in the 30 days preceding the survey. While only 10% of students admitted to being truly cyberbullied, up to 43% of middle schoolers reported an incident that likely was cyberbullying given the description. This points to how difficult it is to classify the situation or define it in people's minds.

In response to being bullied, 25% of kids blocked the bully, 22% logged off, 10% changed their screen name or e-mail, and 10% did nothing. Fifty-four percent of kids reported telling a friend about the incident, 41% mom or dad, and 29.7% a teacher. Twenty-six percent of victims were bullied by someone they knew from school, 21% were bullied by a friend, and 20% an "exfriend."[4]

Similar statistics have been found by other groups. I-SAFE surveyed 1,500 kids in grades 4 through 8 in the 2003–2004 school year and found that 43% of kids reported being cyberbullied, with 1 in 4 having had it happen more than once. Thirty-five percent of the kids surveyed reported being threatened online, with 1 in 5 having that happen more than once. Fifty-eight percent reported others saying mean or hurtful things to them online, with 1 in 3 having that happen more than once. In this survey, 58% of the kids did not tell an adult.[5]

A cyberbullying study from Samuel C. McQuade III, PhD, at Rochester Institute of Technology was equally alarming. It showed that cyberbullying begins as early as second grade and peaks in middle school, which is when issues such as sexting begin. Dr McQuade's data show a clear dose and response with online time and the likelihood that some sort of cyber-abuse will occur. In other words, the more time our kids spend online, the more likely they will cyber-abuse or be cyber-abused by another kid.

What's even more intriguing about Dr McQuade's data are the many forms of cyber-abuse he was able to define with his study.[6]

- Academic dishonesty
- Cyberbullying
- Acquiring passwords
- Pirating digital files such as music, movies, and software
- Lying about age or identity
- Use of a credit card to commit fraud
- Posting or sending "indiscreet or nude photos"
- Sending unwanted sexual texts or solicitations to others

Pew Internet's 2007 "Cyberbullying" report teased out more characteristics of the cyberbullying experience. The data showed that the teens who used social networking sites and created more content online were bullied more. The most common type of cyberbullying reported was private communication becoming public, followed by the spreading of online rumors. Teens reported that off-line conversations could easily be rebroadcast online and turned into harassment. Others reported what they called the "e-thug," where kids feel invincible and act in a way they wouldn't online and become incredibly mean. Intolerance and ignorance in how to treat others was also mentioned as contributing factors to cyberbullying situations.[7]

How do you know if a child is being bullied? It can be challenging to figure out. Look for subtle signs in behavior—not wanting to go to school or an activity; becoming upset after using the computer or cell phone; seeming unusually sad, withdrawn, or moody; and avoiding questions from you about what's happening. Kids who bully may have similar signs, but you may notice unusual computer activity such as switching screens when you walk in or multiple log-ins that you don't recognize.[8]

As with all childhood changes from normative behavior, anything that's extreme and interfering with home, school, and friends warrants further investigation. Call the school to see if grades are slipping, and call your pediatrician to arrange an evaluation including a discussion of whether it would be appropriate to obtain psychologic input.

Because the numbers are so high, and climbing, this is a situation we all need to be aware of. Bullying expert and psychologist Joel Haber, PhD, notes that bullying is on the rise due to technologic changes in our culture. Dr Haber feels as other experts do that it's the accessibility coupled with technology that is part of the issue. The indirect nature of the Internet allows even good kids to be mean because of the faceless power that the screen builds in. Dr Haber notes that "it's easier to have fun at someone else's expense" and that being online removes the empathy that face-to-face contact creates.

Ross Ellis, founder and CEO, Love Our Children USA, a national nonprofit dedicated to stopping all violence against children, including bullying, agrees: "Cyberbullying is huge." E-mails and calls she receives from families confirm the statistics, and she's learned about cyberbullying by instant message (IM), e-mail, and texting. Her best advice to parents is to take all threats any child informs parents of seriously: "You don't know the hatred of the bully." She is so right about that. It is very important to evaluate all threats a child informs you of to determine the level of intensity and how much danger your child may be in.

Ross's advice is to save all e-mails, IMs, and texts. Try to talk to the other parents and determine what may have transpired. Talk to the schools, although be prepared for the schools not wanting to get involved. If the situation seems to place your child in serious danger with a significant threat, or the other parent will not help you, call the police.

Studies show that the child being bullied often knows the bully. The police can track the IP address to find the bully and keep your child safe, which is the ultimate goal. Even if your child claims to know the bully, knowing for sure by tracking the IP is the best insurance policy, as there have been cases of mistaken identity in the online world with people using other people's computers and cell phones to send harmful messages and bully.

"If a child says he or she was bullied, take it seriously," Ross told me. "That's a form of violence against a child. It must be taken seriously and the child needs help to look into it and the tools to work it out. Adults must listen."

Any child online is at risk for being bullied. Our off-line senses for detecting that something is off with our child will help us pick up that something may have occurred and questions should be asked. And monitoring programs that help you uncover situations that your child may not know how to talk to you about can help facilitate conversations that kids find very difficult to bring up to any adult, including parents. I cover the full array of products available today in Chapter 18.

It's important to keep an open mind and listen without overreacting if your child comes to you with hard-to-hear information. And be on the lookout.

Sexting

Sexting is the sending of sexually explicit pictures electronically to another person. Sometimes also referred to as a "sexty text," the phrase is used to describe the current phenomenon seen with the transmission of these images via cell phones and texting services. See Chapter 13 for a full explanation of sexting and its consequences.

Media Violence

Do you know that many of the video games our older kids play are so violent that they are used by the military to desensitize recruits?

Movies today are much more violent than years gone by; just look at the James Bond series for a case in point. Roger Moore (one of the stars of the film series) has gone on record stating that the newer Bonds are "darker" and "too violent."[9]

Earlier Bond movies like *Goldfinger* and *Dr. No* were rated PG. The newest films, *Quantum of Solace* and *Casino Royale,* are only rated PG-13 even with all the violence and sex. And the earlier movies contain drinking and smoking which by today's standards would not only not be in movies but would lead them to have a higher rating.

It's important we pay attention to the content of any movie or video our kids watch online or in a movie theatre because those exposures do affect our kids. Keep in mind that virtual reality games also need to be monitored, given the nature of the graphics and movie-like elements.

Instead of outright banning a movie, talk to your kids so they understand what it is about the movie that concerns you. That will help them tune into the content themselves and build in their own barometer for avoiding those movies in the future. It will also help them learn what questions to ask of video and movie options in the future.

Putting Risks in Perspective

These are the major risks, but others are important as well. We live in a world where media affects our kids in direct and indirect and positive and negative ways starting at a young age. Our job is to help our kids understand these influences so they can mitigate them as they grow up and learn to negotiate the world around them on their own.

References

1. Do they have something like myspace and facebook for tweens? Yahoo! Answers Web site. Available at: http://answers.yahoo.com/question/index?qid=20081026152 652AAY3RD4. Accessed March 12, 2010

2. *Enhancing Child Safety & Online Technologies: Final Report of the Internet Safety Technical Task Force to the Multi-State Working Group on Social Networking of States Attorneys General of the United States.* Berkman Center for Internet and Society at Harvard University Web site. Available at: http://cyber.law.harvard.edu/ sites/cyber.law.harvard.edu/files/ISTTF_Final_Report.pdf. Published December 31, 2008. Accessed March 12, 2010

3. Wolak J, Finkelhor D, Mitchell K. 1 in 7 youth: the statistics about online sexual solicitation. Crimes Against Children Research Center Web site. Available at: http://www.unh.edu/ccrc/internet-crimes/factsheet_1in7.html. Published December 2007. Accessed March 12, 2010

4. Hinduja S, Patchin JW. Research: downloadable data images. Cyberbullying Research Center Web site. Available at: http://www.cyberbullying.us/research.php. Published 2009. Accessed March 12, 2010

5. Cyber bullying: statistics and tips. I-SAFE Web site. Available at: http://www.isafe. org/channels/sub.php?ch=op&sub_id=media_cyber_bullying. Accessed March 12, 2010

6. McQuade SC. *Survey of Internet and At-risk Behaviors Undertaken by School Districts of Monroe County New York: May 2007 to June 2008: October 2007 to January 2008: Report of the Rochester Institute of Technology.* Cyber Safety and Ethics Initiative Web site. Available at: http://www.rrcsei.org/RIT%20Cyber%20 Survey%20Final%20Report.pdf. Published June 18, 2008. Accessed March 12, 2010

7. Lenhart A. Cyberbullying. Pew Internet and American Life Project Web site. Available at: http://www.pcwinternet.org/Reports/2007/Cyberbullying.aspx. Published June 27, 2007. Accessed March 12, 2010

8. Hinduja S, Patchin JW. Cyberbullying warning signs: red flags that your child is involved in cyberbullying. Cyberbullying Research Center Web site. Available at: http://www.cyberbullying.us/cyberbullying_warning_signs.pdf. Accessed March 12, 2010

9. Roger Moore slams Bond movies for becoming too violent. *The Insider* Web site. Available at: http://www.dailymail.co.uk/tvshowbiz/article-1085074/James-Bond-violent-says-007-Roger-Moore.html. Published October 23, 2009. Accessed April 5, 2010

Chapter 21

Online Parent Traps

Have you noticed that some people seem born to be parents? They seem to have that natural touch and innate instinct to know what to do. If the truth be known, they just roll with the ups and downs better than the rest of us who wear our hearts on our sleeves a bit more and are more comfortable showing the outside world our anxieties over not having all parenting answers at our fingertips right away. We all start off with the same clean slate as we enter the world of parenting for the first time. Despite feeling ready and having read every single book on the subject, nothing in the world can prepare us for that moment when our child is born.

American author Joyce Maynard once wrote: "It's not only children who grow. Parents do too. As much as we watch to see what our children do with their lives, they are watching us to see what we do with ours. I can't tell my children to reach for the sun. All I can do is reach for it, myself."[1]

As we go about our journey in raising our children, we forget that we, too, are on a journey and are growing. Our children recognize this far earlier than most of us ever do, by the way. They see us evolving at times and struggling at others. They are the ones who reap the benefits when we grow and are confident in our parenting styles, and they feel the pinch when we become anxious and uncertain.

When I look at my own journey as a person, there is a definite divide in the type of person I was before I became a mother and since. As a human being and a pediatrician, my views on life and the type of advice I am able to give have been profoundly affected by being a mother and having children of my own to raise and bear witness to developmental achievements.

Parenting styles cover the gamut from the very rigid to the very permissive. Many parents seem to have one style, while I find my own seems to molt as the situation dictates. "Never say never" has played out so many times, my husband and I find that attempting to predict what we might do ahead of time with either of our daughters simply doesn't make sense. The best we can do is to make the best decision at the time.

Have you ever stopped to think about the messages you send to your kids through the decisions you make? Have you thought about the effect of your parenting style on their development? These are not issues we often think about. They go beyond the scope of this book but are important to consider because they come into play when making decisions about the online world. Many times parents will do things online they would never do off-line, and the slippery slope has incredible moral implications for their kids!

Whether it's using a digital camera, learning to blog, mastering chess or a musical instrument, or becoming competent at a sport, parents today become quite taken with their kids' prepubertal successes, to the point of being blinded to the fact that they are just kids doing what kids love to do—explore new activities. There is absolutely no evidence that prepubertal achievement correlates to postpubertal achievement. In fact, it's just the opposite—there are many stories of kids who peak early and plateau while other kids come into their own in high school and college and start to take off in areas they didn't even know they had an interest and skill set in.

Our society has become consumed with overspecialization at a young age and this has trickled into all areas of life, including the digital world. Once a phenomenon in sports and the arts, we now see it in fashion with teen and tween clothes that are totally inappropriate for their young bodies, especially young girls. Likewise, we see this in the digital world when parents convince themselves that rules are made to be broken and look the other way as their tweens put themselves on social networking sites well-identified as being for much older kids.

Stopping this madness is as easy as recognizing that our kids are the ages they are and nothing more, and as simple and difficult as recognizing that the issue isn't with our kids' development but our fear that we may not be doing the right thing for them.

Think about the issue of going onto Facebook too young, at age 11 or 12 years. Facebook's terms of service clearly state that 13 is the minimum age to join. To sign up, a child has to be represented as older than he or she truly is and everyone has to be OK with it. The parents are actually saying to the child, "It's OK to lie here."

Up until that moment, however, those parents had spent countless hours reinforcing to the child that lying was not OK, that honesty and integrity are highly valued in society. Those parents had explained how rules and laws had to be valued because

1. It's the right thing to do.
2. We have to follow rules created by authorities whether we agree or not because of how our society is set up.
3. Not following rules and laws is not only unethical and immoral but illegal and in violation of posted laws and rules.

What we have to understand is that online rules are there for our kids' safety because of the social climate of these sites. We may feel somehow that our kids are "missing out" by not being on Facebook or MySpace like their friends, but looking the other way at the posted law is really like letting your child swim in a pond where "no swimming" signs are posted. When kids do that, eventually someone slides off a rock or falls into the water and a big accident occurs.

As a parent, our kids look to us as role models. By breaking these rules at one time and not another, we are tipping our hat that our own moral compass is not so steady and showing off our own anxiety.

Psychiatrist Michael Brody, MD, explains that by doing this, "parents lose credibility of moral influences" and kids will essentially stop listening when the stakes get higher. This is clearly what we don't want to happen.

Psychologist Joel Haber, PhD, agrees: "Kids follow what you do, not listen to what you say. If your behavior shows duplicity, your child will follow that role model."

So what's the solution? Dr Brody explains that it's the parents' fear of their kids not socializing and keeping up with other kids that's driving them to continue this crazy age compression online. What needs to happen is for parents to leave the socialization to the kids because they know what they want to do. Instead of putting them on Facebook or Twitter, for example, find off-line social activities that kids are more interested in.

Dr Haber goes a step further; he told me that allowing kids to do things such as Facebook when the age is much older is a sign of the breakdown of family values and parenting. Instead of living through our kids, parents need to regain control and reassert family values, he explained.

In fact, studies show that we give mixed messages about this already off-line all the time.[2] Our kids really do look to us to learn the moral compass of the world. If we break the rules, they learn that lying is OK.

I'm reminded of a few times in my daughters' elementary school lives when they turned to their teachers for help with some social situations, only to be told to "work it out" themselves. A couple of years later when some bullying occurred in the schools, the administration seemed surprised that my girls and their friends did not turn to any teachers for help. We were not. They were clearly given the message that no help would be given.

We are great as adults with coming up with rules such as "No dangerous or destructive activities allowed," or "Zero tolerance for bullying," but time after time we hear stories of kids not being heard. The one truism of kids we can bank on is that they do not lie when they are stressed and in trouble. As parents and educators, that is something we can always count on and should always listen to. But we have to set the stage early for them to keep coming to us. If we tune them out young, they will tune us out and stop coming. If we given them mixed messages about rules, they'll stop following the rules and find more to break and lie about. This is how good kids start pushing the limits.

The other issue is developmental—we have to allow ourselves to evolve as parents. And we have to recognize that tweens are not teens and that there will be changes of which we have to admit we do not know the implications. To confidently state that our 10-year-old will be a "good" teen is the voice of anxiety, not reality.

Society: The Trap Setter

Comparing our childhoods with our children's would be like comparing apples to oranges. Dorothy's famous line, "Toto, I've a feeling we're not in Kansas anymore," from *The Wizard of Oz* comes to mind immediately when I think of the differences in the 2 experiences.

Every generation wants more for its children, but our generation has gone a step past that natural parental need and wants to see the next generation shine. We've taken our desires for our kids to succeed to an epic level that practically begins with conception. From parents pondering the "right" preschools to bragging on Facebook of their kids' accomplishments, we have lost sight in every plane of the fact that these are children trying to live out their childhoods.

I have a vivid memory of working in an emergency department a few years back when a high school athlete was brought in with a knee injury. She was a junior at a local high school and injured her knee during a playoff soccer game. I recall her father pacing as soon as they came in. Before I could even examine his daughter he asked, "When can she go back, Doc?" I noticed his daughter, my patient, looking at me wide-eyed and quickly shaking her head "No." I simply told him I needed to examine her knee first and would know better then.

The dad left the room to make a phone call and I examined my patient's knee. No sooner had her dad left the room than she said to me, "I know this is likely not that serious, but can you make it a season ender? The thing is, I like soccer but don't love it. My dad's the one who loves it."

I looked over at her mom and simply said, "What do you think?"

Her answer was, "It's important to him that we have a soccer player."

When her father returned I explained to him that her knee needed 6 to 8 weeks of rest, which put her out past the end of the season (2 weeks' time). He just nodded and said, "Well, if that's what it takes."

I turned to my patient and said, "Go ahead, tell your dad what you just told me." She did.

He looked at me and said, "I don't understand."

"Your daughter sounds like a great athlete," I said. "But if her passion isn't soccer, shouldn't you allow her some time in childhood to figure out what that is?"

He just looked at her and said, "Wow, I feel like a heel. I really thought you loved the game."

He thanked me on the way out. Another dad likely would have been very upset, but this one could see that there was more to life than soccer.

And that's the point. We all get caught up in childhood sometimes— sports, the arts, music. And we're allowing our kids to be that way with how they act, dress, and behave online. What we have to do is find a middle ground and let them be kids. We have to listen and let them be the guides to their childhood online and off while still being involved so we know what's happening.

For the off-line world, you would never just write a check without knowing what about it was for and who was involved. So don't write a check or allow your child to cavalierly sign up to online sites.

For the off-line world, you would never disregard an age requirement or change your child's birth date to participate in an activity or allow them to get fake IDs to drink in bars. So you shouldn't do the same bad behavior with online venues or activities.

But we don't know the online world as well as our kids, so we have some catching up to do! What do you do if your kids seem a bit ahead of you? You are the parent; hit the pause button until you are ready and feel they are ready. There is no rush, no pressure. The only pressure you feel is artificial coming from a society that makes us feel we must keep up with each other and compete all the time with everything online and off.

Let Your Inner Parent Sing!

We all came to wear our parenting shoes differently, and we all wear them differently. What we all do similarly is focus a great deal on our kids' development and accomplishments. Part of this is instilled in us by our pediatricians, who help us focus early on certain milestones to help us gauge if our children are developing on track.

What none of us really pay attention to, at all, is our own development as parents. We recognize on some level that this occurs but don't really talk about it or even acknowledge that we evolve and develop as parents just as our kids do as children.

Given that experience is our guide, it makes sense that over time we'll become more confident and make parenting decisions more easily. It also makes sound sense that we'll have an easier time adjusting to child number 2 than we did to child number 1 and be less rattled when any child after the first tosses curveballs our way. We pay most of our dues the first time around.

It can be helpful to recognize that when put in new situations, we still have some growing to do; that will ease our anxiety and prevent us from making decisions under the umbrella of "best interest of our kids" that are really designed to ease our uncertainty or help us not lose face with our peers.

Not surprisingly, the stages of parenting match the stages of our children's development.[3] Here's a quick summary.

- **Infant:** A parent's goal at this stage is to learn to read the baby and meet her needs.
- **Toddler:** This is the stage parents must learn to separate from the child and deal with some of the child's more frustrating moments.
- **Preschool:** At this stage, parents learn to set limits and allow emotional expression but help the child control his actions.
- **School age:** This is the first stage parents have to accept a child's independence and learn to separate out their feelings from the child's. This is a "be there when needed" stage.
- **Teen:** Parents have to work on allowing growing independence and establishing a life separate from teens. Communication and flexibility are key to this stage.

The Great Age Debate: Straddling the Fence of the Law

Do you remember in Chapter 8 when I asked you to consider the following simple questions?

1. Would you allow your 11- or 13-year-old to attend a weekend party with 16- or 18-year-old kids?
2. Would you let your teen operate a car without a valid driver's license?

As we've seen, some families are allowing their tweens to go on Facebook. We could argue about the merits of this decision based on "maturity" and "development," but it really is much simpler than that. It boils down to ethics and teaching our kids right from wrong.

By going online and letting our tween pretend to be someone older, we are violating personal and stated rules of ethical behavior. First, we're going against our own instincts for doing what's right in most situations. Second, we are blatantly violating the stated terms of use for each and every site on which we practice this improper registration, which is a form of breaking the law.

Facebook's terms of use could not be clearer.[4] The site has clearly posted: "Children under 13 years old are not permitted access to Facebook. In addition, parents of children 13 years and older should consider whether their child should be supervised while using Facebook." The Facebook team also notes: "Remember that while Facebook has always been based on a real name culture, and using fake names is a violation of our Statement of Rights and Responsibilities, people are not always who they say they are.

Use caution when accepting or sending friend requests, and keep in mind that it is always risky to meet anyone in person whom you don't know through real world friends."

Facebook is serious about this. On the Privacy Policy page[5] is a section called "No information from children under age 13" that states: "If you are under age 13, please do not attempt to register for Facebook or provide any personal information about yourself to us. If we learn that we have collected personal information from a child under age 13, we will delete that information as quickly as possible."

This holds for Twitter as well, although not as clearly delineated as with the other sites. According to Twitter's Privacy Policy: "Our Services are not directed to people under 13. If you become aware that your child has provided us with personal information without your consent, please contact us at privacy@twitter.com. We do not knowingly collect personal information from children under 13."[6]

We are essentially giving our tween the keys to the car without a license, or permission to go to a party with much older kids who will be doing much older kid stuff. Given we would not allow this off-line, we shouldn't be allowing this online.

It's the job of tweens to look and act more mature than they are. Regardless of how technically savvy they are, we have to remember they are still their stated ages at their core. We have to be the ones to put on the brakes and let some digital activities stay reserved for when they are older, just as some off-line activities remain reserved for when our kids are older teens. Facebook is smart to point out that young teens may be the appropriate age for Facebook but may still not be ready for unsupervised Facebook. We're dealing with the online world, complete with virtual people who are not always who they represent themselves to be.

What's odd to me is that by falsifying the age of a child younger than 13 years, a parent is actually violating that child's own protection under the Children's Online Privacy Protection Act of 1998 (COPPA). Web sites are required to comply with COPPA and most work hard to make sure that our youngest digital natives are protected online.

By playing around with our own kids' birth dates, however, that protection becomes faulty. We are now putting our own kids at risk and undoing the progress that so many groups have made in ensuring the success of COPPA to protect our kids online and help people understand where true risks lie.[7] As parents, we have to be online more and manage our kids' digital imprints, and we also have to be the ones to keep the keys out of reach until they are ready and make sure rules are not broken. Breaking them ourselves is creating a secondary problem with implications much farther-reaching than allowing our tween to go online. We're now telling our kids it's OK to break rules if we don't like them or they are uncool.

References

1. Quotations about parents. The Quote Garden Web site. Available at: http://www. quotegarden.com/parents.html. Accessed March 12, 2010
2. Bronson P. Learning to lie. *New York* magazine Web site. Available at: http:// nymag.com/news/features/43893. Published February 10, 2008. Accessed March 12, 2010
3. Stages of parent development, kids health, Available at: http://www.kidsgrowth. com/resources/articledetail.cfm?id=1110. Accessed May 10, 2010
4. Facebook safety. Available at: http://www.facebook.com/safety. Accessed March 12, 2010
5. Facebook's privacy policy. Available at: http://www.facebook.com/home.php#/ policy.php?ref=pf. Updated December 9, 2009. Accessed March 12, 2010
6. Twitter terms of service. Available at: http://twitter.com/privacy. Accessed March 12, 2010
7. Kids' privacy. OnGuard Online Web site. Available at: http://www.onguardonline. gov/topics/kids-privacy.aspx. Published January 2009. Accessed March 12, 2010

Conclusion: We Live in One World—Let's Parent That Way!

Watch any movie today and you'll know just how digital we have become. There's a scene from *He's Just Not That Into You* in which a woman says: "I had this guy leave me a voice mail at work, so I called him at home, and then he e-mailed me to my BlackBerry, and so I texted to his cell, and now you just have to go around checking all these different portals just to get rejected by 7 different technologies. It's exhausting."

Art doesn't always imitate life, but it did in that scene! Whether dating, working, parenting, or connecting with family and friends, we are all checking our many accounts many times a day.

Producer Rachel Dretzin knows how digital our lives have become, having filmed the documentaries *Growing Up Online* with PBS and *Digital Nation* with Frontline. Dretzin's mission is to document the effect of digital technology on our kids. Her concern comes not just from being a journalist; she's also a parent of 3. "We remember a time when we had to get online and had a big choice," she told me. "It was different for us."

As she talked, I couldn't help but remember my first online experiences back in the 1990s. I recalled how long it took to get online and what those early Web sites looked like. I remember the experience of searching being somewhat maddening and often not worth the time. And I recall the book we had, *Easy Web Searching*, being not at all easy to understand. It's no wonder we have trouble thinking about the online world as naturally as our kids do. We may have adapted well, but somewhere in our beings we recall a time when it wasn't always so automatic and breezy.

For our kids, however, this is the only world they know. "It is breathing for our kids," Dretzin mused, and I'd have to agree.

Dretzin's *Digital Nation* is one of the first documentaries to help us not only record where we are today but what we hope we want for the future.

It's an interesting notion to consider since we are truly the last generation of parents to recall the unplugged world. One can't help wonder if we "should" be less digital, at least once in a while, and whether we should be encouraging our kids to be a bit less digital at times in their evolving lives. What's interesting is how digital we all have become despite our protests. I recall my husband bucking the trend for businessmen to get cell phones back in the early 1990s; now he is almost as connected as one of our kids, with lightning-fast fingers.

I remember thinking e-mail would never last; now I check and send it a few times a day from my iPhone, almost more than my kids, who are online with social networking sites.

As she's been working on *Digital Nation,* Dretzin has been in an interesting position to observe and talk with parents as they work through their digital issues. I asked Dretzin what sort of awareness parents seemed to have of their digital lives and the concept of trying to be less digital at times. She noted that parents didn't seem to give much direct thought to the fact that we've all become quite wired and are trending toward a state of inattentiveness to the world around us at times, especially in our interactions with each other. What I found intriguing was Dretzin's observation that once this issue was pointed out to people, they were able to express that they would like to have some quieter, less digitally connected times and have more face-to-face contact.

"People haven't given it thought," noted Dretzin, "but then seem relieved when it's pointed out to them, particularly parents who are aware they are modeling for their kids."

She noted that in her own life she didn't think much about her own online use until she realized she was using technology more for work and when her 3 kids (ages 6, 8, and 11) were around. "It's a profound moment when you carry the Internet with you," she said. "I realized I have to walk the talk," ie, not always use technology when her kids are around, like texting when they get in the car. Many parents do this, and studies have shown it really upsets kids.

Dretzin's observation is a common one among parents and kids today. There is a growing awareness in families of the need to be unplugged when together. I had a dawning moment at a restaurant as I was finishing this manuscript. I was answering a media call from a reporter. My teenage daughter was texting a friend. My tweenaged daughter was on her cell phone texting a friend and listening to music. And my husband was replying to an e-mail. When our food arrived, we had a collective aha moment and put our handhelds away simultaneously; a new family rule was created—do not use handhelds at any dinner table!

Pediatrician and author Bryan Vartabedian, MD, FAAP (known as Dr V online), had a similar moment. He recognized he was beyond addicted to his iPhone and tuning out his family. He didn't want to be one of those dads who was not involved, so he set a rule for himself and even blogged about it to hold himself accountable. Now he doesn't allow his iPhone at the family dinner table or when on any family vacation.

Dr V told me about a post from a mom on his Twitter page. Her daughter asked for the family to be completely unplugged each evening from dinner to bedtime. Talk about an insightful girl![1]

So Dretzin is 100% accurate that families are struggling with how to effectively balance technology and parenting. Moreover, experts in the medical and Internet fields have made similar observations.

While being online and connected is part of our lives, it's clear we do not desire to do it more. Perhaps being so online actually fuels the inner fire to be more off-line. We also have to wonder if we are truly as off-line as we think with so much technology now in the palm of our hands.

Today we are increasingly online and even seek it out. While early Web sites were interesting, the move to Web 2.0 and social networking has made the World Wide Web a virtual coffeehouse where we can connect, chat, and interact to our heart's connect…and so too can our kids.

The question to ask is this: If we are experiencing the off-line world while always plugged in to something, are we really experiencing it? If our kids are multitasking and trying to experience a slice of life while texting, calling, and snapping photos, are they experiencing the real world the way we did? Will their learning suffer from being so plugged in?

There are a number of issues for us and our kids to consider.

- We have to recognize that if we are with our family and also texting or checking e-mail or doing anything online, we are not really in the moment with our kids.
- Kids and teens walking with earplugs in and heads buried in phone screens are not experiencing the world around them. In fact, just the opposite—they are tuned out.

- Kids online do not have the filter that adults have.
- Not all Web sites and blogs that claim to be PG- or G-rated in content, really are.

Parents can take 2 messages away from these observations. First, parents must be off-line and in the moment themselves to raise healthy children, to provide a healthy role model for appropriate media use, and to monitor kids' online use. Second, parents must be involved with their kids' online lives actively and passively, and help them be part of the greater digital world.

From Home to World

When Joan Ganz Cooney asked, "How can emerging media help children learn?" in 1969, the seeds of the Children's Television Workshop and *Sesame Street* were planted. Once added to TV, the media of the day, they were quickly watered, took root, and grew to what we know now as one of the most innovative and landmark shows ever created.

But it was more than a show. The entire Children's Television Workshop industry showed us how media can affect lives for the good, first with TV and now with digital media. It brought us shows such as *Sesame Street, Zoom,* and *The Electric Company,* and has kept pace with the digital world by going online and developing games that help kids learn. Now, through the Joan Ganz Cooney Center, we have research to help us understand the effect of the digital world and games on our kids. It's a true coupling of promoting the good while being mindful of possible harm.

Cooney's mission is simple. As she states on her foundation Web site (www.joanganzcooneycenter.org): "If we can harness media as a powerful teaching tool, we can help children grow-up as literate, responsible global citizens." That's it in a nutshell—helping our kids become the best global citizens they can be. After all, we live in one world and that world happens to be digital.

That's why it's so important that we as parents be online and a part of the digital conversation with our kids. Internet safety is part of the issue, an important one. But we are part of this world too. To be truly involved citizens we have to learn the tools of the day, and today's tools are online. As you've seen throughout the pages of this book, there are many resources at your fingertips to help you get where you need to be and get your kids where they need to be. If all goes well, you'll all end up in the same digital space more digitally literate and safer!

We are in a time of transition. Those of us born during the non-digital era need to take a moment at the start and end of each day to remind ourselves that we still live in one world and that the digital world hasn't created an alternate world within a world. This will take a bit of practice for some of us, but we can do it! In fact, we must. It's the faulty thinking that the online and off-line realms are separate worlds that got us into the pickle we are in today with our kids, that closed our minds off to parenting effectively online. Time to regroup and just parent. We are just one person each day, so let's not make our lives more complicated!

Others have a bit more experience with the digital age, so parenting in that realm may not seem as foreign. They feel a bit more comfortable, although they still struggle with how to feel at ease with their kids so online because it is still more than they had as kids.

It truly may take until our digital-born kids are parents themselves for this to settle out. That's a good decade or two away; for them to be effective parents, we want them to really grasp these concepts well. Wouldn't you agree?

So let's help kids today understand their role as digital citizens and how to be more responsible online because someday they may be parents themselves. It may be hard for you to picture that, but there is a circle of life to consider, a big picture and inevitable baton passing as our children grow up and eventually leave home.

As teachers of global citizenship, let's help our kids embrace the best that technology has to offer by providing not just good examples of how to behave but safe places for them to use their skills at home and in the community. To accomplish that, we have to support programs in schools that provide more digital learning and have the resources that kids are actually demanding. The battle cry is there; we only have to tune into the right digital frequency to hear it.

As broadband creeps around the globe and more remote villages and towns become interconnected, our kids should have access to those cultures. The growth of broadband will create a natural explosion in our global reach and ability to explore the world and its amazing cultures, civilizations, and landscapes. Wouldn't it be amazing if our kids could experience those worlds in real time?

The implications for our children are enormous if we help them embrace this positively and help the rest of society not be so fearful, especially schools. That's why programs such as Edutopia (www.edutopia.org), home of some of the digital kids we met earlier in the book, are so important. Edutopia's goal is to show the myriad of amazing ways today's kids can use digital technology. The concept is to mobilize the education world into action to use technology as a learning tool that benefits today's kids because this is how they learn and what they want to use to learn. Why are we still using books when we have so many Internet connections and social networking capabilities that can enhance learning in ways our children already thrive on and actually are wired to think with? Locking kids out of this world is counterproductive to their growth.

Yet the digital world also needs boundaries. Just as we saw with the fictional world of *WALL•E,* we can become too dependent on technology and be incredibly unhealthy as a result. Balance and a healthy media diet are what ward off problems, not irrational restrictions and lockdowns. This is no different than helping our kids have a healthy attitude toward food and teaching them that no food is unhealthy if eaten in moderation. Just as we don't want kids to view food as "good" or "bad" and create unhealthy associations that can lead to later issues, we want kids to learn appropriate uses of technology and how to seek help if an unhealthy situation arises.

Similarly, we know that accidents happen in the non-digital realm and help our kids prepare for emergencies as best they can. We teach them the life skills and give them tools to keep them safe for those what-ifs. But knowing those scary what-ifs are rare, we don't harp on them too much so our kids can get through their day without fear.

That's what we need to do with the digital space. Sure, digital "accidents" sometimes occur and we have to know what to do just in case. At the same time, it's important to have a reality check when we list in our minds those what-ifs and understand the scarier stuff isn't necessarily the most likely to occur. At some point, we have to allow ourselves to be reassured by the data and the multitude of expert input about the online world, as we do with the off-line world and things that could occur as we go about our day. If you think about a typical day, we could create a long list of what-ifs that could happen to any one of us, but we don't. We understand that data go against rare accidents happening to any of us in the off-line world, regardless of how frightening they are to think about. We've learned to put those risks in perspective and go about our lives worry-free. What we have to do is adopt this thinking to our digital lives. It will take time, but as we become familiar with the technology, we'll get there.

In *Born Digital*, John Palfrey and Urs Glasser wrote: "Parents and teachers need to start by putting in the time it takes to understand how the digital environment works so that they can be credible guides to young people. It's not that anyone has to use every new technology the minute it comes out....In general, parents are likely to find themselves reassured by what they find in the digital world; they will quickly discover that the challenges of keeping children safe online are not much different from the challenges of keeping them safe in other contexts."[2]

I couldn't agree more! I believe that parents are the key to children's ability to succeed. This is their childhood and it's digital. As good parents, our job is to embrace it, learn it, and allow our kids to thrive in it. Given how easy it is to learn these technologies, we have no excuse not to. It's important for our children's success in the world as well as our own. That is how we grow as a global community, online and off, in the world in which we live.

Don't be fearful of the unknown. Let it energize and empower you to be an amazing parent online and off.

See you soon somewhere in cyberspace!

References

1. Vartbedian B. Are you tuning your kids out? Parenting Solved blog. Available at: http://parentingsolved.typepad.com/parenting_solved/2009/01/are-you-tuning-your-kids-out.html. Published January 6, 2009. Accessed March 12, 2010
2. Palfrey J, Gasser U. *Born Digital: Understanding the First Generation of Digital Natives.* New York, NY: Basic Books; 2008:100

Glossary and Cyber-Dictionary

Glossary

We use the following words and phrases all the time, but do we really know what they mean? If you don't, here's a handy list to get you up to speed.

In addition, I've created and included a few mnemonics to help you with some digital concepts. This isn't meant to be an all-inclusive list but a starting point for your digital vocabulary.

Blog: Shorthand for Weblog, a type of Web site that is very editorial, user generated, and opinion based. Initially thought of as online journals, all blogs have similar characteristics of being user generated, easy to set up and maintain, and listing material in reverse chronologic order. Blog can mean the actual online entity or the act of blogging.

Bookmark: A digital placeholder for information found online. You can accomplish this on your computer's Web browser, which is referred to as local bookmarking; this allows for organization by folders. Or you can engage in one of the many social bookmarking sites (eg, http://delicious.com) to save your favorite links online and organize them by keywords.

Boomers: Young, born from 1955 to 1964; old, born from 1946 to 1954.

Cyberbullying: A form of bullying that takes place in the digital space. This can involve e-mails, instant messages, and texts but has the same elements of off-line bullying in that threats are involved and the victim feels anxious and scared of the bully.

Digital age: The term *digital* is really synonymous with *computer.*

Digital divide: The gap created between the people who have computers and access to digital technology and are users of technology, and those who don't have or don't use technology.

Digital immigrant: Simply put, parents of digital natives. The generation born before the digital and Internet age who have had to become accustomed to digital life as it evolved and new technologies were introduced. Parents of this generation of digital natives are the first to raise all-digital kids.

Digital native: Kids born into the digital age. This generation of kids, our kids, are the first to be completely digital and online.

E-mail: Simply put, shorthand for electronic mail sent by your computer over the Internet.

Facebook/MySpace: The 2 most popular social networking Web sites for the teen and young adult population. They allow people to connect online with others individually or in groups, as well as the ability for members to communicate with each other as well as share information, pictures, videos, and music.

Following/Followers: The term used by some social networking sites to indicate the process people use to subscribe to your profile, feed, or social networking site, and the people behind that process.

Friending/Friends: The term used by some social networking sites to indicate the process people use to subscribe to your profile, feed, or social networking site, and the people behind that process.

FTP: Shorthand for file transfer protocol. Allows files to be sent computer to computer via the Internet.

Generation X: People born between 1965 and 1976.

Generation Y: People born between 1977 and 1990; also called Millennials.

Google: Many search engines exist online today. Google is the biggest and most popular. Others include Yahoo!, MSN, every cable company including Comcast and Verizon, AOL, and countless others.

Googling/to Google: The phrase people use generically to refer to turning to the Internet to do a Web search. The search may not necessarily be on Google itself, but Googling has become interchangeable with Web searching.

Instant messaging: A real-time form of communication that is popular among tweens and teens. This may be computer- or cell phone-based. Lingo and shorthand are popular to keep conversations flowing and sentences short. Many services are available. Texting SMS (simple message services) is becoming standard with cell phones, making the cell phone-based systems very popular with teens.

Internet: A complex, global computer network that allows for the exchange of data; very sophisticated technologies and computer programs.

Kids: For the sake of this book, we'll identify this age group as 4- to 8-year-olds, post-toddler to pre-tween.

Microblogging: A form of blogging that involves brief updates about daily events. Twitter is the most popular microblogging service. It has elements of blogging, instant messaging, and social networking. Update are brief and immediate, go to a wide array of people all at once, and you can respond to people and their updates in real time.

MP3 players and music: MP3 stands for MPEG-1 audio layer 3 and refers to an audio compression technology that revolutionized the entire music industry, transforming it from store-based records and CDs to home computer-based music that can be played and shared on handheld devices.

MySpace: *See* Facebook/MySpace.

New media: Communication modalities since the advent of the Internet and digital age. Examples include everything online, MP3 music, digital videos and players, digital TV, electronic publishing via CD-ROM and downloadable publications, e-mail, and instant messaging. User modification is often expected, with sharing actively encouraged.

Old media: Communication modalities pre-Internet or digital age. Includes pre-digital TV (analog), radio, and all print materials. Prepackaged with little room for user modification.

Profile: Also referred to as a personal profile or online profile. An online description of a person on a social media or social networking site.

RITE: Mnemonic for deciding if a digital message is correct (see Chapter 17).

Is the Digital Message RITE?

Reread your message to be sure it sounds OK.

Imagine if you were receiving the message—would you be upset or hurt?

Think about whether it needs to be sent now or can wait a bit.

Enter button time.

RSS feed: Two popular meanings for RSS are real simple syndication and rich site summary. RSS is a publication process that pulls headlines from your favorite Web sites and blogs onto your Internet browser home page. Very often, the full story view keeps the reader on his or her home page, with the story appearing in a bubble. This allows the reader to not have to click in and out of so many sites and be more efficient with headline scanning.

Search: Search is how we find what we are seeking on the Internet. Uses keywords.

Search engines: The technology behind search.

Social media: Anything online created by people for other people. Social media is also called user-generated content. Examples include blogs, podcasts, Wikipedia, social networking sites (eg, Facebook, MySpace, Club Penguin), and Twitter.

Social networks: Online communities that often focus on shared interests and experiences. Popular social networks include Facebook, MySpace, and Twitter. Most online networks have many Web 2.0 features such as blog-like aspects, instant messaging, and e-mail.

TECH: Dr Gwenn's mnemonic for the new American Academy of Pediatrics policy on social media and sexting (see Appendix F). Talk to your kids about what they are using and what they'd like to use. Educate yourself about the technology so you can use it; your kids about the issues online to be aware of; and our communities about why this is a global as well as a family issue. Check your kids' social media logs and profiles often to be sure they are not getting in over their heads and posting inappropriately. Have a family social media and technology use plan (see appendixes G, H, and I) that everyone in the home agrees to and signs, including adults.

Teens: People 13 to 18 years old.

Texting: A cell phone-based form of instant messaging. *See* Instant messaging.

Tweens: People 8 to 12 years old; also called preteens, this is the group *between* kids and teens.

Twitter: *See* Microblogging.

2 Cs and 2 Es: Mnemonic for summarizing digital native's preferences for features of user-generated content—create, communicate, engage, entertain. This population gravitates toward digital venues that allow them to be creative and create things. They need technology that enhances their ability to communicate together. They need technology that facilitates social engagement and interaction. And they want technology that keeps them entertained.

User-generated content: *See* Social media.

Video-sharing sites: Allow for the sharing and viewing of user-generated videos. YouTube is the most popular.

Web 1.0: First generation of Internet sites that were based on very rigid HTML code. These static sites were not user generated but content generated by a designated Web development team.

Web 2.0: Second generation of Internet sites. Key features include user-generated content and social media abilities.

Web site: Internet destinations designated by a specific URL address.

World Wide Web: A system of Web sites all connected via the Internet via http connections.

URL: Stands for uniform resource locator and is the address for a Web site on the Internet.

YouTube: An example of a video-sharing Web site.

Sources

- Jones S, Fox S. Generations online in 2009. PewResearchCenter Publications Web site. Available at: http://pewresearch.org/pubs/1093/generations-online. Published January 28, 2009. Accessed March 12, 2010
- Webster's New Millennium Dictionary of English. Preview ed (v 0.9.7). Available at: http://dictionary.reference.com/help/wmde.html. Accessed April 5, 2010
- Wikipedia: The Free Encyclopedia. Available at: http://en.wikipedia.org. Accessed March 12, 2010
- *PCMag Digital Network.* Available at: www.pcmag.com. Accessed March 12, 2010

Cyber-Dictionary

The following information was developed by Love Our Children USA to provide a clearer understanding of cyberspace lingo.

A survey commissioned by the National Center for Missing & Exploited Children and Cox Communications found that only about half of the parents interviewed were monitoring their kids' online activity daily or weekly. The other half of the parents said that they don't have or don't know if they have software on their computer(s) capable of monitoring where their teens go online or with whom they interact. Additional findings include:

*42% of parents don't review the content that their teen(s) are reading and/or writing in chat rooms or instant messages;

*Parents are not familiar with the most common IM shorthand/lingo, i.e:

*57% of parents don't know LOL (laughing out loud)

*68% don't know BRB (be right back)

*92% were unaware that A/S/L means age/sex/location

*95% of parents weren't familiar with POS (parents over shoulder) and P911 (parent alert);

*28% of parents don't know if their teens are speaking with strangers online;

*30% of parents let their teens use computers in private areas of the home (e.g. bedroom, office).

Address
A web site's location. Sometimes address is used as shorthand for an individual's personal email address.

Attachment
A file that arrives with an email. You will know if an email has an attachment with it because it has a little icon of a paperclip appearing with the email. Do not open the attachment by clicking on it. If you know who the sender is right click on it and save it on your desktop and run a virus scan to be sure it is virus free before you open it. If you don't know who it is from them don't open it and delete it.

Block
An instruction given to your computer not to allow certain types of activity and emails on your computer, as well as stopping access to particular web pages or chatrooms.

Browser
The address bar which allows you to use the world wide web.

Cable modem
A special device which allows you to access the internet using cable TV.

Compact disc (CD)
Most modern software is now supplied on a CD. CD writers (and re-writers) are very common. This allows you to copy large volumes of material. This can increase the risk of a virus entering your system and also increase the risk of potentially undesirable material coming into your home.

Chat
A means of communicating with people more or less instantaneously by typing messages which then appear on your computer screen, and are transmitted across the internet to be read by everyone else participating in the chat at that time. The conversation continues through the exchange of messages. Chat can either be moderated or unmoderated. In the latter case the conversation will be completely unsupervised and records of it are generally not kept. It is very easy to fake an identity when participating in a chat so be especially wary.

Chatroom
A place where chat happens on the internet.

Chatting
Taking part in a chat.

Click
Pressing on one of the buttons on a mouse to execute a command.

Computer network
A collection or series of computers that are connected to each other and generally can swap information very easily and rapidly.

Conference
Similar to a chat only a conference will probably be arranged for a certain time and on a certain subject. Chatrooms, by contrast, are running all the time and people dip in and out of them.

Cyberspace
Another way of referring to the internet.

Disc
There are several kinds of discs: ordinary floppies, which are plastic squares normally containing up to 1.4 megabytes of data (although newer versions can contain a great deal more). DVDs (digital versatile dics) have enormous storage capacities. Hard discs are generally inside a computer and store your programs and data. These can be huge: their capacity is measured in gigabytes, ie in thousands of megabytes.

E-commerce
Buying and selling over the internet.

Electronic signature
A special, encrypted code that identifies you to the recipient of an email.

Encryption
Software that takes any computer-readable data and converts it into an unreadable code that can only be unscrambled and made readable again by someone with the correct key.

Email
A message sent over the internet. It can be sent only to one person or many. Unsolicited email is known as spam.

Email address
Your personal and unique address on the internet. It is often used as the basic means of identifying an internet user, eg when they subscribe to services or join in chats.

Filter
A means of preventing certain types of material from reaching your computer while allowing others from the same source. You may want to filter out websites that show adult or violent images, but allow sites that show only low levels.

Icon
An image which tells you about a specific function, eg a picture of a printer generally means that if you just click on that picture it will go into the print routine. These icons are alternatives to typing in often long-winded or difficult to remember commands.

Instant messaging (IM)

A form of chat. You can join a service and then whenever you log on to the internet your name will appear in a central register. You can then be contacted by anyone on the register although you will, of course, have to agree to accept their call. With some of the more popular forms of instant messaging you join a club and all members of the club are notified when any other member logs on.

Internet

A global network of connected computers.

Internet café

Public places where computers are connected to the internet. Many places will let you use the machines without having to buy any food or drink. Rarely do these places have filtering or blocking software in place and the levels of supervision and support available can vary enormously.

Internet service provider (ISP)

A commercial company that provides internet access. They charge a monthly fee ... you just pay for the phone calls. Some of the larger ISPs include substantial resources and areas specially designed for children. Check out what is on offer.

Log on

To enter your password and gain access to a computer or a network.

Log off

To sign off from a computer or a network.

Minimize

Most programs allow you to minimize them, usually by clicking once on an icon in the top right-hand side of the screen. This allows you to have several different programs running at once but it also allows you to rapidly hide something that might be on your screen that you don't want prying eyes to see. It's a way kids can switch between homework and games!

Moderated chatroom

A chatroom where, usually, an adult is present to make sure the conversations taking place there do not break the company's policies about online behavior. Some companies do not have a moderator in their chatrooms. They use software which looks for particular words. If the words appear a moderator is notified and goes to take a look. If someone in the chatroom is found to be breaking the rules usually they will first be warned and then, if they persist, they can be thrown out and barred. However someone who is barred can just create a new email address. This gives them a new internet identity and they can get back in.

Moderator

A person who polices and supervises a chatroom, or a newsgroup. Ask your internet service provider if they use moderators and, if they do, how they recruit and train, and what checks moderators go through before being taken on.

Modem

A device for connecting a computer to the telephone system so it can access the internet or other computers.

Mouse

A handheld device used for pointing and clicking as a means of issuing commands to a computer.

Net smart

Being aware of the potential pitfalls of the internet and how to avoid them, or deal with them. It's a modern equivalent of being streetwise.

Network

A collection or series of computers that are connected to each other and generally can swap information very easily and rapidly.

Newsgroups

Like an electronic bulletin board where people with common interests can keep in touch and up to date. You post to the newsgroup using email and you can often include attachments. Much of the illegal material on the net circulates through newsgroups.

Online

If you are online you are live on the internet.

Parental control software

Programs that allow parents or other responsible adults to control various aspects of how a particular computer or network might interact with the internet. Some internet service providers offer free parental control software to members.

Password

A code that gives you access to a computer or a network, or to some functions within a program. If anyone else discovers the password they can pretend to be you or they can override any security settings you might have put in place. Most parental control software uses passwords. If your child reaches a site which you have blocked it will not be visible to the child but you could, by entering the password, allow it to be seen. Obviously therefore, if your child learns the password, they can get through to the site you want to block.

PIN
Personal information number: the same as a password only usually in number form only.

Posting
A posting is a message of some kind, usually in the form of an email sent to a newsgroup or a chatroom.

Search engine
If you do not already know the address of a website you can use a search engine to find it for you. You can type the subject matter you're looking for, eg "England." Some search engines will give you more than you want, as they can bring back thousands of replies, including some which are very far from what you are likely to be looking for. There are specialist search engines specifically for children, eg Yahoo! Kids and other kids sites which tend only to search among child friendly sites.

Site
A specific location on the internet, generally a website.

Software
Otherwise known as a program, which allows your computer to perform certain tasks. Microsoft's Word, for example, is a piece of software which does word-processing.

Spam
Unsolicited and unwanted email. A high proportion of spam is porno-graphic and much of the rest is linked to financial scams of some kind.

Stranger danger
The risk that an unknown person, either an adult or a child, might do some harm to your children, generally through deceiving them or through some other kind of manipulation. In some of the more extreme cases on the internet, children have been persuaded to indulge in illegal sexual acts which they have photographed and sent to the strangers who asked them to do it in the first place. There have been cases where children have gone to meet people they have met on the internet, only to discover they were

not who they claimed to be and were often a lot older. Some children have been raped following such encounters.

Subscribe

When you subscribe to something on the internet it is often free. You give your email address to a site, eg your favorite record club or shopping site, and they send you information about themselves or their activities, events and so on. This can be a valuable service but check to make sure that whoever you are giving your email address to will not then pass it on to third parties, as they will bombard you with offers for commercial goods and services you will never need or want.

Surf

When you are moving around between and within web sites you are surfing.

Surf smart

Being aware of the potential pitfalls of the internet and how to avoid them, or deal with them. It's a modern equivalent of being streetwise.

URL

An abbreviation for uniform resource locator, another way of saying address.

Usenet

This means the same as newsgroup.

Virus

A malicious piece of software which can do great damage to your computer or the programs on it. They often come as attachments to emails or on discs which might have been swapped, in a playground for instance. It is very important to use anti-virus software to prevent them getting into your system and to prevent you from passing them on to anyone else.

Web

The web, or the world wide web.

Web browser

The address bar on the Internet that allows you to use the world wide web.

Web cam

A camera made specially to work with a computer. It can transmit still or video pictures, with or without sound, across the internet.

Key Points for Interpreting Leetspeak

- **Numbers are often used as letters.** The term "leet" could be written as "1337," with "1" replacing the letter L, "3" posing as a backwards letter E, and "7" resembling the letter T. Others include "8" replacing the letter B, "9" used as a G, "0" (zero) in lieu of O, and so on.

- **Non-alphabet characters can be used to replace the letters they resemble.** For example, "5" or even "$" can replace the letter S. Applying this style, the word "leetspeek" can be written as "133t5p33k" or even "!337$p34k," with "4" replacing the letter A.

- **Letters can be substituted for other letters that may sound alike.** Using "Z" for a final letter S, and "X" for words ending in the letters C or K is common. For example, leetspeekers might refer to their computer "5x1llz" (skills).

- **Rules of grammar are rarely obeyed.** Some leetspeekers will capitalize every letter except for vowels (LiKe THiS) and otherwise reject conventional English style and grammar, or drop vowels from words (such as converting very to "vry").

- **Mistakes are often left uncorrected.** Common typing misspellings (typos) such as "teh" instead of the are left uncorrected or sometimes adopted to replace the correct spelling.

- **Non-alphanumeric characters may be combined to form letters.** For example, using slashes to create "/\/\" can substitute for the letter M, and two pipes combined with a hyphen to form "|-|" is often used in place of the letter H. Thus, the word ham could be written as "|-|4/\/\."

- **The suffix "0rz" is often appended to words for emphasis or to make them plural.** For example, "h4xx0rz," "sk1llz0rz," and "pwnz0rz," are plural or emphasized versions (or both) of hacks, skills, and owns.

It's important to remember that the leetspeek community encourages new forms and awards individual creativity, resulting in a dynamic written language that eludes consistency. However, there are a few standard terms. The following is a sample of key words that haven't changed fundamentally (although variations occur) since the invention of leetspeek. The first series is of particular concern, as their use could be an indicator that your teenager is involved in hacking or the theft of intellectual property, particularly licensed software.

Leet Words of Concern or Indicating Possible Illegal Activity:

"warez" or **"w4r3z"**
Illegally copied software available for download.

"h4x"
Read as "hacks," or what a malicious computer hacker does.

"pr0n"
An anagram of "porn," possibly indicating the use of pornography.

"sploitz" (short for exploits): Vulnerabilities in computer software used by hackers.

"pwn"
A typo-deliberate version of own, a slang term often used to express superiority over others that can be used maliciously, depending on the situation. This could also be spelled **"0\/\/n3d"** or **"pwn3d,"** among other variations. Online video game bullies use this term.

Other Common Leet Words:

"kewl"
A common derivation of "cool."

"m4d sk1llz" or **"mad skills"**
Refers to one's own talent. "m4d" itself is often used for emphasis.

"n00b," "noob," "newbie," or **"newb"**
Combinations synonymous with new user. Some leetspeekers view "n00b" as an insult and "newbie" as an affectionate term for new users.

"w00t" or the smiley character **\o/**
An acronym that usually means "We Own the Other Team," used to celebrate victory in a video game.

"roxx0rs"
Used in place of "rocks," typically to describe something impressive.

"d00d"
Replaces the greeting or addressing someone as a "dude."

"joo" and **"u"**
Used instead of "you." This is also commonly written as "j00" or "_|00."

"ph"

often replaces "f," as in "phear" for "fear" (as in "ph34r my l33t skillz") and vice versa, such as spelling "phonetic" as "f0|\|371(."

Chat, E-Mail, Web, and Chat Room Slang and Acronyms

AAK	Alive And Kicking
AAR	At Any Rate
AAS	Alive And Smiling
ADN	Any Day Now
AFAIK	As Far As I Know
AFK	Away From the Keyboard
AFN	that's All For Now
AOTA	All Of The Above
a/s/l or asl	Age/Sex/Location - (used to ask a chatter their personal information)
AV	Avatar - Graphical representation (a picture) often used in chat rooms to depict a person that is in the room and chatting.
b4	Before
BAK	Back At Keyboard (I'm back)
BBL	Be Back Later
BBS	Be Back Soon
BCNU	I'll Be Seeing You.
b/f	Boyfriend (also shown as bf, B/F, or BF)
BEG	Big Evil Grin
BFN	Bye For Now
BMA	Bite My A**
boot	To get kicked out of a chat room, or have to restart the computer because you couldn't talk in the chat room anymore.
BR	Best Regards
BRB	Be Right Back
BRH	Be Right Here
BSEG	Big S**t Eatin Grin
BTA	But Then Again....
BTW	By The Way
btw	BeTWeen you and me ...

Appendix A: Glossary and Cyber-Dictionary

chat room   A web page where people gather using software that allows them to talk to one another in real time.

CRS   Can't Remember S**t

CU   See You - also posted as cya

CUS   Can't Understand S**t (stuff)

CNP   Continued in Next Post (seen more on message boards than chat)

CP   Chat Post

CUL8R   See You Later

CUOL   See You On Line

CYA   See Ya

dd, ds, dh   Darling or Dear: Dear Son, Dear Daughter, or Dear Husband. Usually exchanged in family chats.

DDSOS   Different Day, Same Old S**t

DEGT   Don't Even Go There (I don't want to talk about it)

DIKU   Do I Know You?

DIS   Did I Say

D/L, DL, d/l, dl   Downloading, or Download it.

EG   Evil Grin

EM   E-Mail

EMA   E-mail Address (example: ?ema or ema? = what is your email address)

EOT   End Of Thread (meaning end of discussion)

ez or EZ   easy (one of the really old ones)

F2F   Face To Face

FAQ   Frequently Asked Question

FISH   First In Still Here (someone who is on line TOO much)

FITB   Fill In The Blanks

flame   to insult someone. Used when a person asks a stupid question, or says something rude to irritate the users of a chat room or message board.

FOCL   Falling Off Chair - Laughing

forum   What today's message boards are called. Often using php as defining language to quickly write "real time" messages and replies to a web site (or page)

FTS   F*** This S***

fu	f*** you (If you can't figure this one out, you shouldn't be online)
FUBAR	"Fouled" Up Beyond All Repair/Recognition
FUD	Fear, Uncertainty, and Doubt
FWIW	For What It's Worth
FYI	For Your Information
GA	Go Ahead
GAL	Get A Life
gest	Gesture…a small multimedia file played over the internet, usually expressing an emotion or comment.
g/f	Girlfriend (also shown as gf, G/F, or GF)
GFN	Gone For Now
GGOH	Gotta Get Outta Here
GMTA	Great Minds Think Alike
GR	Gotta Run
GR&D	Grinning, Running, and Ducking
GTR	Got To Run
GTRM	Going To Read Mail (leaving chat room to check email)
H&K	Hugs and Kisses
hack	person who breaks into software, or disrupts a chat room.
HAGD	Have A Good Day
HAGO	Have A Good One
HB	Hurry Back
Hosts	Refers to the people that are running the chat room, they usually have the ability to kick a person off due to rude behavior.
HTH	Hope That Helps
huggles	Hugs
IAC	In Any Case
IB	I'm Back
IC	I See
IDN	I Don't kNow
IDK	I Don't Know
IDTS	I Don't Think So
IANAL	I Am Not A Lawyer (expect an uninformed opinion)
IC	I See

ICQ	I Seek You. A computer program used to communicate instantly over the Internet.
ILU or ILY	I Love You
IM	Instant Message
IMHO	In My Humble Opinion (or In My Honest Opinion)
IMO	In My Opinion
IOH	I'm Out of Here
IOW	In Other Words
IRL	In Real Life
IYO	In Your Opinion
JAS	Just A Second
JIC	Just In Case
JK	Just Kidding
JMO	Just My Opinion
JW	Just Wondering
k, K, or kk	O. K.
KIT	Keep In Touch
L8R	Later (an early one, kind of outdated with current "young geeks")
LMAO	Laughing My A** Off
LFFAO	Laughing My F***(freak)ing A** Off
LOL	Laughing Out Loud
LTNS	Long Time No See
LTS	Laughing To one's Self
LY	I Love Ya
LYL	Love You Lots
Message Board	A web page where people write comments, and those comments are than added to that web-page for others to view. Used to carry on conversation, request information, and relay messages.
MUG	Refers to a new user of that chat program, goes back to Excite VP days when the AV (or icon) that represented someone new was a picture of a coffee mug.

NE1	Anyone
newbie	refers to a person who is new to an area or technology. Also seen as nube, nooby, nubie, nb, etc.
NFW	No Feasible (or F***ing) Way
NIMBY	Not In My Back Yard
nm, or NM	Never Mind
NP, np	No Problem
NRN	1. No Response Necessary
	2. Not Right Now
NT	No Thanks
OBTW	Oh, By The Way
OIC	Oh, I See
OF	Old Fart, someone who has been around for a while
OJ or OK	Only Joking or Only Kidding
OL	the Old Lady
OM	the Old Man
OMG	Oh My Gosh (although it's usually used with the Lord's name in place of "gosh")
OT	Off Topic
oth or OTH	Off The Hook: Something is really popular, or hot. Very exciting.
otr or OTR	Off The Rack: Saying that something is outside the ordinary.
OTE	Over The Edge (beyond common sense or beyond good taste)
OTOH	On The Other Hand...
OTOMH	Off the Top of My Head...
OTW	On The Way ... I've sent a file to you, it's "On the way"
P911	My parents are in the room. P=Parents, and 911=emergency, in other words either drop the subject, or watch the language.
PANS	Pretty Awesome New Stuff (often referring to computer technology)
PCMCIA	Personal Computer Memory Cards International Association
PCMCIA	People Can't Master Computer Industry Acronyms (slang)

PEBCAK	Problem Exists Between Chair And Keyboard
peeps	People. example: "There sure are a lot of peeps in this room" - meaning a lot of people are in the chat room.
peep this	Hey, listen to this, I've got some interesting news.
PITA	Pain In The A**
PLZ	Please
PMJI	Pardon Me for Jumping In (when you enter into a new conversation)
poof	when someone leaves a chat room, often seen as *poof* as in boy he *poofed* in a hurry.
POTS	Plain Old Telephone Service
POS	Parents are looking Over my Shoulder.
POTS	Parents Over The Shoulder - (My parents are watching, I can't really talk)
PPL	People
QT	Cutie
RFC	Request For Comments (used more in newsgroups, a page or pages that supply technical information)
rl or RL	Real Life (as opposed to being online)
r m or RM	Ready Made: pre-existing
ROFL	Rolling On Floor, Laughing
ROTF	Rolling On The Floor (laughing is implied)
ROTFLMAO	Rolling On The Floor Laughing My A** Off
ROTFLMFAO	Rolling On The Floor Laughing My F(***ing) A** Off
RSN	Real Soon Now
r/t	Real Time (also: RT, or rt)
RTFM	Read The "Flippin" Manual (response to beginner question on net, chat, newsgroups, etc.)
RU	aRe yoU?
SEG	S**t Eating Grin
SH	Same Here
SMS	Short Message Service (more cell phones and pagers than chat rooms and the Internet)
SN	Screen Name. The name or moniker selected by person in an IM or chat program. ex: My "SN" in vp was "-lone.wolf"

SNAFU	Situation Normal , All "Fouled" Up
SO	Significant Other
SOL	S**t Out Of Luck
SOS	Same Old S**t (stuff)
SOTA	State Of The Art (latest technology)
SPST	Same Place, Same Time
SSDD	Same S**t, Different Day
STR8	Straight (can refer to sex, or DSTR8 as in Damn Straight)
STW	Search The Web
SY	Sincerely Yours
SYL	See You Later
TAFN	That's All For Now
TC	Take Care
TFH	Thread From Hell (a topic or discussion that won't stop - esp. newsgroups)
TGIF	Thank Goodness It's Friday
THX	Thanks!
TIA	Thanks In Advance
TM	Text Message (often refers to communications with text over cell phones)
TMI	Too Much Info. (information)
TNT	'Til Next Time
TPS	That's Pretty Stupid
TPTB	The Powers That Be (can sometimes refer to the people that are running the chat room or server)
TRDMF	Tears Running Down My Face: Can be with either laughter, or due to saddness.
TS	Tough S**t
TSFY	Tough S**t For You
TTFN	Ta-Ta For Now
TTTT	These Things Take Time
TTYL	Talk To You Later
TY	Thank You
TYT	Take Your Time
TYVM	Thank You Very Much

US	You Suck
usa or USA	Until Sides Ache: Usually used with one of the laughter acronyms such as "lolusa" Laughing Out Loud Until my Sides Ache. I've also heard that some folks substitute ush for "Until Sides Hurt". rotflolush = rolling on the floor, laughing out loud, until my sides hurt.
UV	Unpleasant Visual
UW	yoU're Welcome
UY	Up Yours
VPPH	Virtual Places Page Host
WB	Welcome Back (you say this when someone returns to a chat room)
WC	WelCome
WEG	Wicked Evil Grin
WEU	What's Eating You?
WFM	Works For Me
WIIFM	What's In It For Me?
WTG	Way To Go
WTF	What The F**K
WT?	What The ...? or Who the ...?
WTGP?	Want To Go Private? (move to a private chat room)
WWJD	What Would Jesus Do?
YAA	Yet Another Acronym
YBS	You'll Be Sorry
YL	Young Lady
YM	Young Man
YMMV	Your Mileage May Vary
YR	Yea, Right. (sarcastic)
ys	You Stinker
YVW	You're Very Welcome
YW	You're Welcome

Emoticons: (symbols used to display feeling)

Note: For these little things called "emoticons" often the idea is to turn your head sideways, and it makes a picture on a lot of the smiley faces. ;-) for example where the ; (semi-colon) are the eyes, the - is the nose, and the) is the mouth. Also, you see some people use the hyphen (-) to show the nose, while others will show the same expression without the nose. Example: ;-) and ;) signify the same thing.

s, *S*, <s> smile	[_]> Cup of coffee
g, <g> grin	@@@ Cookies
xoxo hugs and kisses	@--/-- a rose
hugggggggsssss hugs	:-) smile
w, <w> wink	;-) wink
g giggles	<:-| curious
k, *K* kiss	:~) cute
;-)~~~~~~~~~ giving someone the raspberries.	:-(sad
(((((person))))) giving them a virtual hug.	8-) wears glasses
\~/ glass with a drink. (usually booze)	:-} embarrassed
^5 high five	:-/ perplexed, confused
?^ What's Up?	:,-(or ;`-(to cry
_/? a cup of tea	:-< pouting

>:-(angry	**&-(** crying
0:-) angel	**!:-)** I have an idea
:-| bored or no opinion	**;-{)** person with a mustache
:-> grin/mischievous	**;-)~** sexy tongue - or drunk
|-) dreaming	**;~)** being cute
:-O shouting, or shocked	**c["]** coffee mug
:-o talking, or surprised	**[_]>** another cup or mug
>:-|| mad/angry	**:->** grin/mischievous
:-D big grin or laugh	**<:-|** curious
=:-O scared	**|-|** sound asleep
:-x keeping mouth shut	**:-x** I'm keeping my mouth shut
:o) smiles (w/nose)	
:-))))))) lots of smiles	
;-P sticking tongue out	
:P sticking tongue out	
# 8 -) nerd, or person with glasses and crew cut	

Another Few Side Notes

0 can be O or vice versa, (the letter and the number are often interchangeable)

1 = won or one, (1dr = wonder)

2 = too, to, or two,

3 = the letter E, (so 's33 U' means See you)

4 = for, four, or a prefix of suffix of 'fore. (b4 = before, 4warned = forewarned),

8 is usually either a pair of eyes, glasses, or ate, although it gets used a lot for making pictures,

9 is a good thing (he was dressed to the 9s means he was all dressed up),

B = be

C = see (IC means I see)

G = gee

K = OK (so k, or kk means I'm OK)

M = am

N = in

O = oh

R = Are

U = You

g = grin

s = smile

Digital Media Use Pyramids

Desired Digital Media Use Pyramid

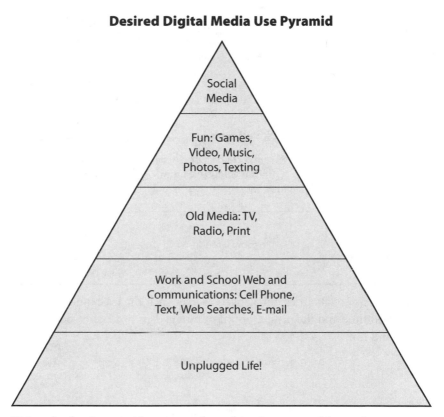

Using the food pyramid as a template, this gives a possible road map to follow. Our goal is to maximize off-line time by making online time more efficient. In an ideal world, we'd use technology to communicate with people and maximize our connections with fun being the smallest component.

Today's Teens' and Kids' Digital Media Use Pyramid

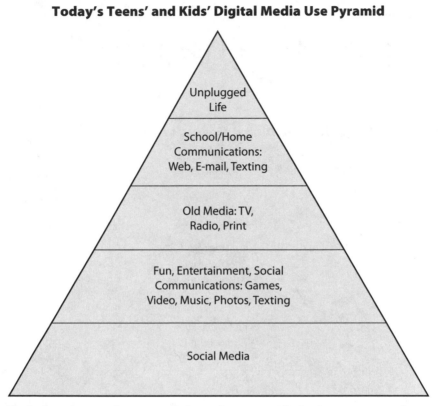

Today's teens are about as unbalanced as ever with the least amount of unplugged time and the most amount of plugged-in time with social media and fun.

Following is what we do online today in roughly the proportions we use daily:

What We Do Online Today

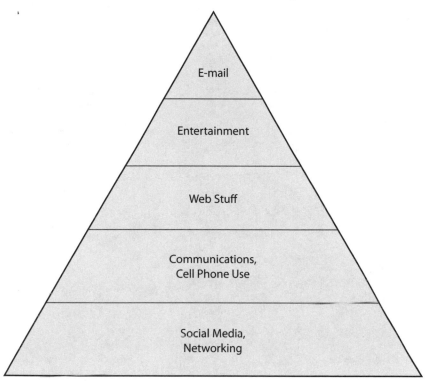

Social Media Use Table

Group	Purpose	Privacy Policy (PP) and Terms of Service (TOS)	Web Site
Facebook	Social networking	• TOS: 13 and older • PP: Encourages 13- to 18-year-old kids to "ask their parents' permission" before sending information over the Internet.	www.facebook.com
MySpace	Social networking	• TOS: 13 and older	www.myspace.com
Twitter	Microblogging Social networking	• TOS: 13 and older	http://twitter.com
Webkinz	Social networking with virtual pets Games	• TOS: Any child younger than 18 must have parent's permission to register.	www.webkinz.com
Club Penguin	Social networking in a virtual world Games	• TOS: All ages • PP: Must have parents' e-mail to confirm permission to play on site.	www.clubpenguin.com
Neopets	Virtual pet reality game	• TOS: If younger than 18 years must have parental consent to use. • PP: Users younger than 13 years must have parental involvement for privacy issues.	www.neopets.com
Shining Stars	Virtual world Games	• TOS: Requires user code from a purchase of Shining Star toy and parental consent if younger than18 years to register. • Web site designed for ages 4 to 12 • Chat limited to preset phrases • Charitable component:"glowing points" are converted to real cash donations by company.	www.shiningstars.com
Millsberry	Virtual world Games	• TOS: All ages. E-mail is required for kids younger than 13 for registration then deleted. • PP: Does not routinely collect information of kids younger than 13.	www.millsberry.com

Teen Use and Abuse of Today's Web 2.0 Technologies

Media Venue	Purposes	Advantages	Pitfalls or Health Risks
Web Sites (1.0 and 2.0) **(See Chapter 12.)**	• Research • Product information • Entertainment • News Content-only sites are known as Web 1.0. Web sites with all the bells and whistles of social features such as blogs, chats, discussion boards/rooms, and shopping zones are referred to as Web 2.0.	• Gather information. • Stay up-to-date. • Relaxation • Reading or studying breaks if entertainment value	• Misleading information if author of Web page is not a true expert • Too much distraction from other important tasks such as work and homework • Interfacing with inappropriate material or people • Exposure to ideas, topics, and images not appropriate for age and development
Instant Communication • **Instant Message (IM)** • **Cell Phone Texting** • **Sexting** **(See Chapter 13.)**	• Quick communication • Online conversation • Uses a code that can be fun and entertaining. • Cell phone texts can be used for 911 situations.	• Quick • Can be done from anything with an Internet connection.	• Code can be used to talk about dangerous topics such as sex and drug use.

Appendix D: Teen Use and Abuse of Today's Web 2.0 Technologies

Media Venue	Purposes	Advantages	Pitfalls or Health Risks
Social Networking Sites (Facebook/ MySpace) (See Chapter 14.)	Sites that allow for connection of people and sharing of contact information, ideas, videos, pictures, and links.	• Stay connected with family and friends. • Communication • Networking • Scheduling	• Cyberbullying • Harassment • Stranger danger is real, but there is a privacy feature to make the profile private. • Easy to create dummy profiles and hide true identity • Facebook depression
YouTube (See Chapter 3.)	Video sharing Web site	• Sharing of videos • Entertainment • Public service and health announcements	• Inappropriate content depending on age of viewer • Ability to learn risky behavior • Reinforcing of dangerous behaviors
Podcasts (See Chapter 3.)	A series of audio or video media shows made available via an Internet syndication service or feed. Typically available for free, but some are fee-based.	• Entertainment • Public service announcements • Health messages	• Inappropriate content depending on age of viewer • Ability to learn risky behavior • Reinforcing of dangerous behaviors
Chat and Discussion Rooms (See Chapter 13.)	Interesting way to have a discussion with a virtual group of people about any topic you can think of	• Information • Opinions	• Can't be sure you are getting expert advise. • Advise can be misleading. • Are not sure who is on other end of chat or discussion, which can lead to dangerous situation if personal information is given out.

Media Venue	Purposes	Advantages	Pitfalls or Health Risks
Blogs (See Chapter 3.)	Also called Weblogs. Similar to traditional Web sites, they Provide information, links, and resources. • Have a similar appearance. • Have a specific URL and site name. Unlike traditional Web sites, blogs • Are editorial-like. • Run in reverse chronologic order. • May allow reader comments to give a pseudo-discussion feel. • Are very user-friendly and easy to set up and maintain. • Can be hosted for free on sites like Blogger and WordPress.	Many people find the editorial nature of blogs refreshing because it provides opinions and ideas. When the comment feature is enabled, a blog is interactive and this unites people together through their blogs and makes them social, unlike static Web sites.	Opinions may not be factual and can be misleading. Depending on the topic, this can get kids (and adults) into trouble, especially if the topic is about health issues. A huge pitfall is not realizing the blog author is not a true authority or expert. Many bloggers are fantastic writers. It is easy to misinterpret well-written posts for authoritative ideas.
Microblogging (Twitter) (See Chapter 15.)	This new technology is a cross between blogging and IM. Limited to 140 characters. Conversational. Can post pictures and links.	• Quick communication • Networking • Gathering ideas • Traffic driving to Web sites and blogs • Can follow groups and people.	• Limited in word count • Stranger danger is real, but there is the ability to make profile private. • More informal than other communications venues—easier to be tempted to tell more personal information

Appendix E

Risk Table

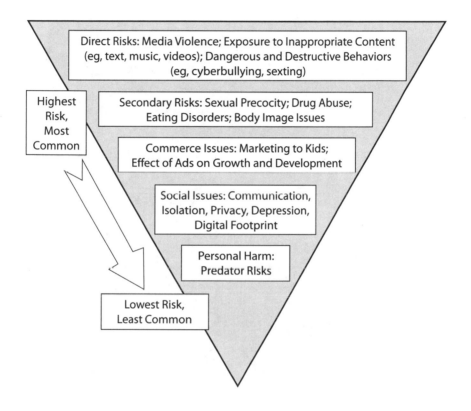

Direct Risks: Media Violence; Exposure to Inappropriate Content (eg, text, music, videos); Dangerous and Destructive Behaviors (eg, cyberbullying, sexting)

Highest Risk, Most Common

Secondary Risks: Sexual Precocity; Drug Abuse; Eating Disorders; Body Image Issues

Commerce Issues: Marketing to Kids; Effect of Ads on Growth and Development

Social Issues: Communication, Isolation, Privacy, Depression, Digital Footprint

Personal Harm: Predator Risks

Lowest Risk, Least Common

American Academy of Pediatrics Talking to Kids and Teens About Social Media and Sexting

Social Media

Today's teens and "tweens" are connected to one another, and to the world, via digital technology more than any previous generation. Recent data suggests that social media (SM) venues like Facebook and MySpace have surpassed e-mail as the preferred method of communication in all age groups. While today's tweens and teens may be more digitally savvy than their parents, their lack of maturity and life experience can quickly get them into trouble with these new social venues. For this reason, it is imperative that parents talk with their children of all ages about SM and monitor their online SM use to help them navigate this new online social world. How parents talk with their kids and teens will vary slightly by age depending on the topic being discussed. These tips will help you start that journey with your family.

- Learn about these technologies firsthand. There is simply no better way than to have a profile yourself. It will also enable you to "friend" your kids and monitor them online.
- Let them know that their use of technology is something you want and need to know about.
  - For kids of all ages, ask daily: "Have you used the computer and the Internet today?"
  - Technology use will vary by age. Tweens are likely to be using more instant messaging (IMing) and texting, while teens use those technologies and also networking sites such as Facebook. (These tools often are referred to as "platforms" for social networking.) Ask daily how your family used those tools with questions such as: "What did you write on Facebook today?" "Any new chats recently?" "Anyone text you today?"

Appendix F: American Academy of Pediatrics Talking to Kids and Teens About Social Media and Sexting

- – Share a bit about your daily SM use as a way to facilitate daily conversation about your kids' online habits.
- – Get your kids talking about their SM lives if you can just so you know what they are doing.
- Keep the computer in a public part of your home, such as the family room or kitchen, so that you can check on what your kids are doing online and how much time they are spending there.
- Talk with other parents about what their kids of similar ages are using for SM. Ask your kids about those technologies as a starting point for discussion. If they are in the same peer group, there is a good chance they are all using the same platforms together. For example
  - – For teens: "Mrs Smith told me Jennifer uses Facebook. Is that something you've thought of doing? Do you already have a profile? If so, I'd like to see it."
  - – For tweens and older elementary schoolkids: "Are you planning on meeting up with kids on Club Penguin today? I'd love to see how that works." Or, "Let's look at your text log today together. I'd like to see who's been texting you."
- For all ages, emphasize that everything sent over the Internet or a cell phone can be shared with the entire world, so it is important they use good judgment in sending messages and pictures and set privacy settings on social media sites appropriately.
  - – Discuss with kids of every age what "good judgment" means and the consequences of poor judgment, ranging from minor punishment to possible legal action in the case of "sexting" (see page 299) or bullying.
  - – Remember to make a point of discouraging kids from gossiping, spreading rumors, bullying, or damaging someone's reputation using texting or other tools.
  - – To keep kids safe, have your kids and teens show you where the privacy features are for every SM venue they are using. The more private, the less likely inappropriate material will be received by your child, or sent to their circle of acquaintances.
  - – Be aware of the ages of use for sites your tweens and older elementary schoolkids want to use, including game sites such as Club Penguin and Webkinz. Many sites are for age 13 and older, and the sites for younger kids do require parental consent to use.

- Be sure you are where your kids are online: IM, Facebook, MySpace, etc. Have a policy requiring that you and your child "friend" each other. This is one way of showing your child you are there, too, and will provide a check-and-balance system by having an adult within arm's reach of their profile. This is important for kids of all ages, including teens.
- Show your kids you know how to use what they are using, and are willing to learn what you may not know how to do.
- Create a strategy for monitoring your kids' online SM use, and be sure you follow through. Some families may check once a week and others more sporadically. You may want to say, "Today I'll be checking your computer and cell phone." The older your kids are, the more often you may need to check.
- Consider formal monitoring systems to track your child's e-mail, chat, IM, and image content. Parental controls on your computer or from your Internet service provider, Google Desktop, or commercial programs are all reasonable alternatives.
- Set time limits for Internet and cell phone use. Learn the warning signs of trouble: skipping activities, meals, and homework for SM; weight loss or gain; a drop in grades. If these issues are occurring due to your child being online when they should be eating, sleeping, or participating in school or social activities, your child may have a problem with Internet or SM addiction. Contact your pediatrician for advice if any of these symptoms are occurring.
- Check chat logs, e-mails, files, and social networking profiles for inappropriate content, friends, messages, and images periodically. Be transparent and let your kids know what you are doing.

The New Problem of "Sexting"

"Sexting" refers to sending a text message with pictures of children or teens that are inappropriate, naked, or engaged in sex acts. According to a recent survey, about 20% of teen boys and girls have sent such messages. The emotional pain it causes can be enormous for the child in the picture as well as the sender and receiver—often with legal implications. Parents must begin the difficult conversation about sexting before there is a problem and introduce the issue as soon as a child is old enough to have a cell phone. Here are some tips for how to begin these conversations with your children:

Appendix F: American Academy of Pediatrics Talking to Kids and Teens About Social Media and Sexting

- Talk to your kids, even if the issue hasn't directly impacted your community. "Have you heard of sexting?" "Tell me what you think it is." For the initial part of the conversation, it is important to first learn what your child's understanding is of the issue and then add to it an age-appropriate explanation (see next bullet).
- Use examples appropriate for your child's age. For younger children with cell phones who do not yet know about sex, alert them that text messages should never contain pictures of people—kids or adults—without their clothes on, kissing, or touching each other in ways that they've never seen before. For older children, use the term "sexting" and give more specifics about sex acts they may know about. For teens, be very specific that "sexting" often involves pictures of a sexual nature and is considered pornography.
- Make sure kids of all ages understand that sexting is serious and considered a crime in many jurisdictions. In all communities, if they "sext," there will be serious consequences, quite possibly involving the police, suspension from school, and notes on the sexter's permanent record that could hurt their chances of getting into college or getting a job.
- Experts have noted that peer pressure can play a major role in the sending of texts, with parties being a major contributing factor. Collecting cell phones at gatherings of tweens and teens is one way to reduce this temptation.
- Monitor headlines and the news for stories about "sexting" that illustrate the very real consequences for both senders and receivers of these images. "Have you seen this story?" "What did you think about it?" "What would you do if you were this child?" Rehearse ways they can respond if asked to participate in inappropriate texting.
- Encourage school and town assemblies to educate parents, teachers, and students.
- Watch the ABC Good Morning America segment from April 15, 2009 (http://abcnews.go.com/GMA/story?id=7337547&page=1), featuring a town hall meeting with teens who have sent and received "sexts," parents, and experts.

Resources

American Academy of Pediatrics SafetyNet (http://safetynet.aap.org)

Girl Scouts lmk life online (http://lmk.girlscouts.org)

Federal Trade Commission Social Networking Sites: Safety Tips for
Tweens and Teens (www.ftc.gov/bcp/edu/pubs/consumer/tech/tec14.shtm)

UC Berkeley School of Information "I School Researchers Discuss
'Sexting' Statistics" (www.ischool.berkeley.edu/newsandevents/news/
presscoverage/20090407sexting)

Dr Gwenn's Media Time Family Pledge

- Kids and Teens
  - I will never give out personal information online or by text and will avoid all chat rooms except ones my mom and dad have looked at and approved.
  - I understand my parents have a right to check into my media history on my computer and phone and other devices such as iPod Touch, games, and whatever else I use regularly. I will try and keep my total screen time to 2 hours a day except when doing a project for school, or when my parents give me permission.
  - I will not watch shows or play games that are inappropriate for me or for friends and family watching or playing with me.
- Parents
  - I will check what my kids are doing online and on their phones, consider using parent controls, and use them judiciously.
  - I will let my kids know before I check their computers or enable parent controls on their computers or gaming units.
  - I will take the time to be interested in what my kids are doing online and in the digital world and talk to them about that world.
  - I will help them make good media choices.
  - If my child makes a mistake, I will ask questions and learn what happened before I punish or take away technology.
  - I will only take away technology as a last resort for defying our family pledge when other consequences have failed to work, such as reinforcing the rules and increase off-line chores.
- Entire Family
  - We will talk as a family at a meal a day with no technology in sight!
  - We will agree to technology-free times such as meals, weekends, and vacations.
  - We won't sacrifice important family time for media or digital use of any kind. If media gets in the way, we need to recognize we are using it too much or in a way that is not helping our family.

- We agree to use technology responsibly by not
  - Texting or talking on a cell phone while driving
  - Using cell phones in a public location where it may annoy others
  - Using technology to harm others by engaging in bullying or slanderous actions
  - Listening to music with earbuds in a manner that prevents us from hearing passing cars or pedestrians, and never while in the car as the driver

Date: _____

Signed

Parents: _____

Kids and Teens: _____

The Safe-Surfing Contract: My Agreement About Using the Internet

I want to use the Internet. I know that there are certain rules about what I should do online. I agree to follow these rules and my parents agree to help me follow these rules:

1. I will not give my name, address, telephone number, school, or my parents' names, addresses, or telephone numbers, or anything else that would help anyone find me offline (like the name of my sports team) to anyone I meet on the computer.
2. I understand that some people online pretend to be someone else. Sometimes they pretend to be kids, when they're really grown-ups. I will tell my parents about people I meet online. I will also tell my parents before I answer any e-mails or instant messages I get from, or send e-mail or instant messages to, new people I meet online.
3. I will not buy or order anything online or give out any credit card information without asking my parents.
4. I will not fill out any form online that asks me for any information about myself or my family without asking my parents first. This includes forms for contests or registering at a site. I'll also check to see if the sites have a privacy policy and if they promise to keep my private information private. If they don't promise to keep my private information private, I won't give them any private information. (I will talk to my parents about what "private information" is.)
5. I will not get into arguments or fights online. If someone tries to start an argument or fight with me, I won't answer him or her and will tell my parents.
6. If I see something I do not like or that makes me uncomfortable or that I know my parents don't want me to see, I will click on the "Back" button or log off.
7. If I see people doing things or saying things to other kids online I know they're not supposed to do or say, I'll tell my parents.

8. I won't keep online secrets from my parents.
9. If someone sends me any pictures, links to sites I know I shouldn't be going to, or any e-mail or instant messaging using bad language, I will tell my parents.
10. If someone asks me to do something I am not supposed to do, I will tell my parents.
11. I will not call anyone I met online unless my parents say it's OK. (Even then I will block caller ID on my phone.)
12. I will never meet in person anyone I met online, unless my parents say it's OK and they are with me.
13. I will never send anything to anyone I met online, unless my parents say it's OK.
14. If anyone I met online sends me anything, I will tell my parents.
15. I will not use something I found online and pretend it's mine.
16. I won't say bad things about people online, and I will practice good Netiquette.
17. I won't use bad language online or threaten anyone, even if I'm only kidding.
18. I know that my parents want to make sure I'm safe online, and I will listen to them when they ask me not to do something.
19. I will help teach my parents more about computers and the Internet.
20. I will practice safe computing, and check for viruses whenever I borrow a disk from someone or download something or open any attachment, even from someone I know.
21. I will tell my parents when something bad happens online, because they promise not to overreact if something bad happens online. And I will remember that it's not my fault if others do bad things online!

I promise to follow these rules.
(signed by child/teen)

I promise to help my child follow these rules and not to overreact
if my child tells me about bad things that happen in cyberspace.
(Signed by parent)

Appendix I

Family Internet Safety Gameplan

InternetSafety.com's
Family Internet Safety Gameplan™

The following Gameplan establishes the online ground rules for our home. We will display this Gameplan and update it periodically as our children grow older.

1. **We will never give out personal information such as our last name, address or phone number.** We should also not give out the name of our school, our city, our siblings, our sports team or our parent's workplace.

2. **We all agree to not give our passwords to anyone outside of our family.** We have all agreed upon user names to use while we are on the Internet. I will not change the settings for my computer or my password without my parent's permission.

3. **We all agree to limit our online time so that it doesn't interfere with other activities.** We agree to follow the time limits that our family sets and not let the Internet take time away from homework, sports, face-to-face interactions or family time.

4. **I will never meet an online friend in person.** Just as I stay away from strangers on the street, I will be careful about strangers on the Internet. If anyone ever asks to meet with me off line, I will notify my parents immediately.

5. **I will tell my mom or dad right away if I come across something that makes me feel uncomfortable.** If anyone uses bad language or mentions things that make me uncomfortable, I will immediately log off and tell my parents.

6. **I will not remain on or click on a page that says, "For Over 18 Years Only."** If this happens, I will log off and I will let my parents know. I understand that I'm only a click away from bad sites and that these pages are definitely not for kids.

7. **I will only download pictures and files with my parent's permission.** Some of these files may contain inappropriate pictures or dangerous viruses that could mess up our computer.
8. **I will not send pictures of my family or myself to anyone online.** The only way that I am allowed to do this is if my parents say it is all right.
9. **I will be safe everywhere.** I will follow the same Internet safety rules at my friends' houses, at school and at the library that I do while I'm at home.
10. **I understand that nothing is private on the Internet.** I agree that my mom or dad can read my mail or check the sites that I have been visiting—not because they don't trust me but because they just want to make sure that I am safe.

We agree to the above InternetSafety.com Gameplan:

_____

Child's Signature

_____

Parent's Signature

(Used with permission, www.internetsafety.com)

Resources

Computer Operating System Safety Features and Parent Controls

Apple Mac OS security controls
www.apple.com/server/macosx/technology/security-controls.html
www.apple.com/macosx/security
(Free, comes with computer OS)

Microsoft Windows computer safety and security information
www.microsoft.com/security/pypc.aspx
(Free, comes with computer)

Microsoft Windows information on safety settings
www.microsoft.com/protect/familysafety/default.aspx
(Free, comes with computer)

Popular Internet Service Provider and Social Networking Site Safety Features and Parent Controls

AOL
https://parentalcontrols.aol.com

Ask.com
www.ask.com/webprefs

AT&T
http://worldnet.att.net/general-info/kidsafe.html

Bing
www.bing.com/settings.aspx?ru=%2f&FORM=SELH

Comcast
http://security.comcast.net

Facebook
www.facebook.com/help.php?page=937

Google
www.google.com/support/websearch/bin/answer.py?hl=en&answer
=35892#safe

iTunes
http://support.apple.com/kb/HT1904
(For all digital downloads from the iTunes store)

MySpace
www.myspace.com/index.cfm?fuseaction=cms.
viewpage&placement=safety_pagehome

Napster
http://home.napster.com/info/terms.html
*(Parent control password can be set up to prevent explicit-lyric songs
from being downloaded.)*

Verizon
http://parentalcontrolcenter.com

Yahoo!
http://help.yahoo.com/l/us/yahoo/search/basics/indexing-07.html

YouTube
www.google.com/support/youtube/bin/answer.py?answer=126289

www.google.com/support/youtube/bin/request.py?contact_
type=abuse&hl=en-US

*(Video-based safety information for staying safe on YouTube as well as
general information on overall Web safety for teens on privacy, digital
citizenship, and related topics)*

Popular Cell Phone Carrier Safety Features and Parent Controls

AT&T
- **Smart Limits**
  www.att.com/gen/landing-pages?pid=6456
  www.att.com/gen/sites/smartlimits?pid=8949
- **MEdia Net**
  www.wireless.att.com/learn/articles-resources/parental-controls/
  media-net.jsp

Sprint
www1.sprintpcs.com/explore/ueContent.jsp?scTopic=parentalControl101

http://support.sprint.com/support/pages/tutorialArticleDetails.
jsp?articleId=2362

www1.sprintpcs.com/explore/ueContent.jsp?scTopic=webAccess

T Mobile
http://support.t-mobile.com/doc/tm23350.xml
(Subscription)

Verizon
- **Content filters**
  https://wbillpay.verizonwireless.com/vzw/nos/parental-control_
  learn_more.jsp
  (Free; prevents downloading of content under a certain age.)
- **Usages controls**
  https://wbillpay.verizonwireless.com/vzw/nos/uc/uc_home.jsp
  (Monthly subscription fee)

Internet Monitoring and Parent Control Programs

CA Internet Security Suite Plus 2010
http://shop.ca.com/malware/internet_security_suite.aspx

($69 for 3 computers; full computer protection plus parental controls)

K9 Web Protection from Blue Coat
www.getk9.com

(Free Internet filter with monitoring and protection against common Web threats)

McGruff SafeGuard
www.gomcgruff.com/m/index.asp?Visits=1

(Internet monitoring, filtering, and parent controls by the National Crime Prevention Council and Parents on Patrol; free basic service; upgrade available for data storage)

Norton Online Family
https://onlinefamily.norton.com/familysafety/loginStart.fs

(Free service by Norton that allows you to monitor your child's online life and facilitates discussion with your child; recommended by product reviewers and Internet safety experts.)

Optenet
www.optenet.com

(ISP-based Internet security system that will be rolled out in United States throughout 2010)

Safe Eyes
www.internetsafety.com/safe-eyes-parental-control-software.php

($49.95 for the download, $59.95 for the CD; top-rated Internet filtering and monitoring software program; includes controls for instant messaging, YouTube, Web sites, blogs, and social networking sites; parents can also install time limits for Web use.)

Spector Pro 2010

www.spectorsoft.com

(Award-winning Internet monitoring and recording program that captures all the information needed by law enforcement if a what-if occurs; highly recommended by leading Internet safety experts because the information collected is what law enforcement officials need if they need to pursue a situation; the program does not provide filtering and other computer protection; $99.95.)

Cyber-Help Resources: Fraud, Identity Issues, Crimes, Concerns

Computer and IP crimes

www.usdoj.gov/criminal/cybercrime

(Includes a comprehensive law enforcement list by types of cyber-crimes.)

CyberLawEnforcement.org

http://cyberlawenforcement.org

CyberTipline

www.cybertipline.com

Federal Trade Commission

www.ftc.gov/bcp/comsumer.shtm
www.ftc.gov/idtheft

Internet Crime Complaint Center

www.ic3.gov/default.aspx

(Includes e-mail scams.)

National Center for Missing & Exploited Children cyber-report form

https://secure.missingkids.com/missingkids/servlet/CybertipServlet?
LanguageCountry=en_US

OnGuard Online

www.onguardonline.gov/file-complaint.aspx

314

Chat, Instant Messaging, and Texting Acronyms and Translators

Chat acronyms and abbreviations by i-SAFE
http://isafe.org/imgs/pdf/Acronyms.pdf

LG DTXR (Dee-text-er)
www.lgdtxtr.com
(Includes a comprehensive glossary of terms and phrases; can translate text lingo to English or English to text lingo.)

NetLingo
www.netlingo.com/acronyms.php
www.netlingo.com/top50/acronyms-for-parents.php
www.netlingo.com/top50/top50parents.php

TransL8it!
www.transl8it.com/cgi-win/index.pl
(English to lingo or lingo to English)

Translators from WiredSafety
• Acronym: www.wiredsafety.org/internet101/acronyms.html
• Emoticon: www.wiredsafety.org/internet101/emoticons.html
• Chat: www.teenangels.org/scrapbook/translator/index.html

General Internet Safety Resources and Information for Parents, Kids, and Teens

bNetS@vvy
http://bnetsavvy.org/wp
(Resource for parents from Sprint, National Association for Missing & Exploited Children, and National Education Association Health Information Network)

Campaign for a Commercial-Free Childhood
www.commercialexploitation.org/index.html

ChildSafe International
www.childsafe.com

(International group striving to educate families about the dangers of the Internet and promote better use of iWatchDog)

Common Sense Media
www.commonsensemedia.org

CyberAngels
www.cyberangels.org

(Cyber-safety program of the Alliance of Guardian Angels)

Cyberbullying Research Center
http://cyberbullying.us/index.php

Enough Is Enough
www.enough.org

(Adult internet education)

Family Cell Phone Agreement
www.wirelessfoundation.org/WirelessOnlineSafety/family_cellphone_agreement.cfm

Federal Trade Commission Children's Online Privacy Protection Act
www.ftc.gov/privacy/privacyinitiatives/childrens.html

(US Federal Trade Commission privacy laws affecting our children can be found on this Web site with an explanation of what they mean; these laws are designed to protect kids younger than 13 years.)

4NetSafety
www.sprint.com/4netsafety

(Resource for teens founded by Sprint and produced by the National Center for Missing & Exploited Children's NetSmartz Workshop)

GetGameSmart.com
www.getgamesmart.com

(From Microsoft)

GetNetWise

www.getnetwise.org

(Public service educational Web site resulting from a collaborative effort from the main technologic groups and leaders in the Internet fields including Google, Microsoft, Verizon, Yahoo!, Comcast, Adobe, AOL, and many others)

Hoax Busters

www.hoaxbusters.org

(Looking for a Web site to track down a potential online hoax? This site has a fairly comprehensive list of most online hoaxes traveling through cyberspace and ending up in many of our inboxes and cell phones.)

i-SAFE

http://isafe.org/channels/sub.php?ch=op&sub_id=4

Keeping kids safe from drugs

www.drugfree.org/Parent/ConnectingWithYourKids/Articles/
Technology_and_Your_Teen.aspx

Love Our Children USA

www.loveourchildrenusa.org

(Nonprofit organization dedicated to the prevention of all types of violence and neglect against children, online and off)

Microsoft Online Safety and Privacy Education

www.microsoft.com/protect

National Crime Prevention Council

www.ncpc.org

NetSmartz Workshop

www.netsmartz.org

(National Center for Missing & Exploited Children Internet safety educational Web site to help parents and kids learn to be safer online)

Norton Family Online Safety Guide by Marian Merritt
www.symantec.com/norton/familyresources/
resources.jsp?title=online_safety_guide

OnGuard Online
www.onguardonline.gov

(Internet fraud tips from the federal government and technology sector; some of the partners include Homeland Security, Federal Trade Commission, US Department of Justice, Internal Revenue Service, US Postal Service, Federal Deposit Insurance Corporation, Securities and Exchange Commission, GetNetWise, StaySafeOnline.org, i-SAFE, WiredSafety.org, National Association of Attorneys General, Better Business Bureau.)

Point Smart. Click Safe.
www.pointsmartclicksafe.org/flash.html

Respect U, the Bully Coach
www.respectu.com

(Joel Haber, PhD)

SafeSurf
www.safesurf.com

(Internet rating system site with educational information on safe surfing)

SafetyClicks Blog
www.blog.safetyclicks.com

(Safety information from AOL)

StaySafeOnline.org
www.staysafeonline.info

(National Cyber Security Alliance public education Web site)

STOP Cyberbullying
www.stopcyberbullying.org

Web Wise Kids
www.webwisekids.com

WiredSafety.org
www.wiredsafety.org

(Nonprofit headed by Internet safety lawyer, Parry Aftab, Esq)

Wireless Foundation
www.wirelessfoundation.org

Yahoo! Safely
http://safely.yahoo.com

(Yahoo!'s site on helping kids stay safe online with information for parents, teachers, and teens)

Gaming System Parental Controls

GetGameSmart.com
www.getgamesmart.com/tools/setcontrols/

Microsoft Xbox 360
www.esrb.org/about/parentalcontrol-xbox360.jsp

Nintendo DSi
www.esrb.org/about/parentalcontrol-DSi.jsp

Nintendo Wii
www.esrb.org/about/parentalcontrol-wii.jsp

PlayStation 3 and PlayStation Portable
www.esrb.org/about/parentalcontrol-ps3psp.jsp

Gaming Information

Entertainment Software Rating Board
www.esrb.org

GetGameSmart.com
www.getgamesmart.com

Media Literacy

America Academy of Pediatrics SafetyNet
http://safetynet.aap.org

Center for Media Literacy
www.medialit.org

Center on Media and Child Health
www.cmch.tv

Media Literacy Clearinghouse
www.frankwbaker.com

Media Literacy Tool Box
www.medialiteracytoolbox.com

National Association for Media Literacy Education
www.amlainfo.org

National Institute on Media and the Family
www.mediafamily.org

New Mexico Media Literacy Project
www.nmmlp.org

Online Sites for Tweens and Teens on Cyber-Issues

CyberSleuth Kids
http://cybersleuth-kids.com

NetSmartz Workshop
www.netsmartz.org
(National Center for Missing & Exploited Children Internet safety educational Web site to help parents and kids learn to be safer online)

NSTeens

www.nsteens.org

*(Site for tweens and teens from Sprint, National Center for Missing &
Exploited Children, and NetSmartz Workshop)*

Open Directory Project

www.dmoz.org/Kids_and_Teens/Computers/Internet/Safety
(Internet safety)

www.dmoz.org/Kids_and_Teens/Teen_Life/Online_Communities
(Teen online communities)

PBS Kids Don't Buy It

http://pbskids.org/dontbuyit

Books

Palfrey J, Gasser U. *Born Digital: Understanding the First Generation of
Digital Natives.* New York, NY: Basic Books; 2008

Small G, Vorgan G. *iBrain: Surviving the Technological Alteration of the
Modern Mind.* New York: HarperCollins; 2008

Tapscott D. *Grown Up Digital: How the Net Generation Is Changing
Your World.* New York, NY: McGraw Hill; 2009

Weinstein M. *The Surprising Power of Family Meals: How Eating Together
Makes Us Smarter, Stronger, Healthier, and Happier.* Hanover, NH:
Steerforth Press; 2005

Index